SUSAN ROTHENBERG

SUSAN ROTHENBERG

BY JOAN SIMON

HARRY N. ABRAMS, INC., PUBLISHERS, NEW YORK

This book is dedicated with pleasure
to Alan Kennedy and Ani and Kira Simon-Kennedy

EDITOR: Harriet Whelchel
DESIGNER: Maria Miller
PHOTO RESEARCH: Neil Ryder Hoos

LIBRARY OF CONGRESS CATALOGING-IN-PUBLICATION DATA
Simon, Joan, 1949–
Susan Rothenberg / by Joan Simon.
p. cm.
Includes bibliographical references and index.
ISBN 0–8109–3753–0
1. Rothenberg, Susan, 1945– —Criticism and interpretation.
I. Title.
ND237.R72484S55 1991
759.13—dc20
[B] 91–8278
CIP

Published in 1991 by Harry N. Abrams, Incorporated, New York
A Times Mirror Company

Printed and bound in Japan

CONTENTS

ACKNOWLEDGMENTS · 6

SUSAN ROTHENBERG · 8

NOTES · 173

LIST OF ILLUSTRATIONS · 178

CHRONOLOGY · 182

SELECTED EXHIBITION HISTORY · 184

SELECTED BIBLIOGRAPHY · 191

INDEX · 199

PHOTOGRAPH CREDITS · 205

ACKNOWLEDGMENTS

THE EVOLUTION OF ANY ARTIST'S WORK INVOLVES TALENT, TRAINING, circumstance, and, not unimportantly, accident. Having known Susan Rothenberg since the early 1970s and witnessed personally many of the changes on the scene and in the studio, I hope that, with limitations of participant-observer status acknowledged, the details provided here will begin to illuminate both the context and content of her diverse, often enigmatic, and important body of work.

My thanks are first to Susan Rothenberg, who as artist and friend continues to surprise. She provided much new material, including previously unpublished photographs, and many answers to questions she has ducked in the past. Most importantly, my thanks to her for the privilege of argument and the recognition of differences in interpretation.

To Miani Johnson, and her Willard Gallery, for providing the professional circumstances and personal support for an artist's work to develop publicly in its own time and on its own terms, for invaluable archival documentation, and for a sustaining friendship. It is not an understatement to say that Miani, Susan, and I grew up together in the rapidly changing art world of the past twenty years.

To Angela Westwater of Sperone Westwater Gallery, also a longtime colleague and friend beginning in the mid-1970s when we both served as managing editors at rival art magazines, for her gracious attention to the many details of making this book and her lively commitment to Rothenberg's work.

Appreciation is also in order to Ann Cook and Charles Harrison of Willard Gallery; Karen Polack and Joan Hirschhorn at Sperone Westwater, and Kellie Jones and Jessica Reighard for photograph, collection, bibliography and chronology research; to The Museum of Modern Art Library for solace and sources; and to the many museums and collectors who are the stewards of Rothenberg's work. Betsy Baker, Sarah McFadden, and Robert Storr have provided encouragement and inspiration in countless ways over many years. At Abrams, Paul Gottlieb vociferously set the enthusiastic tone for bringing this book to his house and the logistics for it to be a truly collaborative venture—the team of Harriet Whelchel, editor; Neil Hoos, picture editor; Maria Miller, designer—as well as providing the wherewithal to rephotograph many of Rothenberg's paintings, whose surfaces, palette, perhaps even spirit, are often evasive of the camera's capabilities.

SUSAN ROTHENBERG

FROM THE TIME SHE BEGAN TO EXHIBIT HER WORK IN 1974, SUSAN Rothenberg has had the audacity to make paintings that are as inscrutably private as they are publicly accessible, as formal as they are magically expressive, as figurative as they are abstract. They have followed a singularly changeable journey that has merged painterly issues with autobiographical concerns so completely that the artist and her body of work appear to have led several different lives. Stylistically, Rothenberg's paintings have been labeled New Image, Neo-Expressionist, even Neo-Impressionist, Surrealist, or Futurist as her own intuitive search for image, content, and surface handling has matched her consistent desires to "catch a moment, the moment to exemplify an emotion,"[1] and never to "paint things the way they are," to continually challenge herself by painting "exactly the way things can't be."[2]

From her earliest iconic horse paintings, through her isolated body fragments in strange and mysterious fields, to her most recent dancers, spinners, and horses in landscapes, Rothenberg has confronted personal emblems that appear to her as she paints. In an almost Proustian sense of naming, recognizing, meditating on, and looking back at what she has made public, triggering further private memories and painterly corrections, she transforms each subject's literal content into multiple layers of meaning. Following the materials she works with and the stretch of her own reach—both across a canvas and into the recesses of her own consciousness—Rothenberg has made some of the most authoritative and convincing paintings of our time. Her visceral, muscular canvases are about the complex, often serendipitous discoveries in making each painting and equally about a self constantly searching for definition, for truths, for envisioning and understanding the impossible.

Susan Rothenberg was born January 20, 1945, in Buffalo, New York, to Adele and Leonard Rothenberg, completing a typical, upwardly mobile, postwar American family of mother, father, son, and daughter. Her early years were "uneventful, quiet, protected, average, conventional," Rothenberg remembers; "you know, with a basketball net and skating in the backyard."[3] Her father was in the produce business and, by the time his daughter was in high school, had with his partners built the enterprise into a successful chain of supermarkets in upstate New York. Her mother, who had been head of the local Red Cross chapter, was a full-time homemaker and sometime watercolorist.

The young Rothenberg's talents for painting and drawing were recognized early, and she was encouraged by her parents, by family friends, and by teachers. "I think you often become what you are praised for when you are very small," Rothenberg once said, "and I think that was about the only thing I was praised for. I was not a real well-behaved child."[4] Her abilities were ascribed by her father to her mother's father, Papa Cohen, who was a housepainter, but her talents were fostered by her mother, who "provided lots of art materials."[5] Among them were paint-by-number kits, one of which—a so-called "bare-tit kit"—particularly sticks in Rothenberg's mind and is revealing both of the nervy, impish, and constantly testing nature of the child as well as the broad permissions granted by the mother.[6]

Among others in the close-knit family were an aunt who was a ceramicist and an uncle who was a veterinarian. As Rothenberg remembers, "That was another fantasy of mine. I always liked animals." Almost-family was her father's best friend, Dr. Joseph Rosenberg, who lived across the street and was an enthusiastic amateur artist. "From the time I can remember, I would ask if I could go visit. [Dad] would go over to have a drink with Dr. Joe and I would always [go to] see what he was doing in his basement studio. There was plastic sculpture, bronze sculpture, abstract painting, realistic painting. He would sometimes give me paint, give me canvas, give me stuff. Look at what I did. I'd bring back what I did there. And I think I worked there once or twice." Rothenberg would show him her paintings and collages. "He was big on collage—cigar labels, tinfoil, newspaper. The time I remember best was when he was sticking everything into his oil paintings. So I was doing that."

While Rothenberg was still in grade school her mother enrolled her in art classes at the local museum (since 1962 known as the Albright-Knox Art Gallery), which she attended with her friend Margie Hoffman. Unlike the classes, two works of art in the museum made indelible impressions: Rothenberg remembers "loving Gauguin's *Yellow Christ*—that was my painting—and a stone Buddha that was outside the museum. I used to cry to that Buddha, tell it all my problems," she laughingly recalls. "I would somehow get myself to the museum—get someone to drive me—and I thought this Buddha understood all my little problems." She also remembers seeing work by Daumier, and that she first saw Robert Rauschenberg's paintings and a Lucas Samaras mirror box there.

It is hard to imagine any other museum that could have provided the young visitor with the quality and breadth of the collections as well as the radically experimental works of the Albright-Knox. Available to her during her wanderings from the early 1950s through the late 1960s were collections that ranged from antiquity to European and American painting and sculpture and included all varieties of modernist abstraction—from the spiritual and organic to the nonobjectively geometric—as well as Surrealism, German Expressionism, Abstract Expressionism and the European CoBrA School, and the newest Pop and Color Field works.[7]

Rothenberg remembers doing as much art as she could in grade school—actually "smoothing [her] way into the art room," by convincing the art teacher to admit her, presenting herself as sweet and helpful, though she had actually been kicked out of her own classroom for talking out of turn. By the sixth, and for the seventh and eighth grades as well, Susan and her friend Margie joined a group of girls who studied with a neighbor, another friend's mother—on Tuesday evenings, doing charcoal drawings of fruit, cloth, and other still-life subjects.[8]

Rothenberg took none of the high school's art classes (she starred in theatrical productions and was a cheerleader). She did, however, take private lessons with the Hungarian realist Laszlo Szabo. The students had to draw *The Winged Victory*—and an ear and a nose and a plaster mouth—for a year before they could draw from a live model. "Just before I went off to college," Rothenberg remembers, "he was teaching us how to make a palette of red, yellow, blue, white, and some umbers, and he said you could make every color in the world you needed from these colors. I studied with him for two or three years. I only got one painting done before I left: the brass plate with an apple."

Toward the end of high school, Rothenberg considered becoming a veterinarian. "Then I heard what vet school was like and how hard it was. And I was a failure at math. I also realized that I probably couldn't handle doing surgery on an animal. Doing surgery was different from loving animals. I worked for my uncle for a summer and passed out during certain procedures." Instead, she pursued her interest in art and in September 1962 entered the Fine Arts School at Cornell University in Ithaca, New York.

During her freshman year Rothenberg took a variety of liberal arts courses as well as introductory art classes and became good friends with Mary Woronov, who over the years would figure in many ways in Rothenberg's working life—as colleague, sidekick, as well as almost alter ego and subject for some of her early paintings. The two students intended to be sculpture majors and shared a love of dancing. For a time they were both dancers at a local bar in Collegetown called the Alt Heidelberg. "For absolute fun. We were go-go dancers, with black net stockings. Because we thought we were such hot chicks." Rothenberg was also taking modern dance classes as a gym requirement and was encouraged by her teacher to join a performing group, which she declined. (As a child Rothenberg had also studied modern dance and ballet. "The dancing was always there, along with summer waterskiing," Rothenberg remembers. "I was always physically coordinated. And I enjoyed it. I always liked dancing of any sort.")[9] Among the other students she got to know were Michael Singer, Alan Saret, Gordon Matta, and Donald Evans, most of whom were studying architecture officially while actually pursuing their own art-making.[10]

Overall, the teachers and course work left little impression. The exceptions included a course on Proust taught by a Professor Grossfogel and two art teachers. One of them was Robert Richenburg, "whose encouragement," Rothenberg points out, "wasn't unique to me. He was the most positive person on the faculty." She also had "some contact with a strange man named Alan Atwood, who taught drawing classes mostly. Very strange Buddhist kind of guy. Unusual for the Cornell faculty. I remember auditing classes of his. He was teaching about drawing negative space. Teaching you to draw a figure by what wasn't around it—that was interesting."

During the summer following her sophomore year, she continued her sculpture studies at the State University in Buffalo. Halfway through her junior year, Rothenberg flunked a sculpture course at Cornell. She was hurt by the grade, and her reaction to the rejection was swift. "I got on my high horse and decided to quit school." With money she had earned waitressing and some financial help from her parents she left for Greece, where she spent five months on the island of Hydra. She painted a little but mostly experimented with expatriate life, which she decided "was too weird. All these expatriates, all these failed people. It wasn't going anywhere. Ultimately it was very hard to get art supplies. If I was intending to get serious, which I wasn't at the time, it was very hard to get anything there. There was also this intricate island life. Who was sleeping with whom. Drugs. It just seemed I had to get out of there. And so I went back to Cornell."

When Rothenberg returned to Ithaca, the head of the sculpture department, Victor Colby, refused to readmit her. "He said, 'You're not coming back into my department.' I said, 'I got an A in sculpture at Buffalo,' and he said, 'Go back to Buffalo, you're not coming back to my department.' I said, 'Why? I did all the work.' He said, 'I don't think you have any talent whatsoever and I'm not letting you into my department.' This is the first I knew there was any problem between us whatsoever."

The Rothenberg sculptures that had caused such aesthetic and personal offense were "cement alarm clocks with little teeth," Rothenberg recalls. "I was very influenced by Lucas Samaras then, and I saw his boxes with needles and spikes. So I decided to make some dangerous objects. I was making these clay alarm clocks with kind of teeth items—clay cast in plaster—coming off the face. Like a Surrealistic object."

What attracted her to Samaras's work was "it was just weird, obsessive. I probably related it to something Dr. Joe had taught me about collage. Samaras was putting yarn all over boxes and putting needles and pins into chairs. They were very homemade, handmade, obsessive-compulsive objects—and some had birds on them." Rothenberg's generalized sense of connection to Samaras's materials, imagery, and method belies her own more intuitive understanding of their import as well as her transformations of what she gleaned from them. As would become apparent in her later work, Rothenberg had an ability to create, with simple, almost innocent-looking images and intensely worked surfaces, art that could reach into the deepest recesses of her own consciousness and touch viewers in an equally profound way—at times hitting the rawest nerves.[11]

Perhaps the most significant event of her return to Ithaca, where she was accepted into the painting department, was her leaving again. She spent the spring 1966 semester in an independent-study program in New York City, sharing an apartment on St. Mark's Place with Mary Woronov, who by that time had dropped out of school to be a Warhol superstar, appearing in such films as *Screen Test, Hedy, More Milk,* and, later that same year, in *Chelsea Girls.* Rothenberg hung out with her a bit in the back room of Max's Kansas City, Warhol's own clubhouse within a hip artists' bar, went to the Factory a few times, and also remembers going to the Dom, a club on St. Mark's Place where Woronov and Gerard Malanga were performing their whip dance (as part of Warhol's multimedia production

The Exploding Plastic Inevitable).[12] Of the Warhol entourage, Rothenberg liked Malanga very much, knew Ondine and Brigid Polk slightly, but recalls that she "never established a relationship with any of them or with the scene. I didn't have the kind of personality that fitted in comfortably with the kind of dramatic personas that everybody adopted for the theater of Warhol life."

Rothenberg was painting in a studio on Union Square, but the emphasis of the program was to go and see as many art shows as possible. Paul Brach and Alan Solomon, who were the supervising teachers, told the students to go to Max's, "hang out a lot, and see if we were suited for this real New York life. So our homework was to experience the city: 'Go to museums, go to shows. What did you see this week?' All the teaching things were more about what was going on in New York than in our own little piddly work."

She pursued her interest in Samaras during that time and acquired an ongoing admiration for Larry Poons's dots—the ellipses. "I just thought they were completely beautiful paintings," she recalls.[13] Of the Minimal art that was coming to the fore, a Robert Morris box built at the Dwan Gallery remains singular in her memory: "The sculpture was the box and it filled the room, and you only had a small channel to walk around the box and then you had to go out of the gallery. And at first I thought, this was insane. This is ridiculous. This is great. This shoves you right to the wall. I really first got a hit of what Minimal art could be. Instead of seeming real passive to me, suddenly he was making a very aggressive object that forced you to the walls of the space."

The intense psychological pressure of Morris's piece and its visceral as well as theoretical demands on the viewer skewed Minimalism's tenets: his works were emotionally loaded even as they were structurally lean, making them exceptions to an aesthetic of primary form bared of subjective reference. In a similar way, Jasper Johns's impure version of Pop Art—his almost Expressionist handling of popular imagery and the autobiographical connotations of many of his found objects—an approach that also heated up a coolly procedural way of working and imbued his readymade subjects with enigmatic peculiarities if not outright personality, attracted Rothenberg. Johns's images and tangible objects "deserved to be," Rothenberg says, "in a way I'm not sure comics deserve to be painting. The Campbell Soup cans didn't do it for me." Johns's beer cans—the Ballantine Ale can sculpture, *Painted Bronze (Ale Cans)*, 1960, which Rothenberg saw exhibited—and his cast light bulb fascinated her. "Those had much more importance to me than Pop paintings. They must have had what I was looking for—that the work of Samaras must have had too—some kind of gravity and obsession." Johns "just transformed those objects into something that ought to be, that could be, that deserved to be a sculpture, somehow, and one wouldn't have thought it."

Beginning to inform Rothenberg's developing understanding of what art (and, by implication, her own work) needed to be was an obsessive relationship between maker and object matched by an ability to transform the familiar into something if not sublime than at

RUBBER BALLS
c. 1967–68
Aluminum and oil-based house paint on canvas
c. 8 × 5′

least oddly, surprisingly other than itself—something that might have an improbable presence, an eccentricity that was distinctly personal and that would also summarize an immediate, emotionally resonant moment. At its core was almost a moral imperative—words like *ought, could, deserved, needed* turn up regularly in her assessments of what constituted the rightness of subjects and the quality of the works she was attracted to. What was lacking for Rothenberg in the deliberate factuality of most Pop and Minimal work was a rawness, a psychological edge. "That part of Pop Art left me cold," Rothenberg has said. "I understood there was great gravity and seriousness to the Minimal sculptures coming up, but I still don't respond personally to them the way I do to, say, late Gustons, early Johns."

After the semester in New York, Rothenberg made up for her leaves of absence by taking a full year's work load per semester. She graduated in 1967 with a BFA and immediately asked her parents to give her a trip to Europe as her reward. She went to Formentera, an island off the coast of Spain. Her reasons for going were straightforward. "I felt I had come back before knowing what I was supposed to have learned the first time, and I really didn't know what I wanted to do here. I didn't want to go to school anymore. I didn't want to have a regular job. So I think it was seen by my parents as 'let her go one more time,' and it worked. I dragged water from a well, read books, lived with a crazy guy, and came back. I realized there was nothing out there for me to do as an expatriate."

Her memory of her stay in Spain, and of the late 1960s in general, is hazy. "I know I got to Washington, D.C., in the fall." When she returned to Buffalo from Spain, her parents realized she was lost and tried to help her get herself situated. They found out she could apply late to The Corcoran School of Art at George Washington University, which she did, and she was accepted. Rothenberg arrived for school in September 1967 but by November had dropped out. She remembers her teachers Ed McGowin and Thomas Downing visiting her in her unfurnished apartment studio once—but her connection to school, as she puts it, "just collapsed." She continued to live in Washington, D.C., drinking, going to a jazz bar every night, being very lonely and uncertain as to whether she might have had what she refers to as "it"—a nervous breakdown. She remembers almost nothing of the year (nor of the academic year 1968-69).[14] She does, however, remember three paintings she made and felt really satisfied with.

One was "about" a hundred balls in the air, a Poonsian atomization of incremental units in an expansive blue field for which Rothenberg used aluminum paint. The vertical canvas is barely divided on a diagonal with the balls in the upper-right section buoyed up by some clouds or air currents that are implied by whitish-blue underpaint. Each ball, based on the most ordinary of rubber-ball toys, was painted blue with two red stripes. The optical flicker of the multiple red stripes causes the whole blue upper-right section to blush red. The other two works were what Rothenberg calls "weird little suburban paintings." One of them depicted a simplified duck and a suburban house, with "a piece of air-conditioning filter" collaged as a cloud; the other had spray-painted sheep in front of a tract house. (In preparing this book for publication, Rothenberg titled them, respectively, *Rubber Balls, Screen Door,* and *Nine Sheep.*)

Formally, as Rothenberg remembers, "There was this half-and-half thing" in them—the way the balls occupied one half of the diagonally divided canvas; the way the horizon in the suburban paintings separated the top half from the bottom half of the canvas into sky and earth, home and animals, domestic and domesticated. "Even the paintings I did at Cornell had that. I did a black column on one side, a white column on another side. There's always been this dividing a painting symmetrically and then having it be asymmetrical. I didn't know whether I was being a smart aleck, commenting on suburbia—I suppose there was Pop influence in there somewhere with the idea of plastic storks on front lawns."

Looking back to these early works, Rothenberg notes: "I understand now wanting to keep this figure/ground thing and wanting to keep things up in the air and to have no ground lines; and I also picked a blue that I convinced myself was Giotto blue. I remember

SCREEN DOOR
c. 1967–68
Mixed mediums, including
collaged air-conditioner filter
72 × 60″

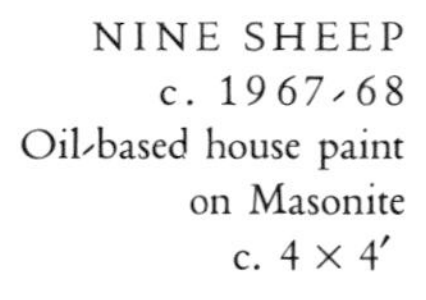

NINE SHEEP
c. 1967–68
Oil-based house paint
on Masonite
c. 4 × 4′

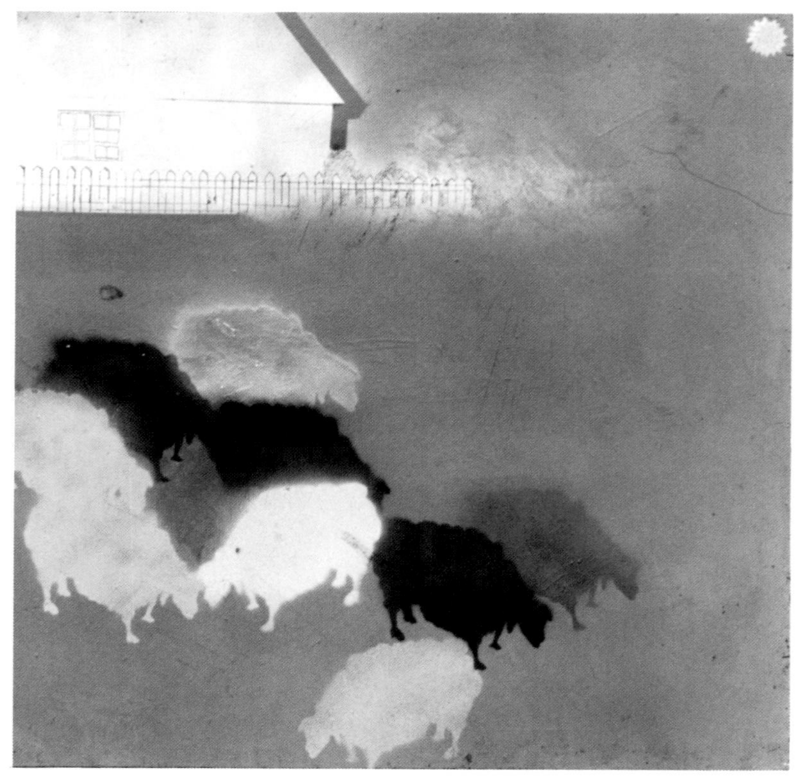

doing them. I remember their pleasing me. And I remember keeping those paintings around for a very long time, until they got moldy and rotted."

You can almost hear Rothenberg asking herself the most basic questions: What subject matter? How to compose? What colors? Whether commenting in her landscapes on her own comfortable suburban upbringing from the grittier surrounds of urban Washington, or finding comfort in the painterly space of the "hundred-balls" painting (and its echos of the works by Poons she so admired), Rothenberg had, with these three works, located the problems that would concern her for the next twenty years: autobiographical reference without explicit detail; imagery drawn both from outside sources and interior thoughts; reinventions of figures, which might take the form of animals, places, or things; arrested motion; a compositional sense that tackled the entire canvas while playing symmetry off of asymmetry; and a vocabulary of recognizable, simplified, abstracted images—fragments located *in* a place, often representing mementos *of* a place.

In these early works Rothenberg's signature palette of muted, almost monochromatic, colors, plus black and white, is evidenced. Also seen for the first time is her own personal blue, a color as hot as it is cool, which has turned up regularly during the course of her career. These blue works, which Rothenberg has referred to as "spirit" paintings (and which she has jokingly said are about as consistent as she gets), often function to summarize intensely important moments and tend to be predictive of new ideas and images to follow. In addition to associating the particular shade with an admired master, Giotto, the color has other, more personal associations as well. Rothenberg's blue connects to an early memory of a wish fulfilled. As a child Rothenberg was hospitalized for a tonsillectomy. She found herself terrified and trapped—almost encaged—in a crib she remembers as being too small for her. She cried for a blue monkey, and her Aunt Pearl managed to find one for her. Filtering such autobiographical information through a variety of imagistic and formal transformations would become the soul as much as the substance of Rothenberg's entire body of work.

When the Washington time "was over," as Rothenberg puts it, she formed a very "half-baked plan to go to the country, to teach English. I was actually heading to Nova Scotia for one reason or another." The idea and direction, she recalls, had something to do with her sitting around and looking at maps. She had heard enough anti-American sentiments during her two trips to Europe that "I thought I probably didn't want to be an American or part of American society." That sense of disconnectedness, of estrangement, a vague sort of unease, was tied to an intense personal isolation, however, rather than to any specific response to the multiple global, racial, and gender tensions that had already begun to politicize an entire generation, and that in fact sent many men her age to havens in Canada to avoid the draft. The year 1968 had become synonymous with violent traumas—of Vietnam, the assassinations of Kennedy and King, of street demonstrations and student unrest countered by police actions from Chicago to Paris—and resistance to authorities of all sorts. Yet Rothenberg's plan to move to Canada in the fall of 1969 was essentially apolitical; her decision allowed her to turn away from an isolating place and go to a familiar one, actually a second childhood home. "It was in the air. I felt comfortable in Canada, having summered there as a child."

She took her leave from Buffalo twice. The first time her trip was interrupted in Toronto by illness in the family (her mother had had a heart attack). After returning home for two weeks, she set out again, this time taking a train to Montreal for the connection to Halifax. During the six-hour wait between trains, an impromptu dinner with two hospitable strangers literally turned her around. Rothenberg returned to the station at midnight and changed her ticket to New York. "I think I was feeling very much alone. I think they must have turned me back towards people. I was going away from people. They played guitar and were kind of like hippies. And somehow the kindness coming from out there turned me back."

If the general direction was set, the particulars were puzzling. Rothenberg doesn't know why she decided on New York. She had lost contact with Mary Woronov and others she had known there during her undergraduate days. Furthermore, her memories of the city were frightening: there were too many late nights, too many drugs. But about a year before, she had run into Michael Singer at the Albright-Knox Art Gallery in Buffalo, where he was having a show of his plastic jewelry—"huge Plexiglas, chunky, strange jewelry. And he [had] told me to come [to New York]. He had bought a synagogue on Ludlow Street."

With her suitcase tied to a skateboard, she got off the train at six in the morning, completely shocked by her own impulsive about-face. She put her things in a locker in Grand Central Station and started walking downtown. At Union Square Rothenberg heard someone calling "Ya Ya," her college nickname, and, turning, saw an architect she knew from Cornell, John Stoumen. If one set of angels had set her in the right direction, here was another fortuitously welcoming her. He gave her the keys to his place, "a beautiful wooden house with plants and stuff," situated on the roof of a building at Sixth Avenue and Twenty-eighth Street. She stayed there for a while, and Stouman updated her on the whereabouts of some of their other friends living in New York. Alan Saret was gaining recognition for his dispersion pieces, cloudlike piles made of chicken wire, industrial steel mesh, electrical cables, and ropes, and for his cornice pieces—architectural fragments isolated as sculpture. Gordon Matta was also recycling urban detritus as well as cooking up vats of algae, pouring his medium into trays and displaying the dried remnants like disembodied skins. Through Matta she met Mary Heilman, who with a number of other artists was about to move to Chatham Square in Chinatown and who turned over to Rothenberg her loft on lower West Broadway. As Rothenberg characterizes the time, "My whole life began all over again."

"NEW YORK WAS A STATE OF GRACE. NEW YORK JUST SAID, 'COME here little orphan.' I met Alan Saret and Gordon Matta, and suddenly I had a home. It was kind of miraculous." Within a very short time Rothenberg was back in touch with a number of college friends—she stayed at Michael Singer's for a time—and through them she very quickly met a good part of the downtown art world, loosely interconnected circles of dancers, musicians, sculptors and performers. Among them were sculptors Nancy Graves, Richard Serra, Robert Smithson, and Keith Sonnier, musicians Philip Glass, Dickie Landry, and Steve Reich, dancers Deborah Hay, Joan Jonas, and artists who worked in multiple mediums, including the youngest practitioners, Tina Girouard and Neil Jenney, as well as the more senior artists Alex Hay and Robert Rauschenberg, and many, many others.

Though very much a loner, Rothenberg was surrounded by and absorbed into a life that centered in the lofts and bars of downtown Manhattan. And if she was immediately in touch with the breadth of possibilities surrounding her in the New York scene, she was also oddly connected with several generations of working artists through the history of her new home, which at various times had been occupied by Robert Motherwell, Richard Lippold, Richard Serra, and Nancy Graves. (Philip Glass, supporting his music by working as a plumber, had installed the toilet.) Her first impression of the place was seeing Mary Heilman's "strange, beautiful, weird process sculptures of thin sticks of clay on shelves with cotton puffs, like clouds, falling off them. I mean very, very funky work. It was presented in a way that it was almost part of the crumbling old building. And that was my first hint of the space—which was gray, peeling, falling down—a totally romantic, 800-foot loft with a huge wooden hoist in it from its time as a textile warehouse."

For a while Rothenberg was very involved with dance and performance, taking classes with Deborah Hay and performing with Joan Jonas. She met the sculptor John Duff and the sculptor/installation artist/painter Neil Jenney and, as she remembers it: "Suddenly I was in the midst of a very, very rich brew—cross-cultural winds floating in and out of all the spaces. It was a wonderful time. And, I had been a painter, although I didn't quite identify myself as such—I had no sense of making a real career for myself, but I soon realized these people weren't partying all the time and going to each other's lofts. They were actually doing work—so I got very involved in things like Process Art. I was looking at Eva Hesse, I was looking at Bruce Nauman, I was looking at John Duff—I was seeing the wryness and humor in Neil Jenney paintings and early paintings by Susan Hall."[15]

After the first few months of getting settled, Rothenberg began to make work inspired by what she saw going on around her—abandoning her interest in painting for a time and trying to figure out what her own kind of process-oriented method might be. She tore holes in plastic; cut holes from wire mesh, which she glued back to the surfaces from which she had subtracted them; and experimented with painted paper, silver paper, and clay paper. She tore bits of paper out and reglued them, following a set of procedures for placing them: "next to," "above," or "below." The pieces were "very formulaic but funky-looking things," she remembers. She started using polyethelene sheets, hanging them up on the wall and tearing segments out. These were the beginning for Rothenberg of "whatever the 'wholes and parts' were."

Throughout her career, Rothenberg has referred to her various series of works with pairs of words that often seem cryptic but that are usually literal descriptions of either the process by which the works were made or the images to be found therein. "(W)holes and Parts," which she finally titled the pieces made from September 1971 to summer 1972, is actually a punning combination of the two. (Later series are referred to by Rothenberg as "hollows and solids" and "Heads and Hands," for example.)

Overall gunmetal-gray fields, sometimes punched with holes, sometimes assembled by overlapping sheets, the (W)holes and Parts have affinities with the surfaces of Serra's lead pieces but also bring to mind various Sculpmetal casts by Johns. Despite Rothenberg's intention to work in a reductive, process-oriented, conceptual mode, these abstractions have a luminosity that diverges from both Serra's and Johns's deliberate opacity. They admit a sensibility and a touch that give them a romantic rather than a programmatic cast.

The last works in the series show that Rothenberg's explorations of process led her to more subtle variations of tonality and to increasingly complicated overall compositions and internal forms. Initially the pieces were titled with a series number and date. The later pieces in the series begin to have descriptively factual or associative titles, as would most of Rothenberg's later paintings.[16] In *Silverstreams,* January 1972, light seems to pour through the space, and in *Blackness,* March 1972, Rothenberg allows a minimal amount of linear white surface to show through, just barely signaling an outlined rectangular figure. With these and with *Single Splice* and *Multiple Splice,* both May 1972, Rothenberg's own sensibility begins to overtake her references to other artists' works and her rules. (She, like many of her contemporaries, had abided by the formalist painting program: maintaining the integrity of the picture plane by keeping the work abstract; referring only to the materials of its own making; and, above all, keeping the surface flat, that is, using no illusionism to disguise or deny the reality of a plane of canvas or paper bearing its skin of paint and distinguished from its surrounds by the specificity of its edges.) With the last works in her W(holes) and Parts series, an airiness pervades the overall surfaces, just barely adding a glimmer of depth to their otherwise flat fields.

Rothenberg supported herself by taking odd jobs.[17] She received some parental assistance with rent but was trying to get by on her own. As part of a process to separate herself from her family, to disengage from the double-edged ease/discomfort of taking money from them, and also to fit in with the funkier downtown scene, Rothenberg in a sense "orphaned" herself from them, and in fact began to develop a persona, which she has often referred to as her "Orphan Annie" act, a kind of down-scale camouflage designed at the time to put distance between her present and her comfortable past, and later, as she began to

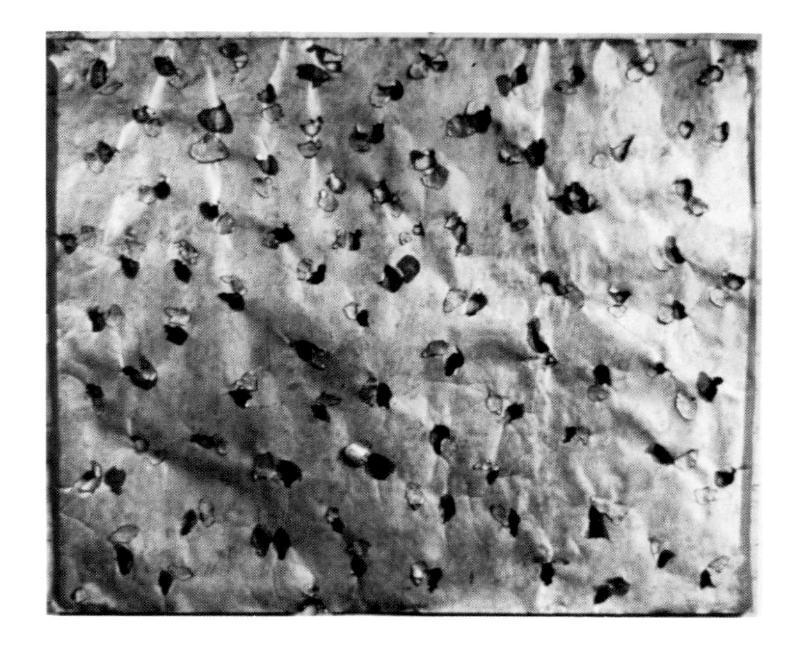

(W)HOLES AND PARTS #4
September 1971
Paper, glue, and aluminum paint
48 × 54″

earn a living from her work, to reduce any overt difference in circumstance between herself and her peers. She was in the center of things, right where she wanted to be, though it was a new and unfamiliar place and she wanted to fit in.

If the modernist impulse was thought to be a precise, linear direction in art-making, a formal and theoretical reach toward purity, reduction, and clarity, then a metaphor for the late 1960s–early 1970s break with the past was the circle, a social and geometric structure that was loosely encompassing rather than delimiting. Emblematic of the time, both in performance and at parties, was the Circle Dance, an inclusive, freewheeling, communal form in which any number of people could take part. Such a lack of formality also marked both the downtown studios and the stylistics of the artworks produced there. Emphasis was on real things, in real spaces, perceived over the course of real time—ordinary gestures deploying egalitarian materials—from readymades for art supplies to unisex work clothes often found in the industrial outlets and secondhand stores along Canal Street (the boundary between the newly named artists' quarters SoHo and TriBeCa).

The lack of a market for such works—nonart in appearance and often ephemeral—was viewed as a fact of the times; further, the very idea of art as a commodity was under fire. Artists and performers waited for no mediator, whether critic, commercial gallery, or collector, to validate work. The spirit was collaborative rather than competitive. Indeed, it was perhaps the very lack of an art market—as well as the widespread influence of dance and performance—that almost imperceptibly, though profoundly, altered the face of the art scene. So matter-of-fact was the exchange between men and women artists, dancers, and musicians, and the free-floating permissions to explore (and alter) what had been traditional men's or women's work, that the uniqueness of the 1970s in general, and the art

MULTIPLE SPLICE
May 1972
Woven canvas, laths, aluminum paint, and graphite
48 × 72″

world in its related ways, was not noticed particularly until the conservative shift of the 1980s brought commerce and its multiple discriminatory pressures to the dominant fore.

In 1969 and 1970 works were shown and performed in artists' lofts, like Alan Saret's—which hosted early painting shows by Jennifer Bartlett, among others, and performances by Joan Jonas—and other loosely collaborative ventures, the generically named galleries 112 Greene Street, 98 Greene Street Loft, and The Clocktower, as well as the restaurant called Food.[18] SoHo was the locus of much of the activity, although there were but two bars and commercial galleries. TriBeCa was also attracting artists, Rothenberg among them.

Post-Minimalism was the term that covered most of the process-oriented, conceptually grounded, three-dimensional works being made at the time. Taking in hand the cool geometries of Minimalism, and messing up its pristine surfaces, the procedural was no longer precisely serial or regularly systematic but allowed for mistakes as well as corrections. Horizontality called into question the authority of the vertical, while the distribution of elements could be overall but equally random or accidental, all of which allowed for the possibility once more of autobiographical incidents—and the evidence of the handmade.

Outright figurative works were not part of the downtown agenda, either in the dominant mode of sculpture or in the formalist, process-oriented abstract painting that still held sway. There were, of course, exceptions: three-dimensional body fragments in works by Johns or Nauman, for example, and live performers in dance pieces and a hybrid medium that would soon be called Performance Art, as well as documentation of those activities in still photographs, films, and videotapes through the newly introduced portable video camera.

The year 1969 also witnessed two exhibitions, at New York's Whitney Museum of American Art, that would both summarize the attitudes in the air and point to new directions. "Anti-Illusion: Procedures/Materials" included the works of the young old masters Robert Morris and Bruce Nauman, Eva Hesse and Richard Serra, while also introducing the beautiful immateriality of Keith Sonnier's neon-light works and the delicate surfaces of John Duff's sculpture. (Alan Saret was supposed to be in the show but withdrew shortly before it opened because of objections to its title.)[19] The show also included two artists who, in different ways, represented the interests of an even younger generation. Joel Shapiro transformed the monumental geometries of Minimalism to intimate scale and affective gesture for his dyed, monofilament wall piece. And Neil Jenney's installation included representational paintings of palm trees (not just painting but especially realist rendering was out of favor with vanguard artists, and these works were certainly an oddity within the show) with bowls of dog food set out below. The contributions of Shapiro and Jenney, though still within the purview of Process and Installation art, were the first hints that Conceptualism bred to craftsmanship and other traditional painterly and sculptural concerns would take contemporary art in a new direction (a decade later to be called New Image, also via a Whitney show).

Also in 1969 at the Whitney was an exhibition even more shocking to an art public somewhat used to the gritty informality of conceptual projects. Three of Nancy Graves's lifesize camels were seen in a solo show. These overall structural analyses, accurate in anatomical detail, from their matted hair to loping poses, were fabricated with the help of assistants in her New York studio. In one blow, a real, full-bodied figure was introduced.

Rothenberg was one of several artists, including the painters Harriet Korman, Jenny Snyder, and Mary Woronov, who worked with Graves fabricating the bones and fossils that she began to make after completing the camels. Having re-created wholes, Graves began a structural analysis of the component parts. "It was a complete factory, producing those parts of camel legs," as Rothenberg remembers the process of making the parts for Graves's *Variability of Similar Forms,* 1970, a freestanding grove of thirty-six isolated legs. "Nancy directed the work very well. She'd give you a couple of lessons, you know, how to make the marble dust and heat the wax. She always made the final decisions. And she liked the way Mary and I worked so we got to do more intricate knucklebone carvings and things like that. But we were also just wrapping wire and dipping things to get armatures. You'd fatten them up for her and then she'd get to work refining. She was finished with the real camels before I even got there," although, as Rothenberg recalls, "there were a couple of them in the studio getting unchunked and undone."

Rothenberg's response to Graves's work was as wide eyed and astonished as her response to other art that she was seeing. "I couldn't believe what people were doing. I had no sense of whether this was great or terrible. I just thought, this is far out. I knew Nancy was shown. I knew she had people's respect. I knew there was incredible drive and dedication there. I knew I was right smack in the middle of a brand-new wave of art-making."

Soon after assisting Graves, Rothenberg began to work with Joan Jonas and appeared in several of her performances. For Jonas's *Jones Beach Piece,* 1970, Rothenberg was rolled down the beach in a hoop, her arms and legs splayed and anchored like spokes, while other performers, also sited far from the audience, clapped wooden blocks together, creating a work that emphasized the rift between actions done (and seen) and sounds being heard. In *Mirror Piece,* 1970, Rothenberg was one of two pairs of performers leaning against each other with a sheet of plate glass sandwiched between them. As they moved, they slowly redistributed their weight so as not to break the glass. And in a piece called *Underneath,* presented at Alan Saret's loft in 1970, Rothenberg was one of a group of performers located in a pit built five feet below the floor; as they lay on their backs a sheet of glass was lowered onto them over which other performers tossed a bucket of water and rolled potatoes, while still other performers stood on the floor at the back edge of the open perimeter holding up large mirrors and shifting their angles so that the audience could see changing glimpses of themselves as well as bits and pieces of walls, floor, and ceiling incorporated into the totality of the work.

Jonas's works, like Graves's, were responding to the prevailing thoughts of the day but were significantly different in conception, in imagery, and in effect. Their works showed that any subject matter, no matter how unfashionable, could be employed, and they emphasized variability of similar forms (to echo the title of Graves's piece), a kind of humanity in repetition and thereby transformation rather than, for example, the machine-made aesthetic of reproduction and repetition that characterized most Pop and Minimalist art or the commonplace literalness of Post-Minimal distributions. In some ways these two contemporaries of Rothenberg extended the gravity and the obsessive reuse of the intensely personal found images that had attracted her to the works of Johns and Samaras. Probably most important, though, they showed that it was acceptable, actually necessary, to use body knowledge, a visceral sense of present and past memory together with formal concerns—whether in the hand-shaping of Graves's fossil-like bones or the internal sense of finding the correct weights and postures in order to maintain the choreographed images in Jonas's performances.

"I loved dancing and I loved rolling around naked on a mirror with Joan Jonas where the mirror might break and cut our bodies in half, and I loved the sound pieces she was doing at Jones Beach; but I guess I have a strong ego and whatever I was going to do—and I wasn't sure that I was going to be a painter—I had trouble working for someone else. I can take orders, but it couldn't go on indefinitely and I wasn't at some point where I wanted to break away and make my own performance pieces. It simply wasn't my arena—my talent. It wasn't my vision to do that. So . . . I don't remember the sequence that well, but in working with Joan I got to know George Trakas, who was building a sculpture and was also helping her build some of the structures she needed for her work, though I had actually met him in a Deborah Hay dance class. We went together for about a year, and at

Susan Rothenberg (in hoop) performing in Joan Jonas's *Jones Beach Piece,* 1970

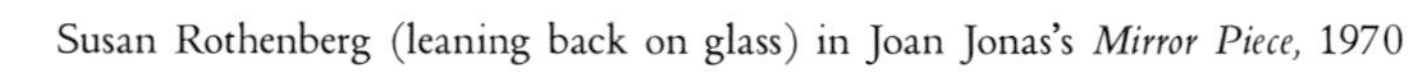

Susan Rothenberg (leaning back on glass) in Joan Jonas's *Mirror Piece,* 1970

some time during that time I got more serious. George is a very committed artist—very, very hardworking, and I was lucky enough to catch some of that ethic."

Rothenberg and Trakas were married at Manhattan's City Hall in 1971. They received a wedding gift of $6,000 from Rothenberg's parents, which Trakas insisted Rothenberg keep so that she could continue to have her own separate work space. (It was a considerable sum at the time; the rent on her studio was less than $250 a month and, in general, fixture fees for lofts—the cost of improvements made to these industrial spaces by previous tenants—usually amounted to no more than a few thousand dollars.) The two maintained a nomadic existence between the two living/working places until their daughter, Maggie, was born in November of 1972.

Rothenberg intensified her efforts as a painter with the birth of their daughter. "It was a way of maintaining my identity as well as being a very good sculptor's wife and a very darling child's mother. I had thought I didn't have any intention of making it a career, but I was isolated because I had a little baby and not many of my friends or any of the people in the art world were having children." In a way, the isolation was a very familiar place from which Rothenberg could work. Having the child, though, put serious constraints on her time and caused her to work in a more concentrated way.

She took her daughter with her to the studio each day and worked around the unpredictable demands of the child, which also necessitated a change in her materials. Rothenberg had been making her own pigments, trying to create a reddish earth color for some large paintings of rocks, but, as she tells it, "When you have a child and when the child cries you have to wash your hands, but then you don't want to put any strong chemicals on them." In experimenting with different mediums, she found that if she used acrylic she could mix sienna with white to get "that reddish, earth color, that sienna/clay, which was just the correct tone for me." The new paints also allowed her to stop and quickly wash up using soap and water rather than harsh solvents, and, since the acrylic dried quickly, when she returned to work she could paint over what she had already done. "So it just became part of my domestic mode to use that," recalls Rothenberg.

With her new materials and focused way of working, Rothenberg approached the end of experimenting with life-styles and testing procedures and materials derived from other artists. As she says: "I had been a playgirl or goof-off before, so the work got more serious when I was with George than it had been before. And I got a lot of support from him, as I had from John Duff, who I went out with before George. I started taking myself more seriously.

"I was cutting up wire mesh and tearing up canvas and using silver paint and lead like Richard Serra. Trying to bring along a Johns touch. It was all abstract work. I was apprenticing, which I think is a very healthy stage in anybody's development, and, as usual, I had reached a point where I knew what I was not. I knew that I was not an abstract artist. I mean, I find things out by stumbling on them. I'm not a clear thinker, but I find things out kind of after they happen, and I saw that I had done a series you could only call pattern painting, gray and green blocks, like checkerboards. And I realized that I had seen Alan Saret do it years before at Cornell. I was painting very similar works, but I didn't know that I was copying until I had seen six or seven of these paintings. I had to see if there was anything for me to do, if there had been anything for me to do, or it was for someone else to do—if it needed to be done at all. So I ditched it and drew a horse."

In 1974, while doodling on a small piece of canvas, Rothenberg intuitively began to draw a horse. When she saw the image that was emerging and subsequently decided to make paintings based on information she found in the sketch, she had a sense she was putting herself "right out of the ballpark in terms of the New York art scene."[20]

The horse itself is a very pale, washed-out pinkish earth color, a figure barely divided in half by a vertical line running down the center of a dirty scrap of canvas. There is minimal differentiation between figure and ground; both are painted with scumbly white patches and earth tones, their edges barely separating yet joining the two into a unified, flat territory. Rothenberg is not quite sure whether she used her own clay pigments or a mixture of pink and white acrylic paint or what she did to get at what she calls that "correct" color. According to Rothenberg, the format of the horse doodle evolved from her process pieces. In ripping her canvases, she had found the central line and subsequently decided to draw where she formerly ripped. What she drew on both sides of the divide, the simplified horse, she attributes to having some relationship to having worked with Graves.

In the doodle Rothenberg experimented with a number of other ideas, which she abandoned as she allowed the horse to grow bigger and the overall conception to become

FIRST HORSE
1974
Tempera, matte, flashe, pencil, and gesso on unstretched canvas
26 × 28″

simpler. One of the notions was that the image "related to a kind of cave painting idea," which was made explicit by adding some grayish arrows, "smudged around" on the rump of the horse and within other muscular contours, almost serving as vectors of mass and energy (and predictive in a sense of the geometries that Rothenberg would later use to emphasize the structural forces of the horses). "I was also getting a lot of talk about inside/outside from Duff," Rothenberg remembers, "and it was about Nauman's sculptures where he focused on inside, negative spaces for his casts. So I think my arrows were trying to see how I would do that—point out this is the inside; this is the outside." She also painted a white border around the whole field and "notched it à la Frank Stella." As she says, "I was trying to figure out exactly what a piece of canvas was and how to put an image on it and how to deal with edges and figure/ground and keep it flat—all the rules."

There had been a previous figure painting, immediately following the checkerboard paintings and preceding the horse doodle, which also featured simply drawn animal imagery on an overall field. *Foxes on a Hill,* 1972, painted in Rothenberg's curious deep blue, is poised right on the divide between the concerns from her college and graduate-school days—involving asymmetrical symmetry, halving the composition, pairing the images themselves—and what would become her signature concerns, recognizable animals and human figures whose spirit and movement are captured on essentially flat though energetically worked surfaces.

Barely noted in black paint on the overall blue field are two tiny foxes at the peak of a mountain, which itself is minimally delineated with one sweeping black curve. Sky, mountain, and animals share the same blue shade. With loosely gestural strokes that sometimes incorporate bits of black or white, Rothenberg unifies highly activated and

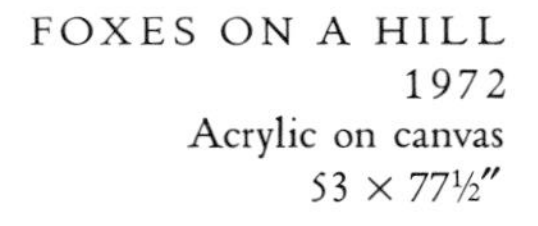

FOXES ON A HILL
1972
Acrylic on canvas
53 × 77½″

oddly differentiated patches. The edges detailing figure from ground are smudged and erased in places, allowing white canvas to show through or white drips to deny the edges even as they emphasize them.

The pair of foxes, caught in stop action as they race toward the descent, are so simply stated and innocent looking as to bring to mind illustrations from a children's book—Jack and Jill tumbling down their hill or a mother pacing her cub. They are grounded on the mountainside, which also appears to be floating in space, its orientation not unlike the vertical placement of elements in Chinese landscape painting, which denies reading in depth while signaling those very same spatial relationships. The overall image, its color, as well as specific passages, has a weathery atmosphere that recalls the abstracted airy locale of Rothenberg's *Rubber Balls,* c. 1967-68, with its drifts of cloudy whites. In *Foxes on a Hill,* the wispy white patches float above as well as simultaneously below the peak and on the mountain itself.

The change from the foxes painting to the horse paintings was a way of simplifying the issues, reducing the painterly problems to barest essentials, and allowing Rothenberg to stick more closely to "the rules." Though she would return many years later to the atmospheres, animated figures, and implied depths of the foxes painting, the horse—initially singular and standing at attention in strict, left-facing profile—presented her only as much information as she needed in order to accomplish the tasks she had set for herself. "The horse was a vehicle for me, I think in the same way Jasper Johns had to use his imagery," Rothenberg recalls. "I think it was a surrogate for dealing with a human being, but at the same time it was neutral enough and I had no emotional relationship to horses, so it really was a powerful object that divided asymmetrically but seemed to present a solid symmetrical presence. I needed something alive, I guess. I couldn't use an object. I'm not a still life painter. The horse was just a quiet image. I was able to stick to the philosophy of the day—keeping the painting flat and anti-illusionist—but I also got to use this big, soft, heavy, strong, powerful form."

As curator Ned Rifkin noted, in 1973 two of Rothenberg's contemporaries introduced the horse image into their work, also to invoke autobiographical reference. Both Joel Shapiro and Robert Moskowitz used the image tentatively, locating diminutive horses within expansive fields (the way Rothenberg herself had situated the foxes). Sculptor Shapiro's small, flat, wooden horse and its back-facing rider were mounted pictorially in profile on a large wall and then spray-painted to deny formally what the artist acknowledged as autobiographical subject matter. Moskowitz felt his own drawing of a tiny horse (and a blur of a rider) on a large, evenly painted field was a way of admitting a self into an essentially abstract work, and he explicitly titled his 1973 painting *Self-Portrait.*[21]

Rothenberg's approach was to allow the figure to share equal weight with its ground. Initially, she drew a skinny, doglike image floating in a similarly tentative space; the

UNTITLED
1974
Acrylic and
tempera on canvas
36 × 45″

second, though still a very awkward horse, was painted somewhat larger; and by the third, *Triphammer Bridge,* 1974, the size of the horse had increased to match her own height. "It interested me," Rothenberg remembers, "to put it to my scale, roughly five feet two—I don't know if it's exactly five feet two, but it's below lifesize. I've always had a strong sense of scale and that it should be a little bit different from what real-life scale is." By taking the horse image to her size, Rothenberg made them formally approximate with the self they were essentially mimicking. The painting matched her reach, her pace, her placement, her body language.

The idea of keeping the figure and ground the same color also came about from ideas of how she located things, including herself, in space. While driving to Jones Beach to take part in a Joan Jonas performance, she had observed that "Everything seemed to have the same color as the rest of the scenery. How can you tell one thing from another? Where does one thing stop and another begin if they're the same color? You would obviously have to have a line, or a bare white space. And I related that directly to the horse images I had begun to paint."

In part, it is this human scale that made the horses read less as animal than as anima—a vital life spirit captured within the horse's silhouetted contours and evoked through Rothenberg's brushwork. But there are other aspects to their making that give them a human presence. The horses lack explicit detail—or even abstracted renderings—of such horse parts as manes and tails. By using only the overall configuration of heads, necks,

TRIPHAMMER BRIDGE 1974
Acrylic on canvas
5′7″ × 9′7″

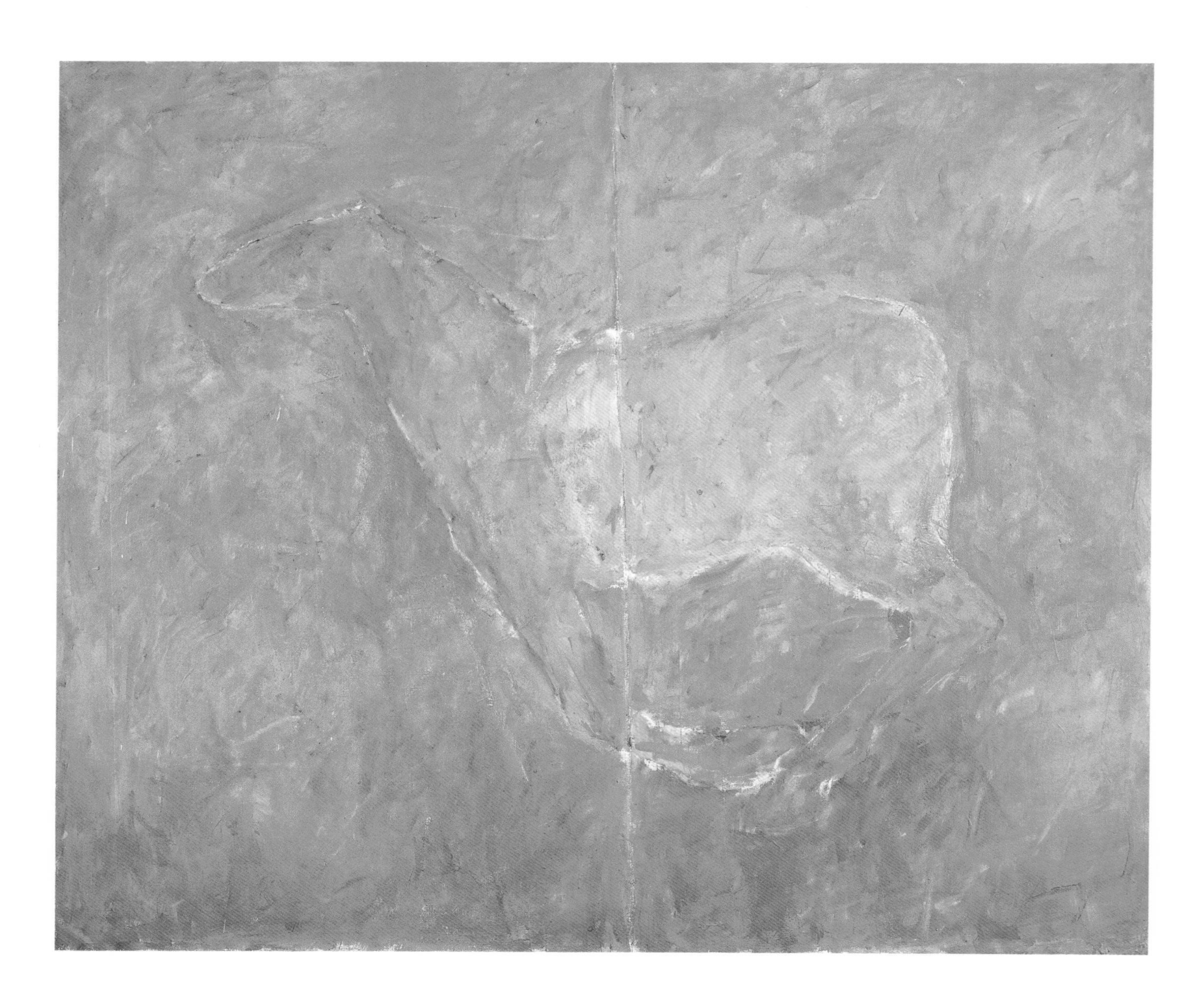

MUKUHARA 1974
Acrylic, tempera, and pencil on canvas
54 × 64″

torsos, and legs, Rothenberg reduced the overall shape to notations of a generalized figure. The human aspect of this horse figure began to become apparent to Rothenberg as one horse painting followed the next. After variations like *Non Mobilier, Mukuhara,* and *Triphammer Bridge,* all 1974, Rothenberg wondered what it would be like to do "a human being in the horse position."

Using as a model her friend Mary Woronov (who frequently worked on her own painting in Rothenberg's studio at the time and with whom Rothenberg also wrote an unpublished novel), Rothenberg tested the proposition. She took some Polaroid photographs of Woronov, nude, in left profile—alternately bending over, crouched, and on all fours. Using her sienna color, Rothenberg then painted from memory a canvas of each posture "to see if the human figure was as strange and compelling to me as the horse was. And it was enough to see that there was much more detail. I got more concerned with the articulation of the figure than painting and was having a hard time keeping them flat, silhouetted. Finally I had to stop it. I didn't do any more figures—that is human figures—in a horse position."

The untitled horse painting from 1974, however, is so close in presence, posture, and painterly surface to the three 1974 *Mary* paintings that it could be seen as part of the series; viewed in conjunction with the three human figure paintings, it also signals how close Rothenberg's image was to a human figure from the start.

Rothenberg was to test out the human figure in the horse position one more time before completely abandoning the idea. She took a series of photographs of herself, mimicking the postures that Woronov had assumed at her direction. Rothenberg chose not to follow up on these studies either. They do, however, serve to complete her own self-discovered version of Muybridgean studies as well as recalling several contemporaneous Conceptual, photographic, and film works (often called Body Art, a close relation to both Performance and Narrative art) in which artists used their own bodies as terrain for analytic scrutiny and material to be manipulated.[22]

Rothenberg continued to take her horse through its paces by giving herself a set of problems, which she verbalized as "What if?" What if it was divided in half? What if side bars locked it into place on the field (*North Wall,* 1976)? As she gained confidence in the image, she allowed it to fully take up its frame, sometimes doubling the horse by depicting two different animals (*Stable,* 1974) or by adding shadows that implied a second horse—or that were actually pentimenti, memory traces of reworkings of the first—creating a third kind of space that was neither figure nor ground and, not incidentally, that offered into her work intimations of depth while paradoxically serving to keep the image as flat as the canvas surface it was painted on (see *Layering,* 1975, page 41). As the horses picked up speed and started to be depicted in stride and full gallop, Rothenberg tightened her geometries, almost as if to rein her horses in—to keep them tensely within their fields and formal parameters. Occasionally, she painted an X across the entire image, as in *Double*

MARY I
1974
Acrylic and tempera on canvas
46 × 78″

MARY II
1974
Acrylic and tempera on canvas
46 × 78″

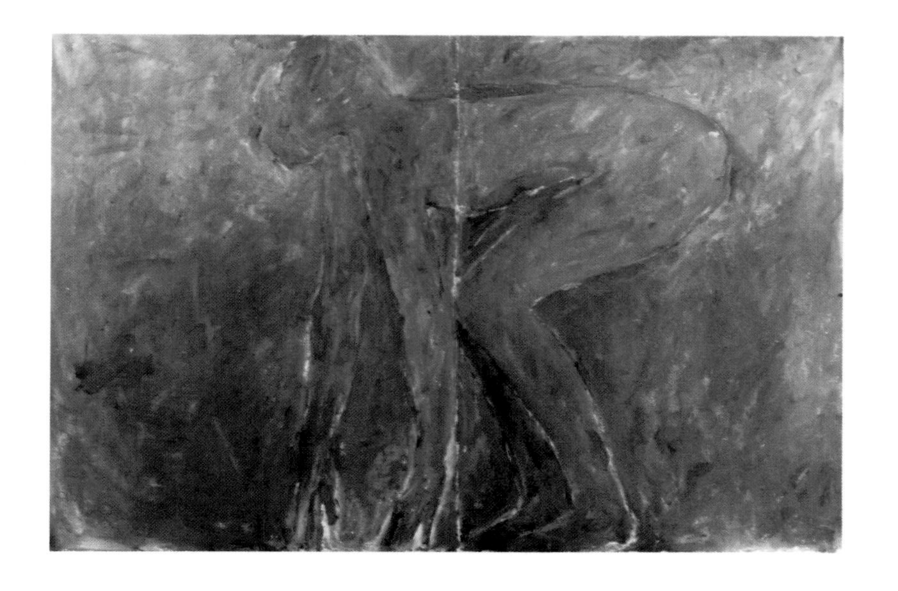

MARY III
1974
Acrylic and tempera on canvas
44 × 66½″

Test photographs,
Susan Rothenberg, 1974

Measure and *I x I,* both 1977, and in *From Buffalo,* 1976-77 (pages 54-56), not to cancel it out in the manner of painters Cy Twombly or Pat Steir, for example, but to emphasize the structural lines of the horses while also locking them into place.

Working with a small brush on a canvas tacked directly to the wall, Rothenberg used no underdrawing or any other preparatory sketches for the horse paintings. For Rothenberg, making drawn works on paper is a parallel activity to painting, though many of the drawings reprise similar ideas and compositional configurations (see the untitled horse drawings from 1976 on page 48, for example). The differences between Rothenberg's paintings and drawings might best be described in terms of two opposing sculptural techniques. The paintings are built up additively, while in her drawings, Rothenberg allows negative space to imbue and define her figures. Rothenberg has, however, often found the germ of an idea for a whole cluster or family of paintings in informal pencil sketches on the backs of envelopes or while doodling in crayon or with paint on small pieces of canvas, as was the case with the horse image.

Confronting the canvas and seeing her image emerge as she tackled each increment of the surface, Rothenberg used a touch both forceful and free. Drips remained where they fell, as did her evidence of stops and starts. She has often said she works "correctively," a method of painting over and fixing images as she progresses on a particular work. Moving back and forth almost like a fencer, hitting the canvas hard to make her marks, she retreats to see what she's done and often spends considerable time in the studio just being with the painting, sitting in a rocker reading a novel and glancing back to check the work in progress.

The overall impression the horse paintings made at the time was one of familiarity—of a recognizable, emotional, warm presence, an expression that was as subtle as it was direct. Akin to cave paintings in their totemic imagery and in their tonality, these works also bore a resemblance, despite their overt figuration, to the more cerebral control of Color Field abstraction. Indeed, Rothenberg's work was considered a bridge between generations: her serial permutations and evident geometries kept her Expressionist impulse in check; yet her images were undeniably powerful and evocative even as they so fully merged with and were integrated into their abstractly lush surfaces. Within each work Rothenberg intuitively linked, indeed synthesized, the polar concerns of the two branches of Abstract Expressionism, joining the often figurative impulse in the gestural, self-revelatory actions of Pollock and De Kooning with the geometrically Minimalist auras of Reinhardt and Newman.

Triphammer Bridge, 1974, was the first of Rothenberg's paintings to be exhibited publicly. Its title comes from "semiconscious, unconscious, preconscious" reactions to what she saw before her. "I was aware that the horse was bridging the center line. . . . I thought of bridge, and 'Triphammer Bridge' was the first name that came into my head," recalls Rothenberg. "It was a bridge over a gorge in Ithaca that I used to cross all the time.

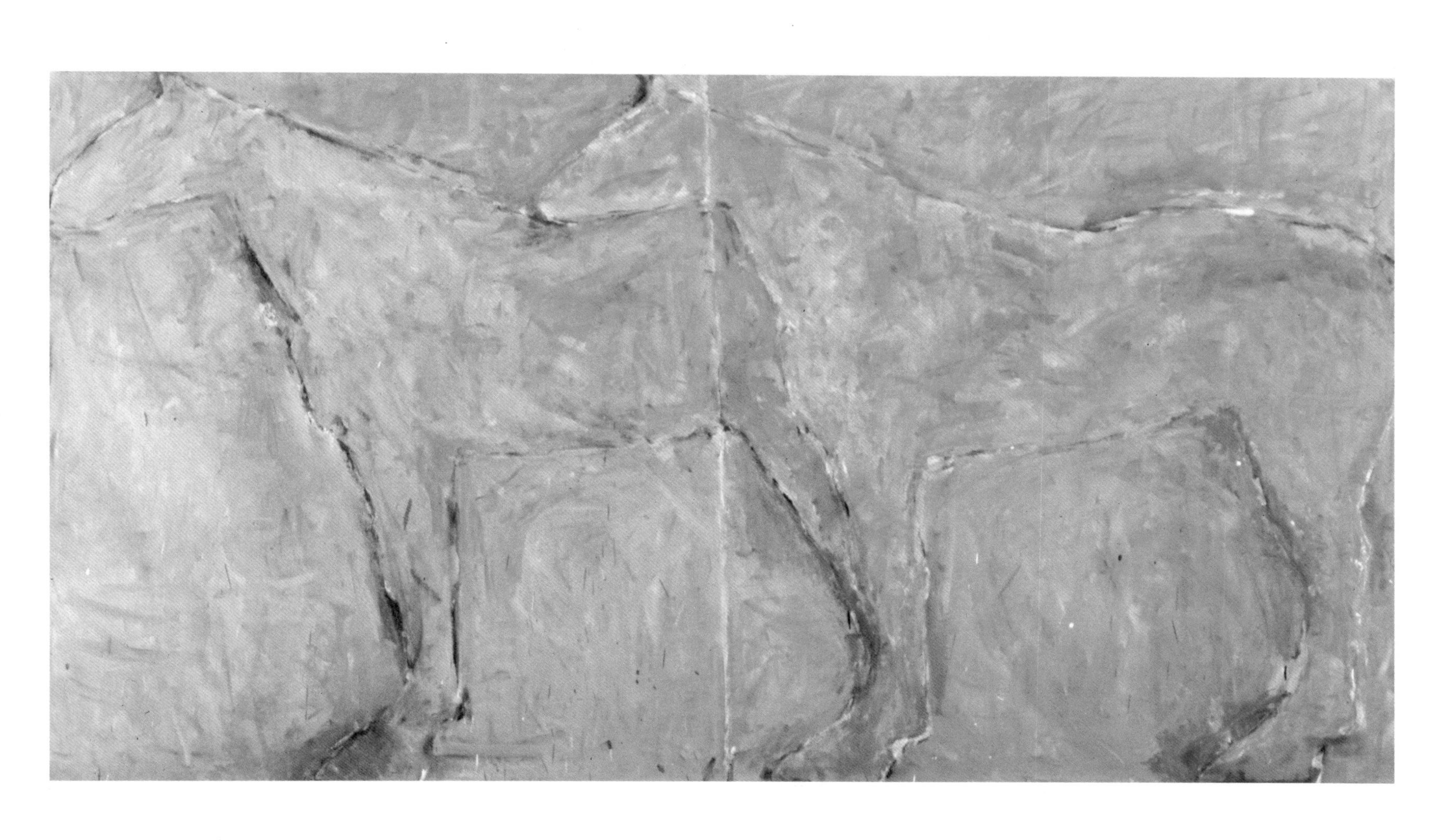

STABLE 1974
Acrylic and tempera on canvas
5′8″ × 10′

WHITE ROBE
1974
Acrylic and
tempera on canvas
64 × 86″

And the head looked like a hammer, too." Rothenberg's method of allowing an image to surface and her subsequent thoughts connecting image to memory to reality—an internal dialogue comparing what she sees and what she knows—is thus an open-ended reckoning of the private and the public. This process is subsequently shared by the audience for her paintings, who at times find in one of her canvases what Rothenberg herself has seen, as often as not finding there something unobserved (as well as unintended) by the artist.

Triphammer Bridge was included in a spring 1974 "New Talent" show at A. M. Sachs Gallery on Fifty-seventh Street, to which Rothenberg had been recommended by a neighbor, the painter Power Boothe, who was represented by the gallery. The painting sold to collector Holly Solomon and was also mentioned in reviews, yet Rothenberg was very disappointed to learn in the fall that the gallery was not going to take her on.

Each painting dictated its own rules, which began to change radically from work to work, from the small, sprightly *Mukuhara,* 1974, suspended in a single bound in midair and midfield, with the barest hint of a vertical divide in its overall sienna surface, to the almost sheeplike image in *White Robe,* 1974, whose blanket appears as a woolly coat. In *Double Masked Heads,* 1974, as its title states, the artist covered the horses heads, subsuming the minimal amount of imagery given. For the most part, Rothenberg used the bare outline of a horse, taking it through formal paces. "The horses suggested so many possibilities of working out these figure/ground relationships. I suppose, though, it's a lot of psychological and personal material."

DOUBLE
MASKED HEADS
1974
Acrylic and tempera on canvas
65 × 78½″

Holly Solomon gave a party to celebrate *Triphammer Bridge* and its maker, and it was there that Miani Johnson, the director of Willard Gallery, first saw Rothenberg's work. After visiting her studio, Johnson offered Rothenberg a solo exhibition. About the same time, Jeffrey Lew, the ringleader of 112 Greene Street, also offered Rothenberg an exhibition. Rothenberg, not yet thirty, was exhilarated by the prospect of two shows, which began to assuage the disappointment of not being asked to join the Sachs Gallery.

It was rare for a painter to show at 112, a regular site for performances by the Grand Union, concerts by Glass and Reich, for example, and installations by Trakas or Matta, who cut through the floors of the space itself, or Bill Beckley, who installed live birds among the rafters. Another friend of Rothenberg's, theatrical designer Bill Katz, encouraged her to do a site-specific project for the space, and she got an "enormous amount of canvas [and] simply proceeded."

Between May 1975 and the opening of the show in October 1975, Rothenberg did three schematic paintings. They were as she planned them, roughly ten by twenty, ten by fifteen, and ten by ten feet. The longest, *Siena Dos Equis,* centered one horse in the elongated field, which she nevertheless bisected into her two more familiarly proportioned rectangles, treating them with their own internal geometries; each rectangle is inscribed with an X. The middle-size painting, *United States,* also bisected the horse—approximately equal in size with the field this time—though one half of the figure is located on a sienna ground and the other on black. And the smallest, the ten-foot-square *Algarve,* depicted but the front half of a horse, outlined in black on a white field. There is something rather comical to this last, also monumental painting. Having halved her utilitarian rectangle, Rothenberg halved the image as well, providing only that portion of the horse that could tightly fit this new format.

The following April Rothenberg had her first solo show at Willard Gallery. Many of the horses in these paintings were depicted in highly improbable if not impossible postures. In *Layering,* 1975, for example, Rothenberg superimposes one horse on another yet has the two sharing one set of forelegs, a confusion of image that in Rothenberg's painting reads as a factual norm. In *North Wall,* 1976, the horse's front half is in a gallop while its hind end is in a stance. Locating their divisible weights and dimensions and locking them into position in her rectangular fields—"parqueting them," a designation she borrowed from the carpenter's term for locking pieces of wood together—took precedence over anatomical accuracy.

Flanders, 1976, whose blackness envelops both figure and ground, is barely detailed within its white outlines. Yet the horse is pushed and pulled both by subtle geometries and distortions of the figure—all within a calm and contained space. The horse's nose presses toward and almost reaches the left edge of the canvas, just over the left vertically painted sideline—while its back half is boxed into the central field by the right sideline, which also functions to keep the horse barred from the right edge of the painting. Its oversize hooves, though, solidly anchor the horse to its bottom-most edge. (Perhaps the most problematic part of Rothenberg's minimal attempts at verisimilitude were the hooves—and, though she once went to observe the police horses at City Hall Park, the hooves kept getting bigger and bigger, despite her cursory attempt at research.)

Hilton Kramer's review in the *New York Times* was the first of many heralding her accomplishment. Kramer declared hers "uncommonly impressive work by a painter having her first uptown solo exhibition" and called her "a painter who we are likely to hear a good deal more about."[23] All the paintings sold. Yet despite being pleased that she could begin to support herself from her work (the highest price of one of her paintings at the time was $1,700, of which she received 50 percent), Rothenberg remembers that both the reviews and the sales "caused an estrangement from myself by what had occurred, which was a kind of instant success."

The Kramer review in particular put Rothenberg in a double bind. Wanting to be taken seriously by her colleagues downtown, she "got the impression that if an establishment critic like Kramer liked the work, you should really feel bad about it." She also began to think that "Kramer had sold the show and I hadn't." In addition, she received little reaction to or comprehension of her work by fellow artists.[24] Yet her overall reaction to the critical acclaim the show received was blunt and self directed: "I began to take what I did in the studio much more seriously because at that point I'd already started competing with myself to see if I could pull this off again."

LAYERING 1975
Acrylic and tempera on canvas
66½ × 82½″

UNITED STATES 1975
Acrylic and tempera on canvas
9′6″ × 15′9″

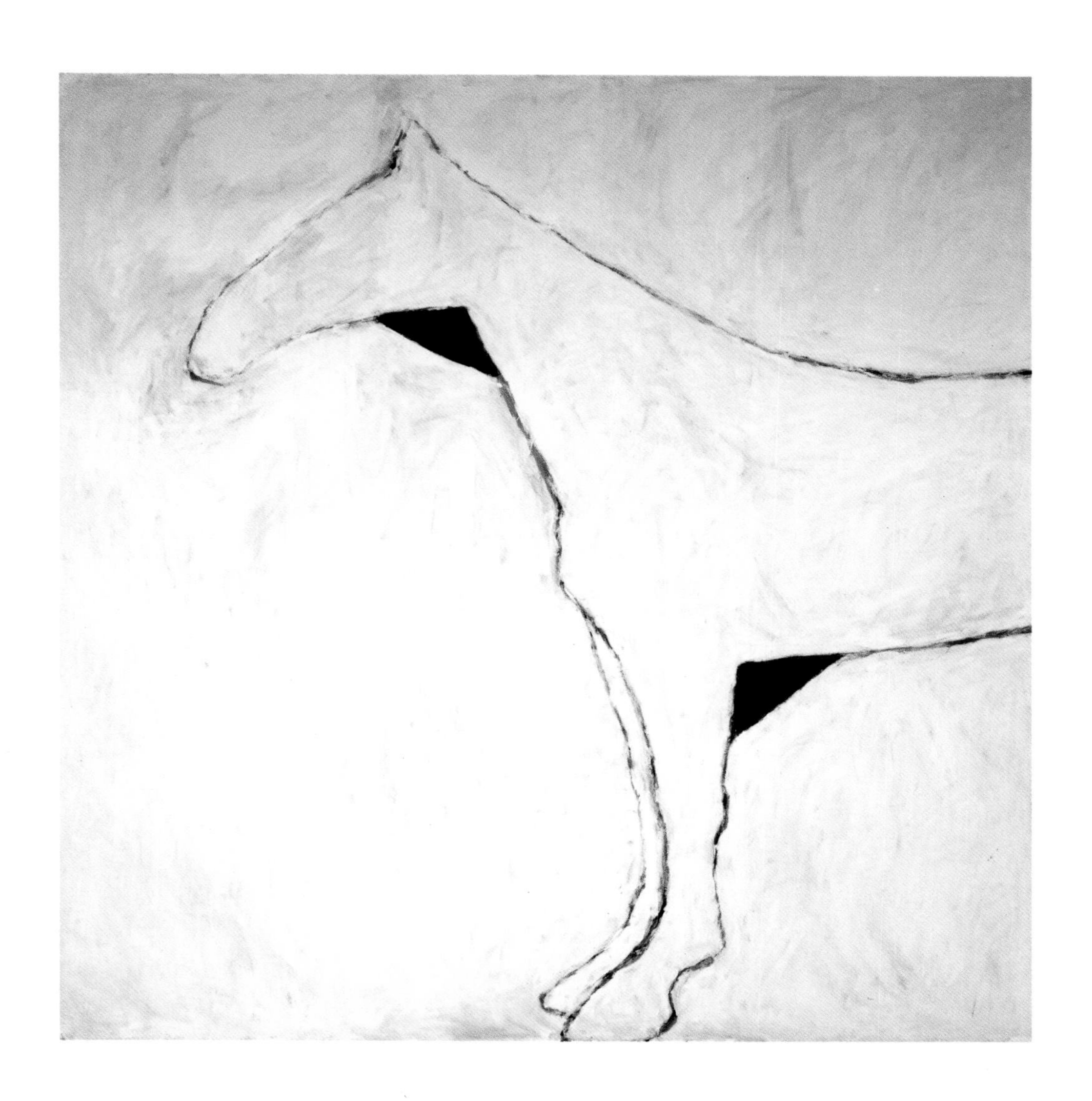

ALGARVE 1975
Acrylic and tempera on canvas
9′6″ × 9′3″

FLANDERS 1976
Acrylic and flashe on canvas
$65\frac{3}{4} \times 98\frac{3}{4}''$

FROM THE OUTSET, AND OVER AND OVER DURING THE YEARS THAT followed, Rothenberg has been continually asked the obvious question, "Why horses?" And her responses have ranged from formal discussions of figure/ground issues, frequently citing Johns's use of imagery as referent, to both acknowledgments and deflections of their implicit mythical, psychosexual, and literary content.

One of her best answers to the question is also one of the simplest: "Well, I can't picture these paintings as giraffes." In the next breath, she complicates that response in a very telling way: "I don't think it could have been an inanimate object either. I like tension. To take something that had implied motion and not use it in that way; to have something that was volumetric and to not use it in that way—there is a certain perversity in the way I use imagery. I don't know if that's the right word, but I have to take something and redigest it and reinterpret it for me to get hooked on it—to get into it."

Curiously, from the time the first horse paintings were shown until 1978, when the images began to break apart under and actually began to reveal, in a rather explicit way, the psychological and emotional freight they had been carrying all along, the blatant image of a horse as well as the perversity of its handling and multitude of issues implied were side-stepped if not completely ignored by critics. Because her works were boldly, plainly, and unembarrassedly painterly, it was Rothenberg's authoritative handling of her lush, overall fields that was seen first and foremost. Rothenberg herself offered no theoretical, ironic, or programmatic underpinnings, or any language whatsoever to interpret them precisely.

The fact that Rothenberg's paintings were equivalently abstract and representational, geometric and organic, formal propositions and emotional evocations, expressionistically inflected while maintaining the flatness of field painting, actually invited a range of interpretations, whether one focused on one or a combination of these properties. There being no immediate precedent in painting for her approach, Rothenberg's work could conveniently be seen as the link between Minimalist reductions and systematic permutations and figurative, Expressionist painting: she took the next logical step of barely adding abstracted imagery to overall reductive fields. Furthermore, her palette was not so far from the tonality of Post-Minimal installations or earth-art projects as to signal traditional, full-color painting. Exactly what Rothenberg added back was seen to be less important than what it was added to. As Kramer wrote, "To say that [this exhibition] consists of horses would be literally correct, but somehow misleading. For it is the quality of the painting that is so impressive—the authority with which a highly simplified image is transformed into a pictorial experience of great sensitivity, even grandeur."[25]

But there were horses, and they were her horses, initially evoked automatically onto her first sketch and later formally probed and poked, placed and displaced. With the horse form, Rothenberg could incorporate all that such a mythical symbol implies while at the same time use it to project something indefinably more: an ambience, a presence of something immediately known and familiar. The image was recognizable by the briefest

JIS 1975
on canvas
0"

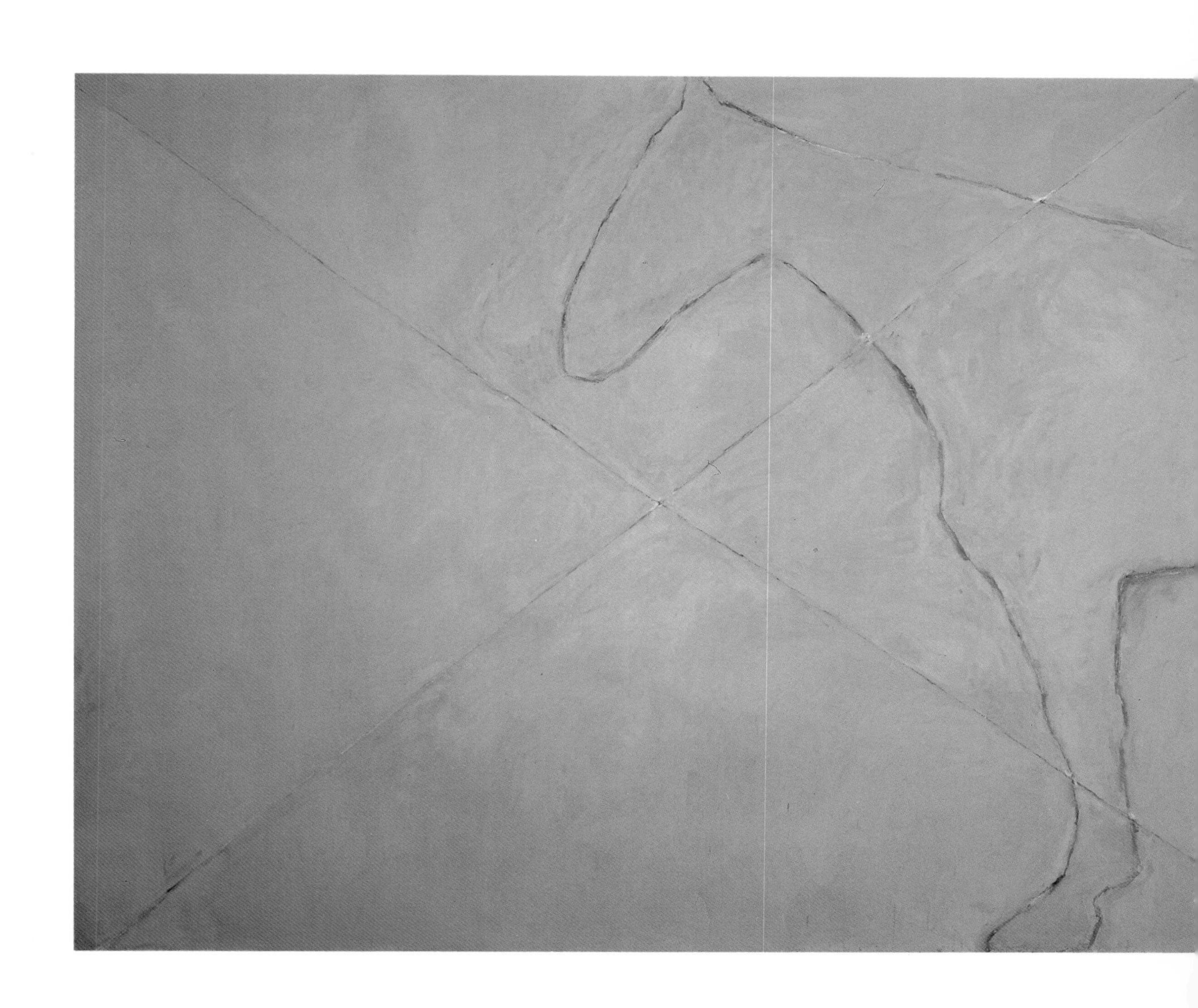

SIENA DOS EC
Acrylic and tempera
9′6″ × 22′

UNTITLED
1976
Acrylic and tempera on paper
39¼ × 50″

UNTITLED
1976
Acrylic and pencil on paper
38½ × 50″

contours, yet its presence was known in the intuitively visceral way that one recognizes someone from afar or at dusk—by the barest notions of silhouette or by the rhythm of a characteristic gait. As Carter Ratcliff later wrote, "They seem to bear some charge of private meaning to her, and not for her alone. Others are drawn to these mysterious creatures as if to half-remembered totems of another time."[26]

By the mid-1970s, when Rothenberg was showing her horse paintings, animal imagery and the ritualistic behaviors and shamanistic relationships between man and animal were also being explored in New York galleries, though in live performances. Joseph Beuys, for example, presented himself with a live coyote for several days in 1974 at the Rene Block Gallery in SoHo. Both man and beast were caged behind a wire-mesh grate through which the audience could see Beuys, amid newspapers dispersed on the floor, holding a crook and bowing toward the animal. In 1975 Jannis Kounellis sat astride a live horse in a corner of the Sonnabend Gallery, whose walls were painted yellow and illuminated by flickering wall-hung lamplight.

This is not to say that Rothenberg shared the specific concerns of these artists—in fact, in the early days she herself always located her own work in formalist terms—but rather to suggest that art-making itself was changing significantly by the mid-1970s. The figure, whether live or invented, was increasingly present, and was often used to focus on the kind of mythological-poetic subject matter that Rothenberg, despite her formal intentions, had incorporated in a de facto way. At the same time, many feminist artists were also approaching the issues of ritual and identity, searching back into primitive symbols to inform their art with both an immediacy and a connection to a larger past involving an intimate entwining of self, nature, and culture, as had many of the Arte Povera artists since the 1960s.

The kinship between Rothenberg's painted images and these other works rests primarily and significantly with her own history in performance. It is this sense of the body doing an action—whether in the arena of painting or the extended field of sculpture, installation, and performance—that critically informs Rothenberg's work and that continued to set hers apart from contemporaneous explorations of representation in painting.

Rothenberg had, at times, looked to sources beyond her invented images. One example was the testing of her "cave painting" idea in the first horse doodle. Another was looking to Native American sand painting for *Four Color Horse,* 1976. After geometrically targeting her horse with an X, she filled each triangular quadrant with a separate color—red, yellow, white, black—filling in the areas with a palette that was similar to the temporal placement of colored sand on ground.[27]

By the time of her second gallery show in 1977, Rothenberg had hit her stride. She seemed at ease with the momentum loosed within each canvas, and her variations on the horse motif, as in *Axes,* 1976, seemed more fluid while her geometries were more subtle and sure. Further, neither her images nor her conflation of abstraction and representation

FOUR COLOR HORSE 1976
Acrylic and flashe on canvas
5′7″ × 9′4″

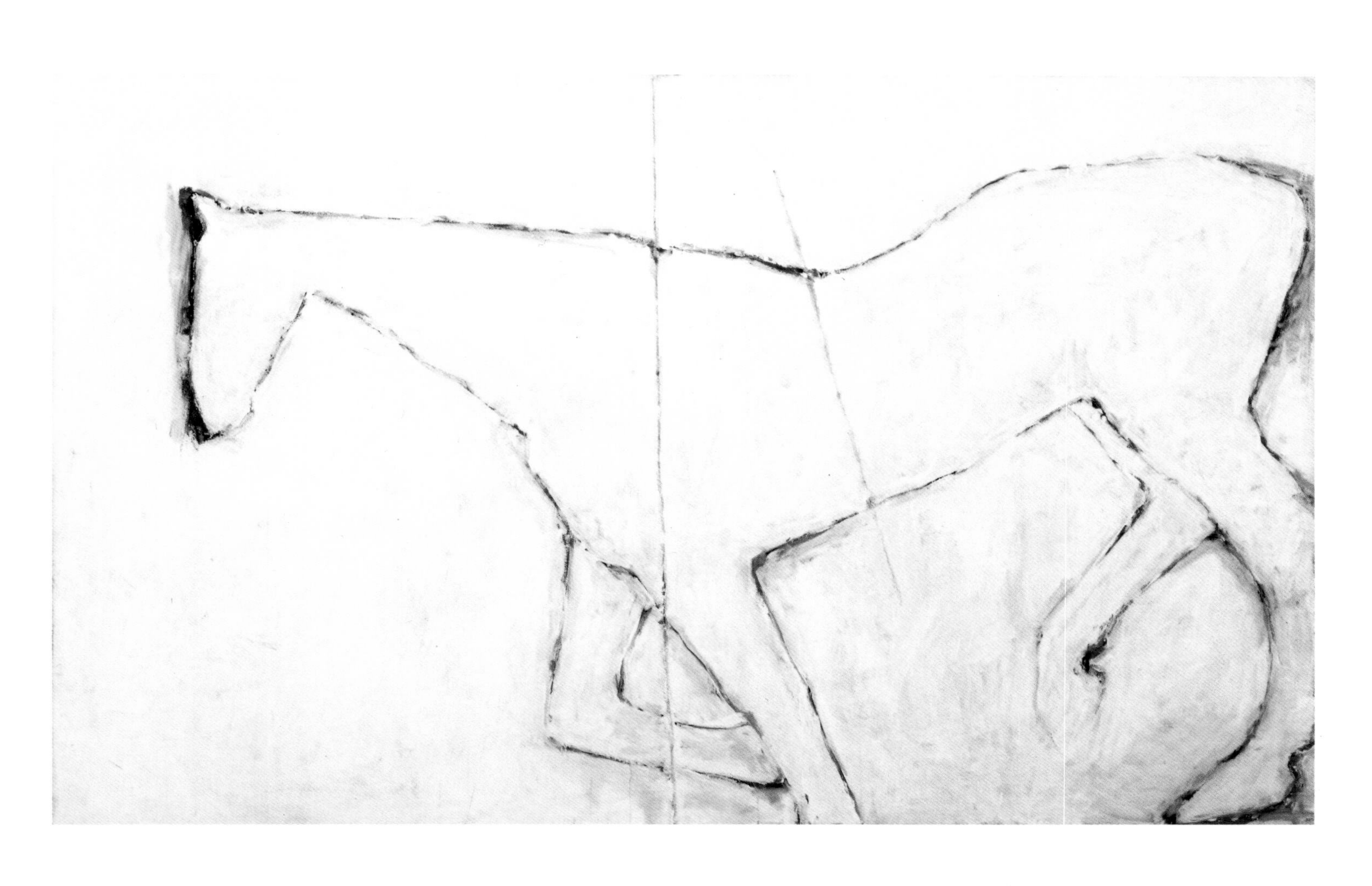

AXES 1976
Synthetic polymer paint and gesso on canvas
5′4⅝″ × 8′8⅞″

seemed so eccentrically novel, as a number of artists, independent of each other, began to exhibit their explorations of abstracted, simplified images. Indeed, the idea of painting itself had returned to center stage. The first museum show to report on this sensibility in art-making, and to give it a lasting name, was "New Image Painting," curated by Richard Marshall at the Whitney Museum in 1978.[28]

Rothenberg was represented in the New Image show by some of her most iconic horses—*United States* and *Layering,* 1975; *Butterfly* and *Flanders,* 1976; and *Double Measure* and *I x I,* 1977. Though all the artists' works were more different from one another's than alike, Rothenberg's stood out from the rest on several counts. Hers were warm rather than cool, painterly rather than illustrational, intuitive rather than conceptual. Most of the

Installation
Willard Gallery,
New York, 1977
Left to right:
Double Measure, 1977
Axes, 1976
Scat, 1977
Untitled # 44, 1977

artists either isolated small images in large fields (Robert Moskowitz, Denise Green, Nicholas Africano, Neil Jenney, Lois Lane) or built large fields from small, often eccentric or conceptually derived increments in or on which they located their images (Joe Zucker's paintings exchanged cotton balls for paint strokes; Jennifer Bartlett's room-size installation was an ensemble of simplified geometric shapes and abstracted images painted on 987-foot-square, gridded, enameled steel tiles).

The New Image show was valuable in many respects, not the least of which was to report on an idea that a number of artists were exploring in isolation from each other even as the ideas were themselves being tested by the artists.[29] It was also useful in demonstrating the great variety of approaches within what became known as a stylistically cohesive group, and in officially declaring that painting was no longer dead but in fact was loosened from the strictures of what had become almost a formalist academy. The field of painting

BUTTERFLY 1976
Acrylic and matte medium on canvas
69½ × 83″

Susan Rothenberg with
From Buffalo, 1976-77,
in progress

FROM BUFFALO
1976-77
Acrylic on canvas
61 × 77½″

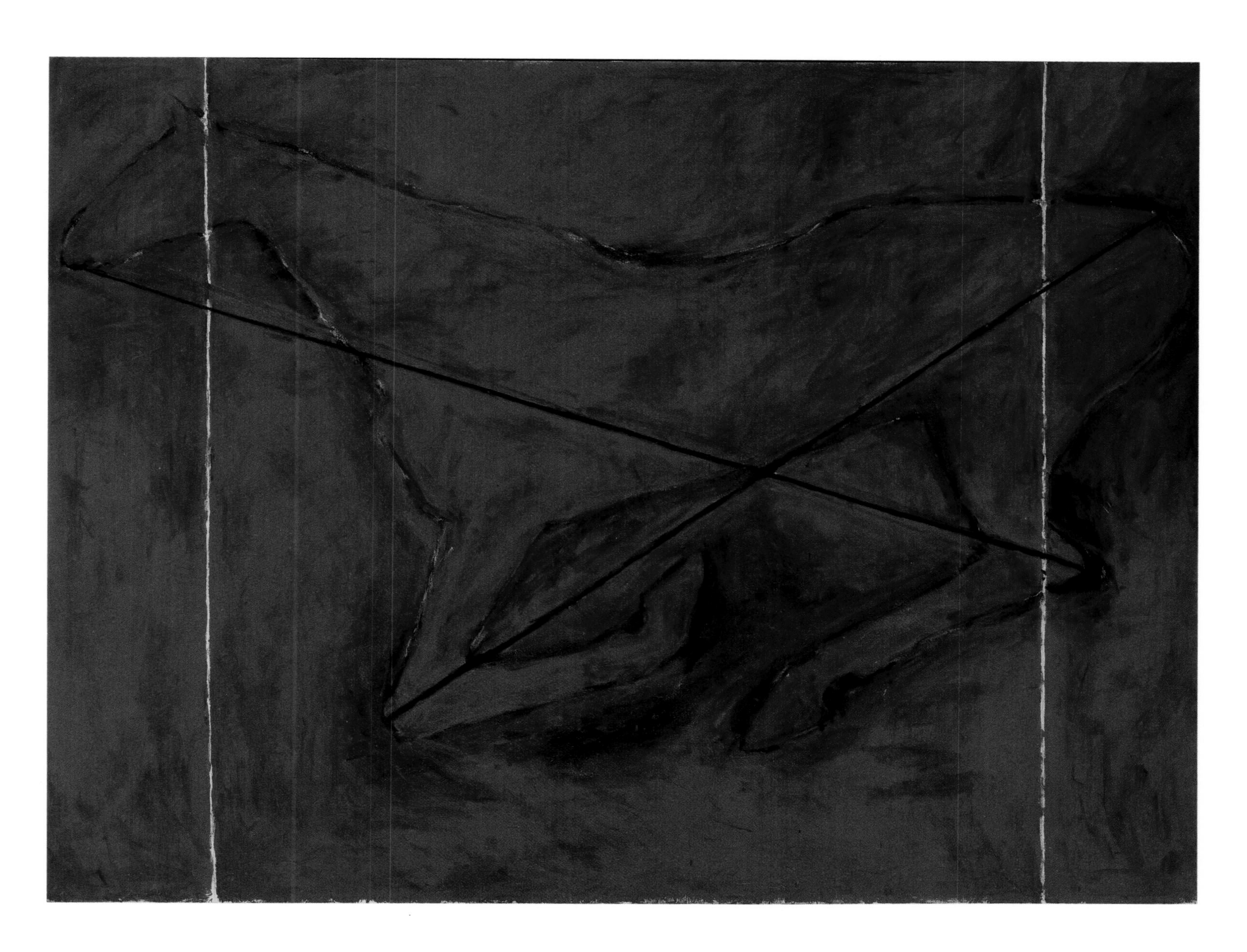

I x I 1977
Acrylic and flashe on canvas
6′5¼″ × 8′8″

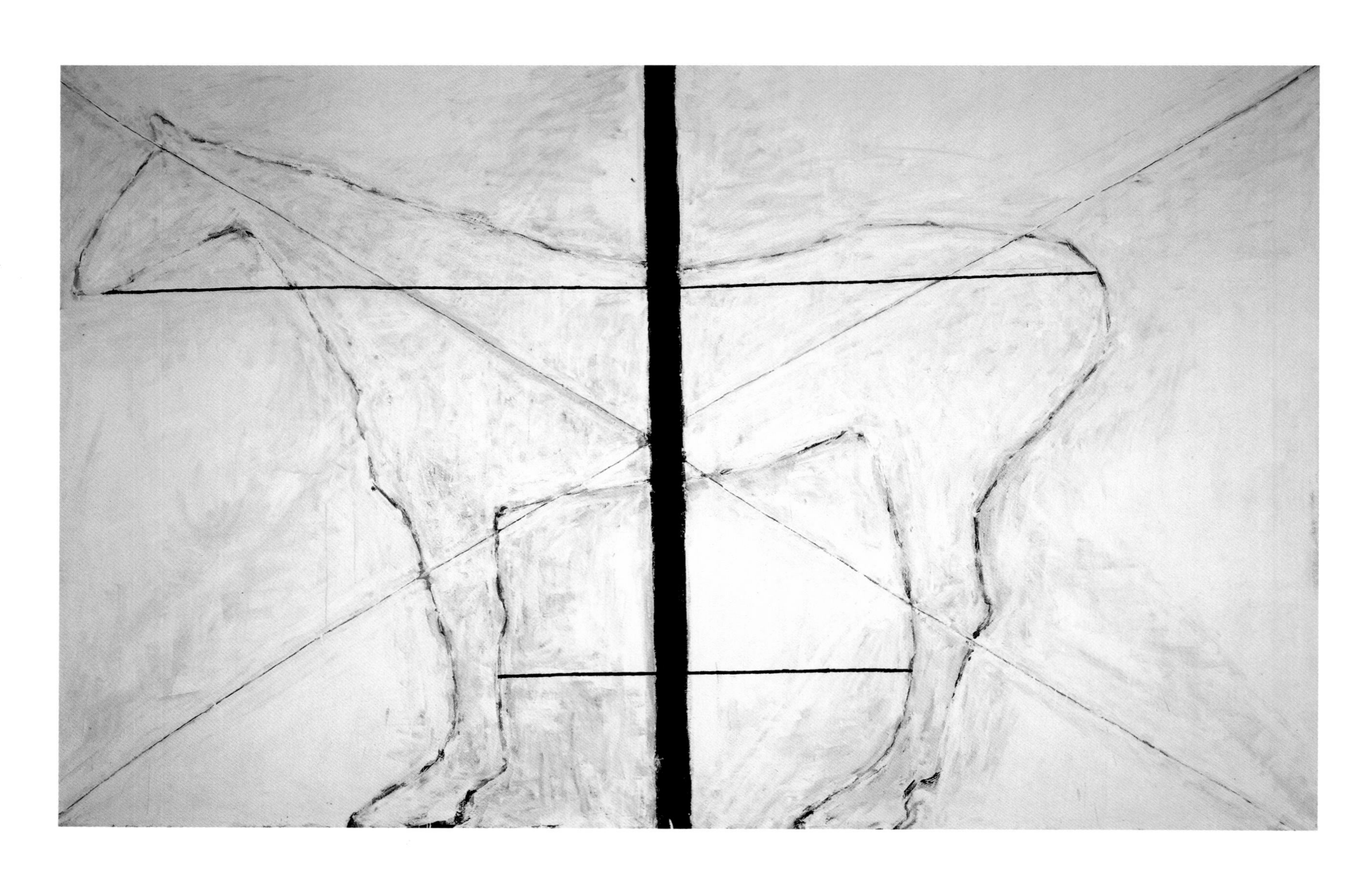

DOUBLE MEASURE 1977
Acrylic and tempera on canvas
6′4″ × 10′

was now open to both conceptual strategy and painterly gesture, narrative content as well as formal rigor, theatricality as well as materiality. The legacy of high formalism and its antithesis, the subjective, autobiographical, and emotional or didactic range of Performance and Conceptual art, were to meet if not merge in these works in curious ways.

The New Image show also signaled a change in the general institutional outlook on contemporary art, which for at least a decade had been dominated by sculptural issues and works made outside of gallery and museum contexts. For the same reasons, the exhibition was also problematic, for it paralleled the art market's eager reception for tangible, salable painting after a decade in which art had often dematerialized into idea alone or, conversely, extended the sculptural field to vast tracts of land in inaccessibly remote places.

By the time the New Image show opened in December 1978, Rothenberg for more than a year had been radically dismantling her signature horse image and refiguring the geometric scaffolding that had so neatly contained it. In the spring and summer of 1977, while making her first print,[30] Rothenberg discovered the pleasurable process and sociable realm of workshop collaboration. The experience provided relief from the isolation of the studio and very likely influenced her to accept her first (and last) teaching job, at Cal Arts in Valencia, California, shortly thereafter.

Taking her young daughter and the family cat with her and leaving her husband in New York, Rothenberg took the job for the 1977 fall semester. The separation of the family was not particularly unusual for them—Trakas had been traveling regularly to build sculptures

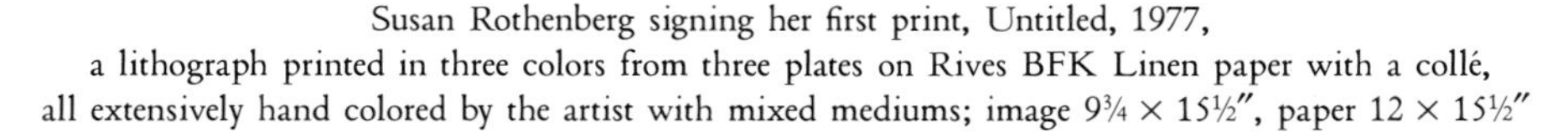

Susan Rothenberg signing her first print, Untitled, 1977,
a lithograph printed in three colors from three plates on Rives BFK Linen paper with a collé,
all extensively hand colored by the artist with mixed mediums; image $9\frac{3}{4} \times 15\frac{1}{2}''$, paper $12 \times 15\frac{1}{2}''$

on site in Europe and elsewhere. This time Rothenberg realized she "wanted to have a chance to go, to leave him for a change." Although she considered herself an enthusiastic traveler, she found herself, on this and subsequent trips, dislocated, detached, and disoriented, missing the domesticity—and perhaps the constraints as well—that she had built into her New York City life. With no experience either in moving or in teaching, she had not realized that she ought to arrive early to find a place to live, and there was no housing to be found.

The college put them up for a brief period in what Rothenberg calls "the naked motel" (it had a swimming pool where students could swim nude)—after which they surreptitiously moved into her studio at Cal Arts. She put up a curtain, bought a mattress and hotplate; they availed themselves of the dance bathrooms to complete their domestic setup. The whole scenario was, as Rothenberg describes it, "like living in a hospital." (According to Rothenberg, the structure was actually built by the Disney Corporation, a patron of Cal Arts, to serve possibly as a hospital.) Periodically they would be found out, move to other facilities temporarily lent to them, then quickly move back into the studio.

Though she met artists Michael Asher, John Baldessari, and Elyn Zimmerman, who were also teaching at Cal Arts, her connection with them was, as she puts it "None. zilch." She had slightly more contact with Jonathan Borofsky, another fellow artist/teacher, but he lived a good distance away and so she saw him infrequently. "It was another one of those grim periods," Rothenberg remembers. "Not many connections to people." In retrospect, there were also intimations that her marriage was coming apart.

As Rothenberg describes the time, "I just got lost out there." She didn't know how to proceed with her work, so she "started doing these heads." They were highly abstracted—but definitely human. Rothenberg remembers them as "quite geometric; they tried to have the same geometric lines through the eyes, down the center of the head," as had the bisected horse image. She had to show them—all of the visiting artists on the faculty were expected to exhibit their work in the school's gallery—but as soon as she took them down she destroyed all but one.

When Rothenberg returned to New York from Cal Arts in 1978, she dropped the geometric head image for a time and started to make drawings of isolated horse fragments as well as an agonized series of head drawings—abstracted human heads whose geometric lines had been replaced by a more fluid black line that was seen in some to be spewing forth; in others, it was something on which the head was gagging. Still others show the head tormented by a hand poking into the eyes or mouth—suppressing whatever might be seen or said—or by an internal hammer.

Blue Frontal, 1978, is a key work from the period. A pair of disembodied horse legs, white and upturned on a blue-black field, encircles and frames a standing, frontal, intensely blue horse. The horse is poised, almost puzzled looking, with its head cocked and looking directly out of the canvas through the legs, ready either to move forward or to retreat.

RED HEAD
(HEAD WITHIN HEAD) 1978
Acrylic on canvas
76 × 60″

BLUE FRONTAL 1978
Acrylic, flashe and tempera on canvas
77 × 88½″

STUDY (THROW-UP HEAD)
1978
Acrylic on canvas
17½ × 17″

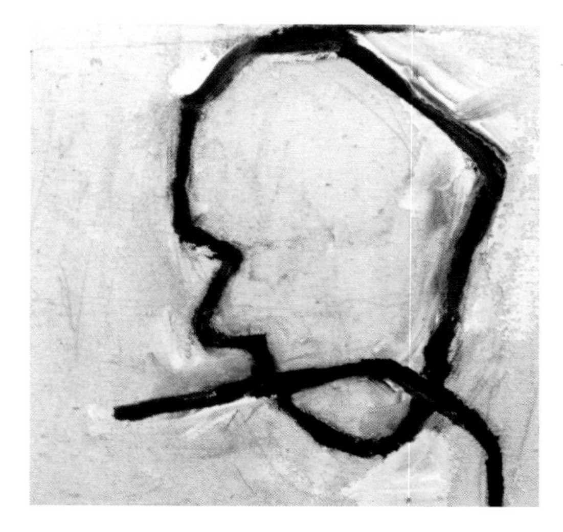

STICK IN THROAT
1978
Acrylic on canvas
7½ × 7½″

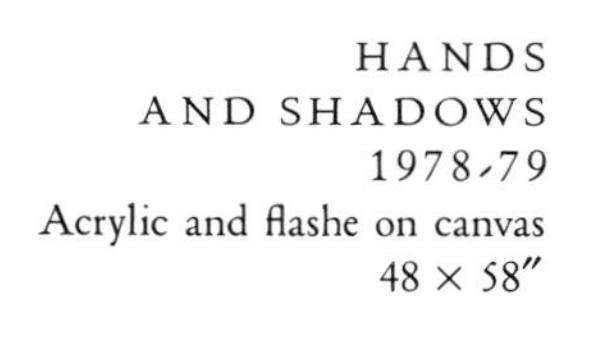

HANDS
AND SHADOWS
1978-79
Acrylic and flashe on canvas
48 × 58″

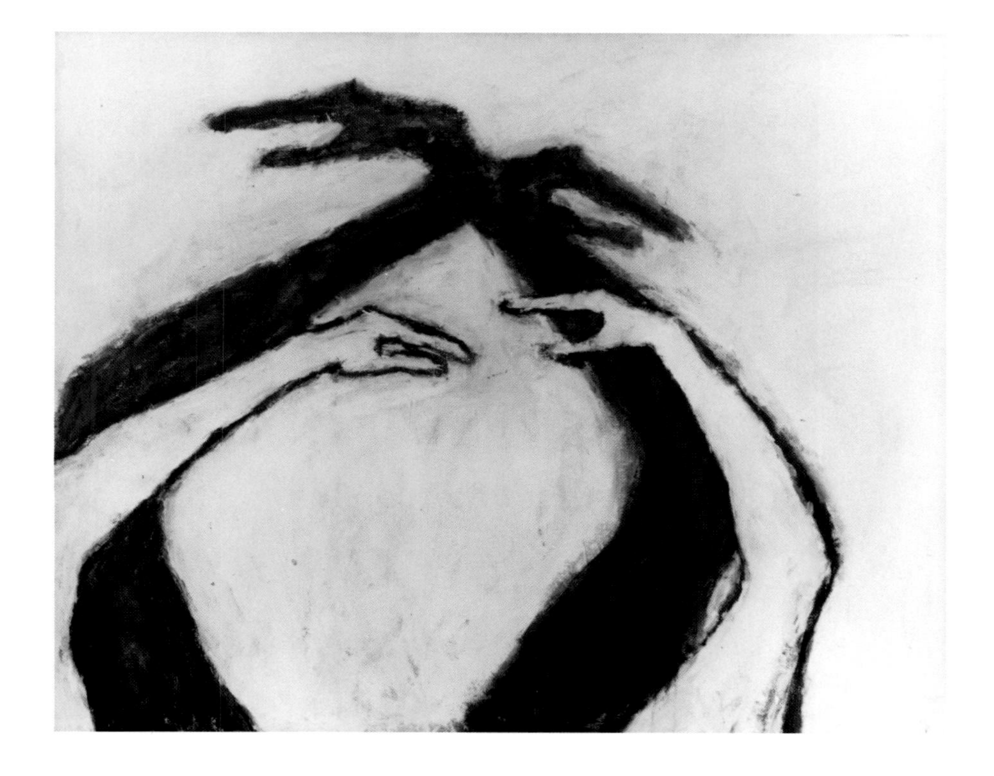

The painting is an odd shift in perspective and point of view from Rothenberg's previous work. While her early horses were flat, left-facing silhouettes, sized to fit the rectangular canvas that contained them, the horse in *Blue Frontal* is seen at a distance through the detached white leg bones that together nearly describe a peephole. If the artist and viewer's points of view toward the early horses were from the outside looking only to the surface on which the horses rested, in this work the point of view began with the very surface of the canvas and then looked farther in.

The point of view in *Blue Frontal* is more specifically that of the artist, locating herself within rather than detached from the work—akin in some ways to Joan Semmel's realistic self-portraits looking down the length of her body. The blue horse is also now more ambiguously figure than specifically horse—seen frontally, only the overall shape of head, torso, and two legs are visible—and the same can be said for the upturned framing legs. Though ending in hooves, their bony knees and fleshy thighs are more recognizably human than horse. The ambiguous relationship of parts in the painting can be read as a birth image; it can also be seen as a sexual image of imminent penetration, with the blue horse as not only phallic symbol but simply phallus.

In its overall configuration, however, it is also like the gentler and more playful images of upraised, curving arms and their shadows—based on the idea of shadow puppets, where simple gestures of hands and arms are transformed into images of animals as they cast their shadows on a wall—that Rothenberg was making at the same time (see *Hands and Shadows,* 1978-79). Yet it also evokes the emotionally grueling, barely outlined circular heads that were spewing black lines (see *Study: Throw-up Head,* 1978) or choking them back (as in *Stick in Throat,* 1978).

Squeeze, 1978-79, and *Cherry Pit,* 1978-79, convey the same extremes of physical and psychological struggle—the sense of compression as repression. In both paintings the tensions are also made visceral and formal. In *Squeeze* (a repeat of the configuration in *Blue Frontal*) the head of the horse is trapped between its upturned thighs, while its hooves are tied together with a black line. Though it can be seen as an animal hung and ready for butchering, for Rothenberg the line was simply a "formal device to pin the legs in space." In *Cherry Pit* an elongated, single upturned leg-cum-neck is distended where a horse skull is stuck, as a throat would choke on a pit.

In a single year Rothenberg went back and forth between the disembodied horse fragments and the full-bodied horse, from excruciating moments of struggle to images of respite, calm, and, sometimes, innocent sweetness. In *Kelpie,* 1978, a black profile horse in full motion is set into and away from its black field by a minimal white outline (one of the many perverse uses of her shadow form, this time a black image casts a white shadow); the entire horse is also encircled by a thickened line forming a loosely organic rather than hard-edged geometric closure. The horse now seems cushioned, protected in this new kind of space—womblike seems an appropriate description if not an interpretation (one that

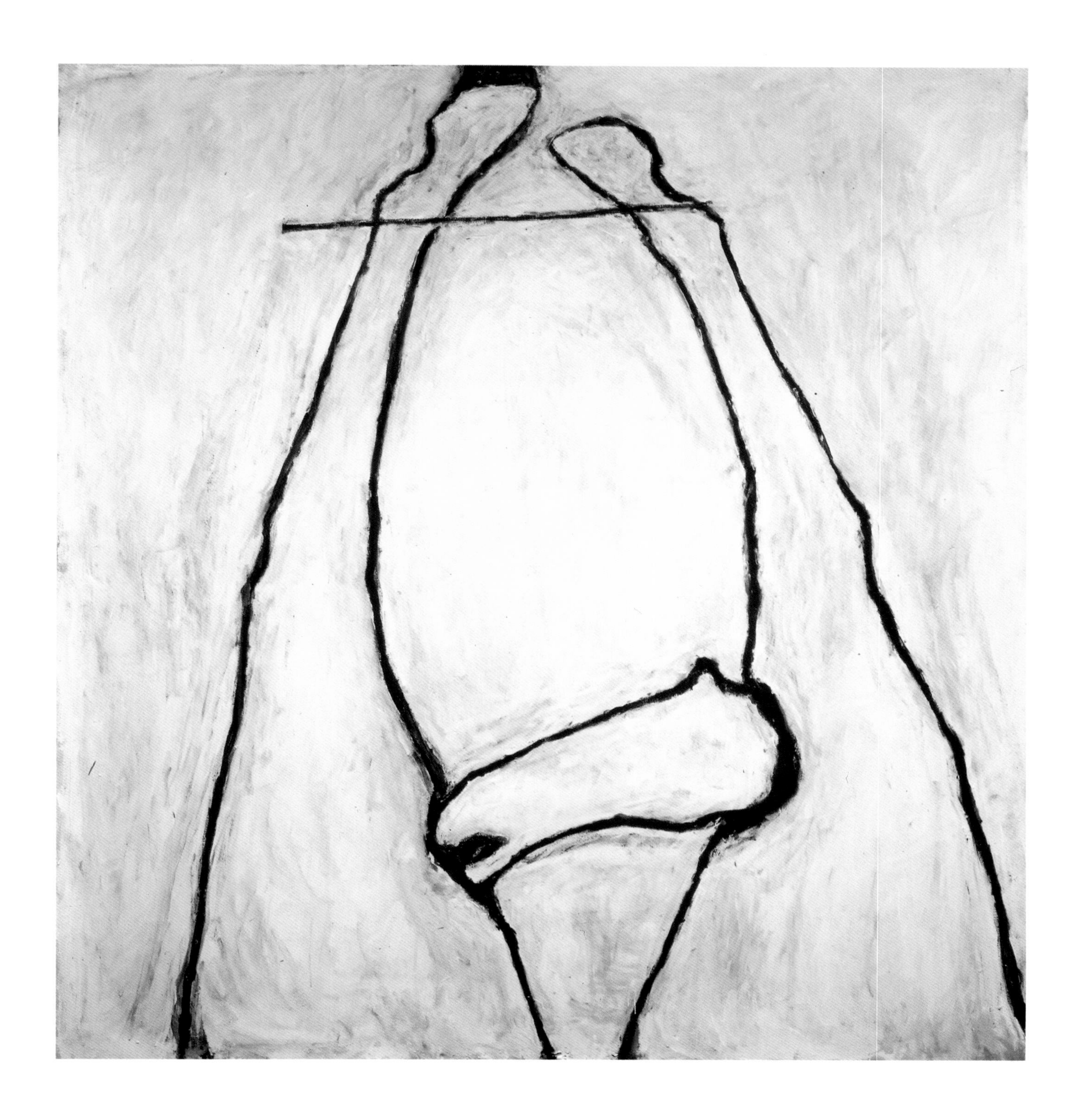

SQUEEZE 1978-79
Acrylic and flashe on canvas
92 × 87″

SOMEBODY ELSE'S HAND
1979
Acrylic and flashe on canvas
21 × 36″

UNTITLED
1978
Acrylic on paper
50 × 38½″

UNTITLED
1978
Acrylic and flashe on paper
14 × 22¼″

KELPIE 1978
Acrylic and flashe on canvas
6′5″ × 9′1″

MR. BEAR 1978
Acrylic and flashe on canvas
95 × 75″

Rothenberg herself does not see and argues with strongly). For Rothenberg, the significance is the very finding of a new formal device itself, the thickened line, which she describes as neither line nor shape but rather a "band," and which would generate an entire series of paintings two years later. *Mr. Bear,* 1978, whose source is Rothenberg's daughter's teddy bear, is painted in bold black outline on a dark red field, its arms and legs pressing against the edges as it pushes out against one of these black elastic bands encircling the whole image. In its forceful pressure against surrounding, encircling form, the image in this painting always reminds me of the photograph of Rothenberg siting herself in the hoop in Joan Jonas's *Jones Beach Piece.*

While many of Rothenberg's horses from this period were gaining both power and momentum, others were dematerializing. In *Outline,* 1978-79, a small black horse head is the only image—isolated in the lower right corner of an overall white field. In works like *For the Light,* 1978-79, and *Pontiac,* 1979, the frontal, fully charging horse, which fills the canvas from top to bottom, is held back against the picture plane by an abstracted bone shape that seems to smack against it and bar forward movement.

The images' fragmentation and cohesion, the forcefulness and emotional upheaval, the visions of birth, death, loss, and sexuality, of separation as well as wholeness, paralleled the wrenching turns of a marriage coming apart and periodically coming back together. In some paintings the emotional spillover seems to have been almost involuntary. In others it is clear that the artist consciously admitted a self into the work, whether indirectly—as the

Installation
Willard Gallery, New York, 1979
Left to right: *Pontiac,* 1979
For the Light, 1978-79
Outline, 1978-79; *Tattoo,* 1979

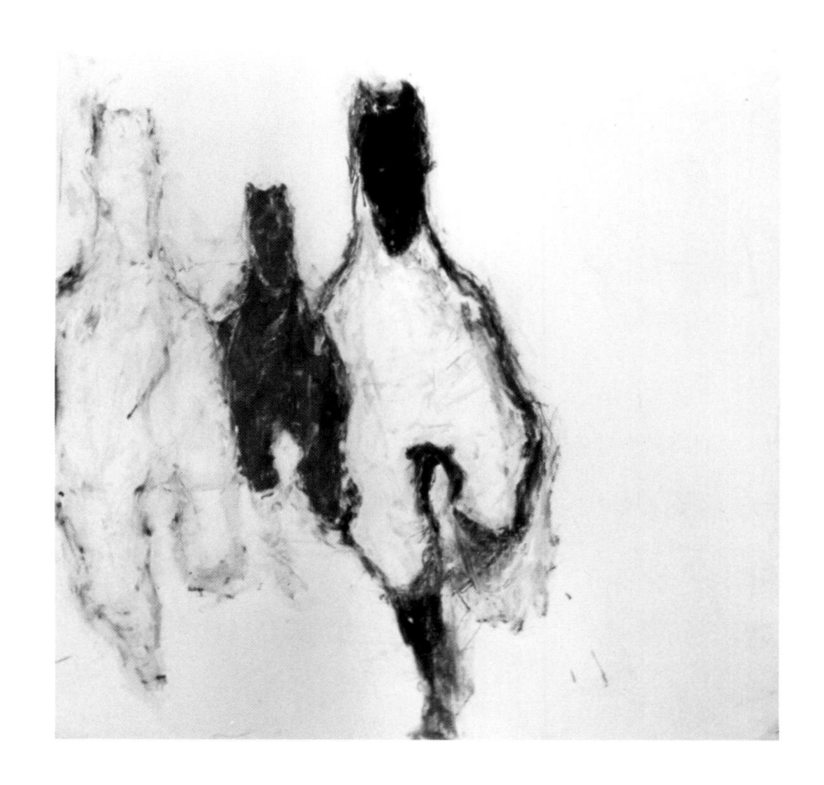

UNTITLED
1979
Acrylic and
flashe on paper
36½ × 36⅝″

FOR THE LIGHT 1978-79
Acrylic and flashe on canvas
8′9″ × 7′3″

OUTLINE 1978-79
Acrylic and flashe on canvas
73 × 50″

UNTITLED
1978–79
Acrylic and
pencil on paper
20 × 20″

horse itself was transforming into shapes that were more ambiguously human than figuratively horse, or as the point of view shifted from outsider to insider—or directly by beginning to make works that appear to be quite evidently self-portraits.

In *Smoker,* 1978–79, a floating blue head is anchored not by its sparely defined, almost suspended torso but by the three white linear elements that connect it to the four edges of the canvas: a white cigarette and smoke at the left; a white bone projecting like a thought from the head to the upper right into the corner where the top- and right-side edges meet; and a wavery white line, which is barely descriptive of the edge of a coat, extending to the bottom. Whether smoke, bone, or line, each is used to both compose and connote. Each of these elements can also be seen as symbolic of the rudiments of what kept Rothenberg anchored during this time of emotional turmoil and intense isolation: the comfort of a cigarette; her own leg/idea to stand on to keep her somewhat grounded while feeling afloat; and her line—the elemental white edge that she early on conceived as the minimal amount of information she could draw or leave bare to define any image, to differentiate one thing or place from another.

Like the many smoker images that Philip Guston incorporated into his work of the 1970s and which served as his alter-ego in his tortured personal inventories of studio props and bad habits, Rothenberg's few self-portrait works also show a smoker (see *Self-Portrait,* 1982). Though their works are very different conceptually and stylistically, Rothenberg, like Guston, quietly exerts a fierce independence both from the expectations of the art world as well as from the comforts of early, untortured, abstractly formal work. They share

PONTIAC 1979
Acrylic and flashe on canvas
88 × 61″

SMOKER 1978-79
Acrylic and flashe on canvas
62¼ × 45″

a blunt poetry as well as sensitively inflected surfaces in both their emblematic and more personally probing works, and both maintained their own signature palettes when their imagery profoundly changed.

For Rothenberg, as well as for many others of her generation, Guston was exemplary not only for his exquisite surfaces and boldly convincing paintings but also for his integrity and truthfulness in revealing, however painfully, the life of the artist as an integral part of a body of work. First shown in 1970, Guston's figurative work initially faced overwhelming critical rejection, both for its grotesque cartoon-like images and its radical turning from his well-known elegant abstractions. Yet it was Guston who set the stage and tenor for Rothenberg's and other artists' figurative and autobiographical explorations throughout the decade.

In adding the solidity of bone to her notion of line in these 1978-79 paintings, Rothenberg shifted from the linear and geometric to the volumetric and organic as an intuitive correction to the emotionally weightier subject matter she had admitted to the work. She also found a weightier counterforce to the physical impetus of the horse's locomotion. As she describes the transformation: "A line is hard and, you know, formal. I could have just as easily tried to paint a stick, but a bone has a more distinctive shape. I could have glued a stick on. I could have gotten into that too. But I just thought a bone makes sense as being—as making—living-tissue sense. To take an element out of the image, to use it in a formal way, turned out to have more of a psychological action than just a formal geometric linear action." Though Rothenberg's destructuring of the horse into fragments and bones recalls Graves's fossils and freestanding legs, for Rothenberg, "It wasn't so much [structural] analysis, it was intuition. It was like a doodle, a thought that, when you try it, if it works, you better believe it, you just go with it." She continued to take the forms of skull and bones through changes, but, as with *Cherry Pit* and *Squeeze,* the horse, Rothenberg says, "transformed itself into other, different kinds of imagery that were no longer connected to the sign of a horse."

In fact, the fragments began to become more and more connected to signs of the self. In *My Bones,* 1979, as the title indicates, Rothenberg sited two of her bones into the horse head shape previously seen in *Outline.* The horse head also appears inscribed on the thigh of one of the legs in *Tattoo,* 1979. In this painting Rothenberg also reuses the upturned leg-bone configuration of *Blue Frontal* as well as the enclosed frontal blue horse—this time opening the legs wide, like framing columns or gateposts (as in her earliest student work), and the horse itself appears contradictorily (evidenced by its small size and relative scale) to be charging forward or receding into deep space. Rothenberg also takes the bones into different kinds of fields, as in the red sweep of *Red Banner,* 1979, and the landscape of *The Hulk,* 1979 (recalling the mountain from *Foxes on a Hill,* 1972, and the almost human hulk of Untitled, 1979).[31] Exploring these images and also, however unconsciously, her own history as a painter, Rothenberg transformed what was left of the horse itself, the

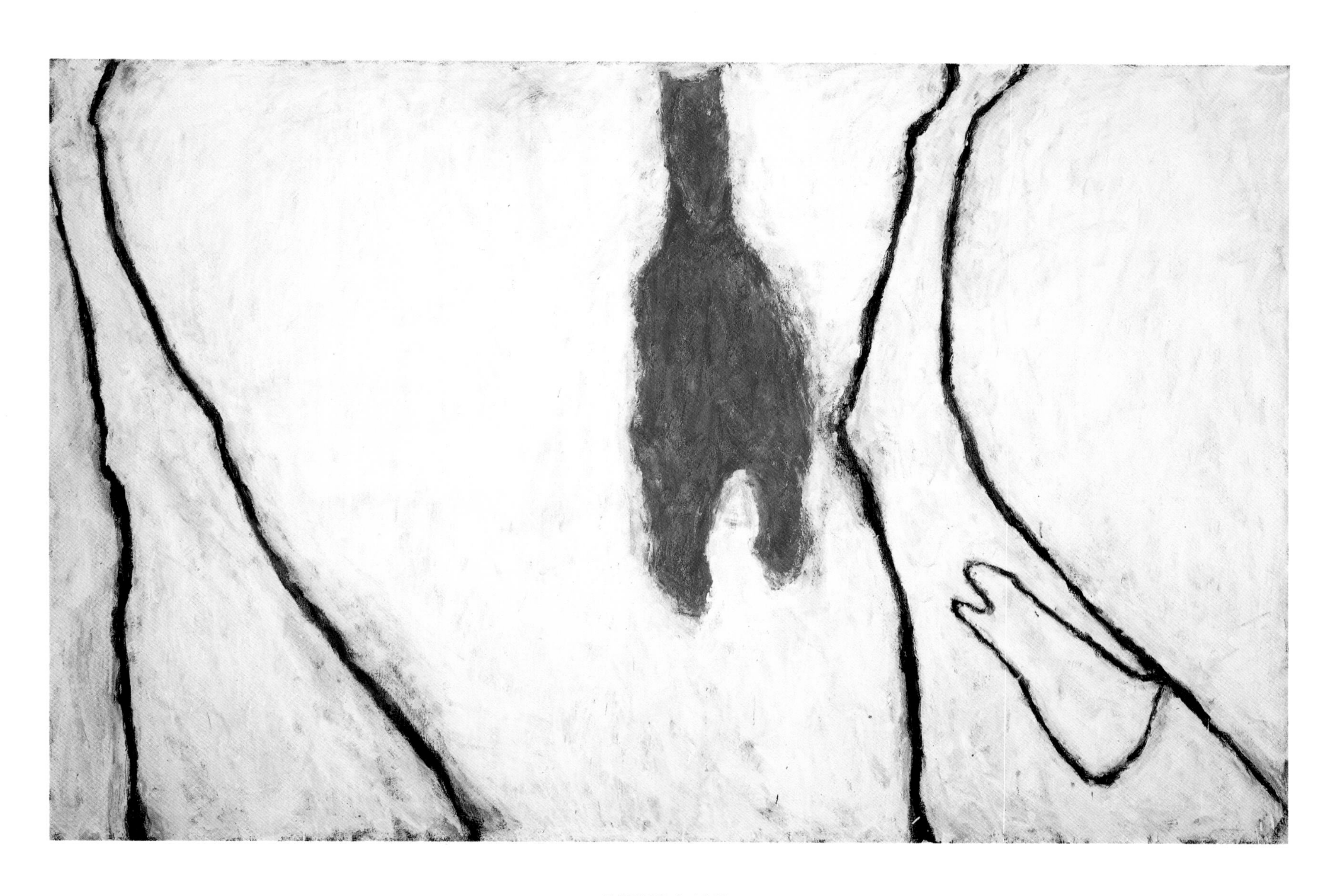

TATTOO 1979
Acrylic and flashe on canvas
5′7″ × 8′7″

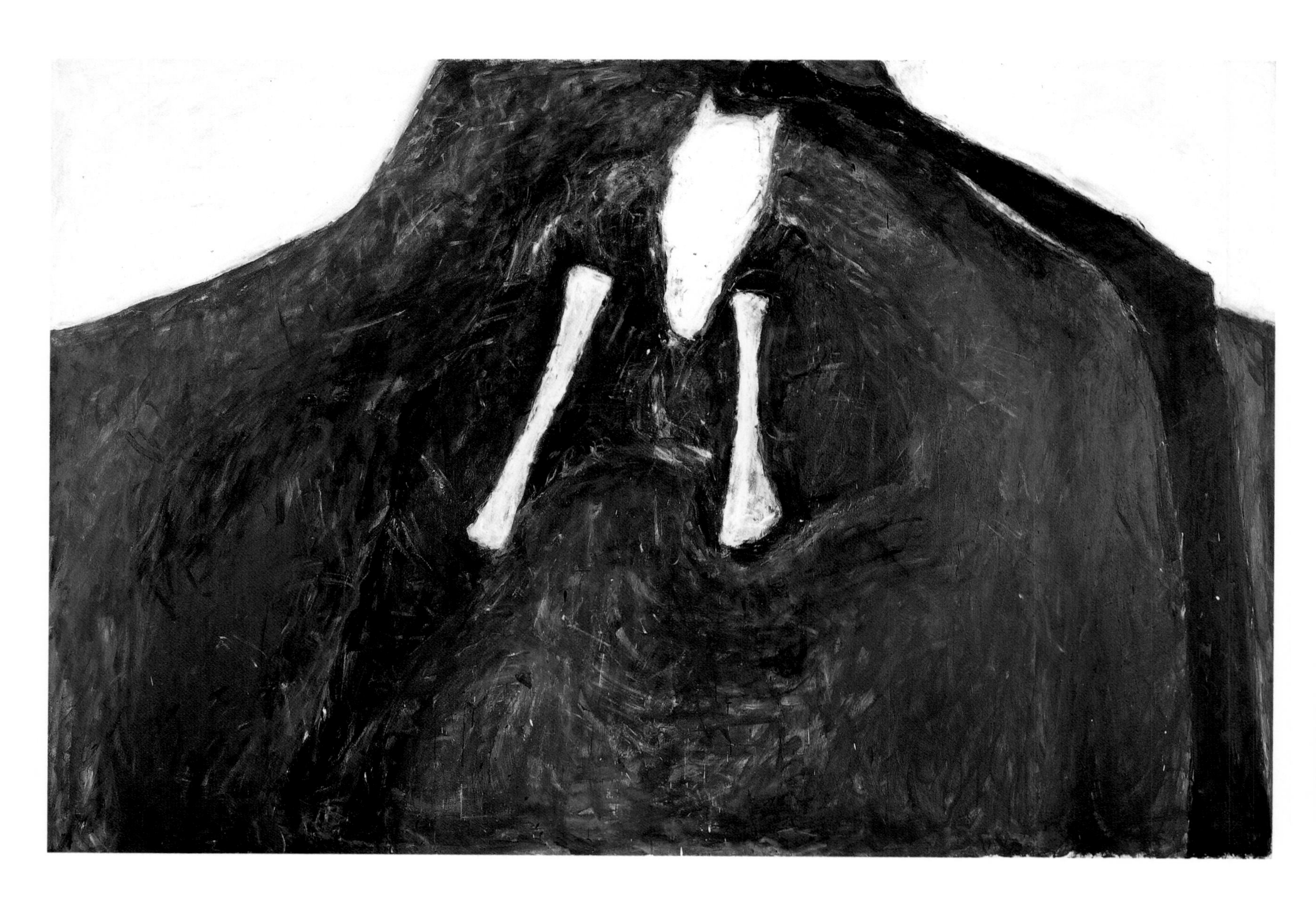

THE HULK 1979
Acrylic and flashe on canvas
6′5¾″ × 8′8″

acknowledged surrogate for a figure and a self, as well as a symbol of power—sexual or mythical—into a recognizable full figure. In *Our Lord,* also 1979, Rothenberg visually decodes the symbol: the blue horse becomes a double human figure of a man with an erection, a man dreaming of himself, or shadowed by himself.

One reading of the painting suggests that the image deals with divorce and separation—the receding image being that of her soon-to-be-former husband (Trakas and Rothenberg formally separated in 1978 and were divorced in 1979). Conversely, the painting could be a projection of the future, of figures as yet unknown but envisioned. That this double figure is also a self-portrait is also plausible. Early in her career Rothenberg often described a fantasy of being the muse of a famous male artist rather than becoming an artist in her own right—being the dreamed of rather than the dreamer. The painting might also hint at the situation she was increasingly finding herself in; often included as the only woman in group exhibitions, she was seen, as the saying goes, as one of the boys. None of these interpretations, however, were part of Rothenberg's intention. She was continuing to allow her imagery to lead her, as did Freud's horse in the anecdote of the Sunday horseman, where it would.[32]

Rothenberg with Untitled, 1979, in progress

UNTITLED
1979
Acrylic and flashe on paper
50 × 38″

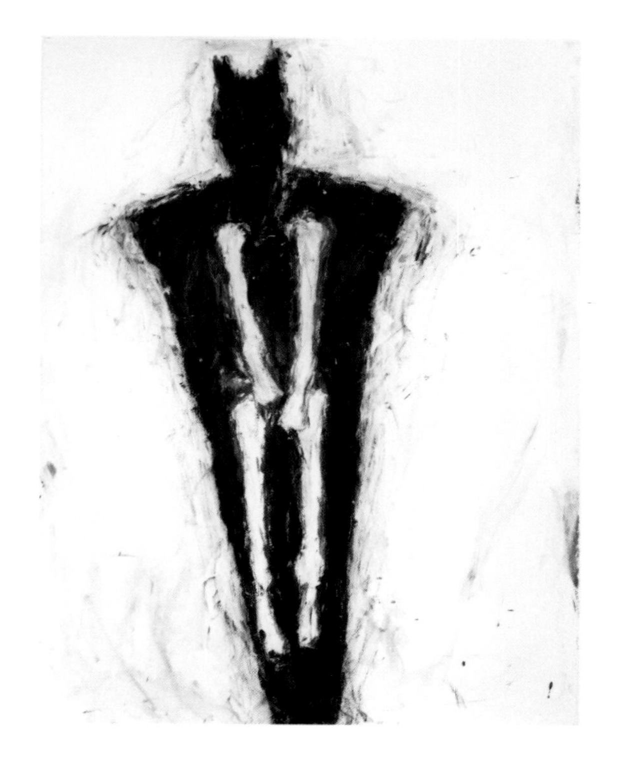

OUR LORD 1979
Acrylic and flashe on canvas
69 × 36″

BLUE BODY
1980-81
Acrylic and flashe on canvas
9′ × 6′3″

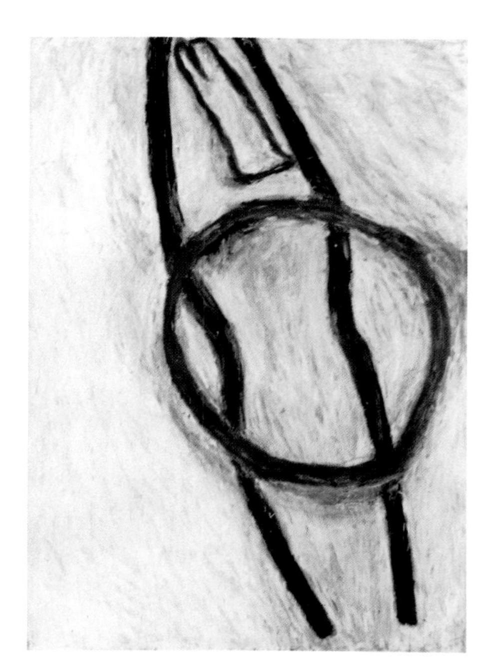

WHITE MOUNTAIN
1980-81
Acrylic and flashe on canvas
8′9″ × 6′3″

Both *Wishbone,* 1979, and *Tuning Fork,* 1980, mark the subtle transformation of horse into figure. In *Wishbone* the legs are no longer horse fragments but literally the extensions of a wishbone, while its shadow is a solid black frontal horse, minus even Rothenberg's minimal horse detail. The doubling of black figures in a black field in this painting overtly states differences rather than similarities. The main figure in *Tuning Fork* also looks like its title, the two pronged legs downturned though topped with a horse head; its shadow, however, perversely solid though cast from an open form, looks like a human figure. In *Tuning Fork,* as Rothenberg has said, "After using the horse sideways, later frontally, it turned almost into a figure. And it turned up in the bare bones. No superfluous geometry dealing with the edges of the painting, but just the bare bones of the frontal horse, which suggested that a figure was appearing—that the horse was metamorphosing into a human figure. I realized that there weren't very many of those images left, that it had absolutely naturally reduced itself to a place where I was going to be forced to continue—differently."

In *Blue Body* and *White Mountain,* both 1980-81, the last remnant of the horse slips away. In *Blue Body* a horse head floats upward to the top of the canvas, defying gravity, as if to ascend out of the dematerialized body that can no longer hold onto it. The figure is barely made up of a pair of framing vertical black lines, which Rothenberg has called an "exoskeleton," and a torso, now also minimally described using only a blue circle. In *White Mountain,* the horse head can be seen to be sliding down a steep road or (as in *Cherry Pit*) slipping down a gullet. This last horse painting reiterates Rothenberg's compositional use of three "things." Now, however, the painting is "about a shadow of a shadow of a shadow." Whether set free into air or absorbed into earthy grounds, the horse, for Rothenberg, has finally been digested.[33]

WISHBONE 1979
Acrylic and flashe on canvas
8′6″ × 6′4″

TUNING FORK 1980
Acrylic and flashe on canvas
83 × 79″

BLUE HEAD 1980-81
Acrylic and flashe on canvas
9′6″ × 9′6″

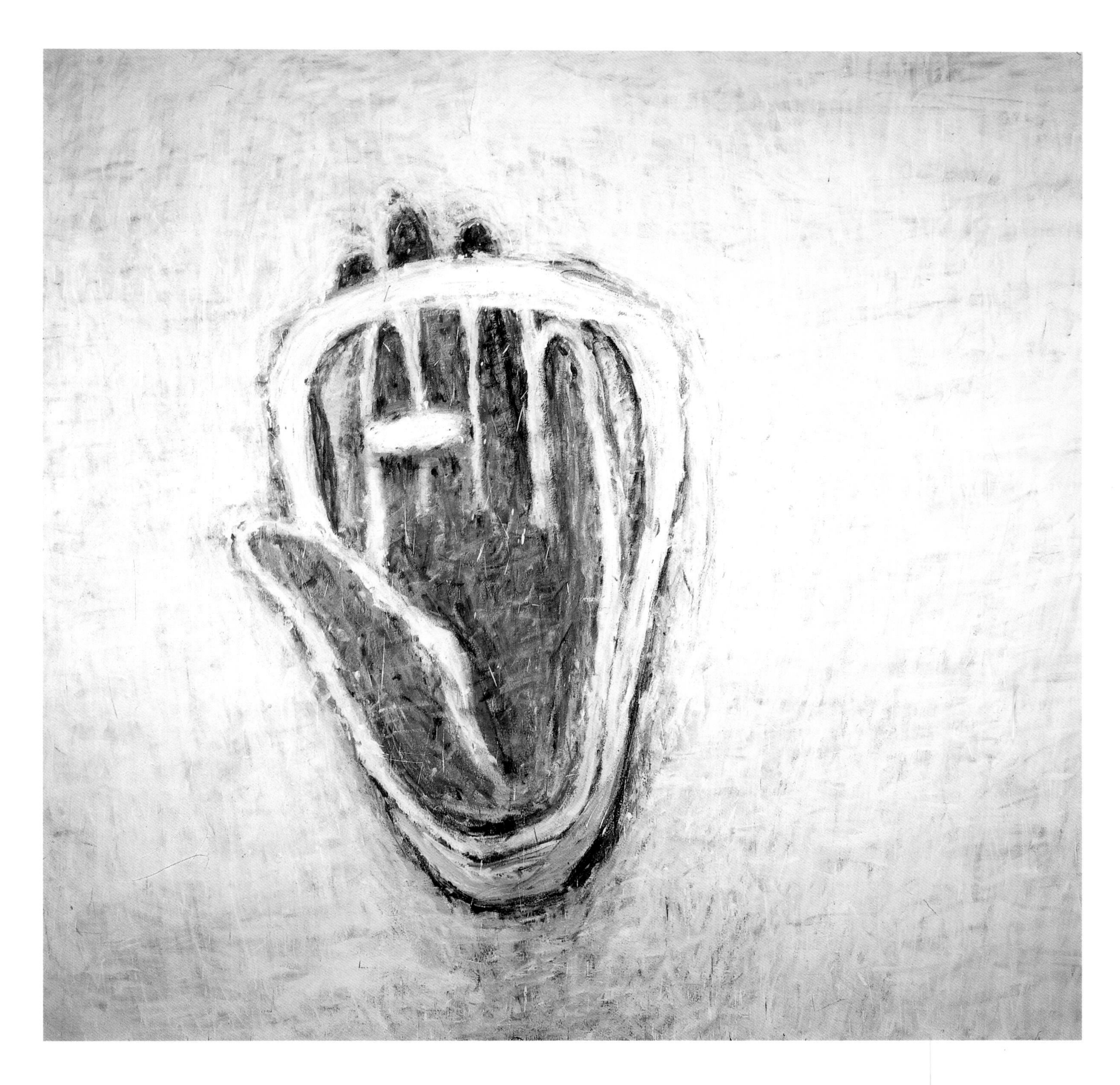

GREY HEAD 1980-81
Acrylic and flashe on canvas
9′2″ × 9′6″

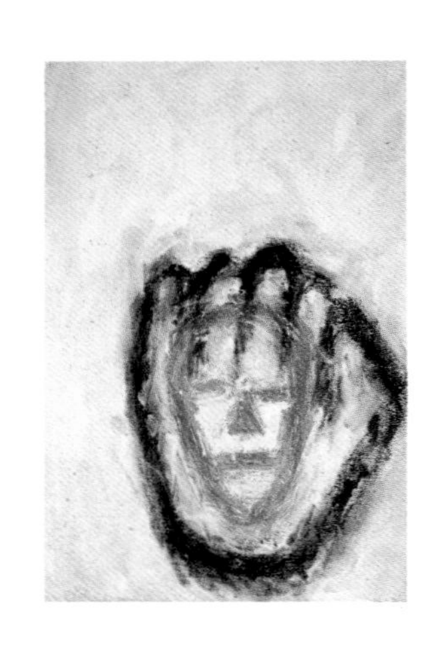

STUDIES FOR
HEADS AND HANDS
c. 1980
Crayon on canvas
Dimensions (clockwise from top left)

14½ × 12¼″
12½ × 11¼″
11½ × 7½″
11½ × 14½″
11½ × 14½″
10½ × 12¼″
11¼ × 7″

BLACK HEAD 1980-81
Acrylic and flashe on canvas
8′8″ × 9′6″

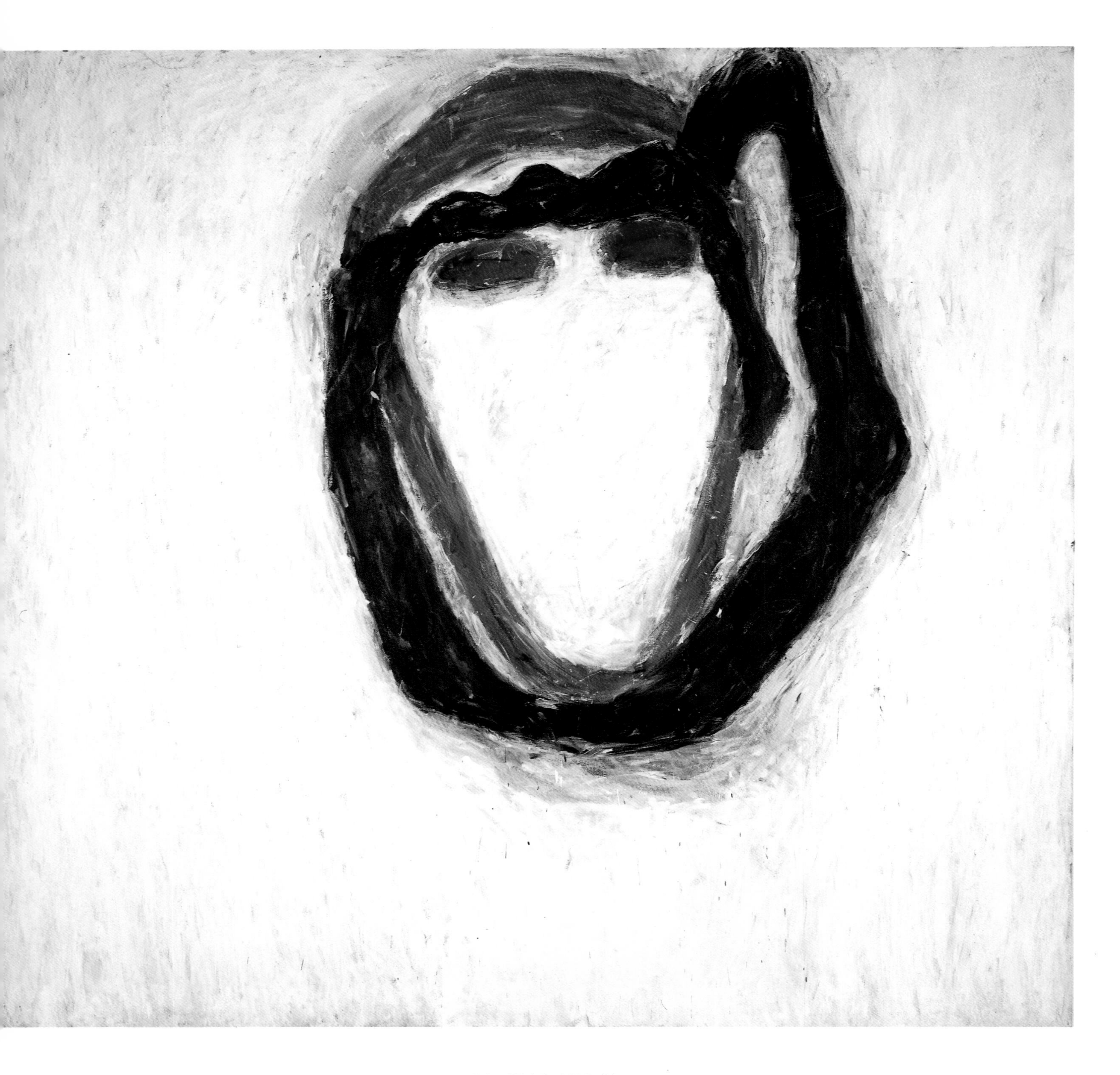

RED HEAD 1980-81
Acrylic and flashe on canvas
8′11″ × 8′11½″

BIG AND LITTLE HEAD 1980-81
Acrylic and flashe on canvas
9′3″ × 9′6″

"THE HORSE JUST RAN OUT," IS HOW ROTHENBERG DESCRIBES THE waning of the image that had sustained her for more than six years. Her approach to painting was to be "scared again" and once more to start doodling. She drew a number of little heads and hands with crayon on small pieces of canvas, and she thought they were odd, that they were good. She also thought they were kind of like a "joke," a child's game "where you draw a face on a hand." Using the closed fist as a head, the movable thumb becomes a movable jaw. Although she had previously experimented with and destroyed a series of geometric heads in 1977 and 1978 and had done the series of throw-up heads, choking heads, and hammerheads (1978-79), which were more like grim occasional poems than sustaining formal subjects, Rothenberg hadn't known where to go with them and both times had returned to the horse image. She worked the earlier heads as she had the first horses, in profile—see *Red Head (Head within Head),* 1978 (page 59). This proved a dead end. "I couldn't get enough out of a facial profile," she remembers. "I couldn't think where else to go with it, except to have paint pouring out of the ears and eyes."

Rothenberg's first thoughts on the new hand-transformed-into-head image on these small sketches were that they were made up of what she calls "bands" of color—a way of using line she had discovered while painting heads at Cal Arts. "Once I started thinking of the line as a band that was halfway between a form or a shape and a line, I started to think of this as something very flexible," and, upon returning to the full horses after both the distraught heads and the destructured horses, she incorporated this band as a new, more elastic kind of geometric device. As they thickened, the bands created interior spaces, almost volumes, that approached form (as in *Kelpie,* 1978).

As a test, Rothenberg enlarged the small studies of the new head image, which she had found "mesmerizing" at diminutive size. *Rose,* 1980, was painted at what she called "door size." She liked the way *Rose* looked and decided to take the head paintings immediately up to a "confrontational" ten feet square—a size in which she had not worked in a sustained way since the 112 Greene Street ensemble in 1975—and to make a series of five of them. She rented a second studio on Franklin Street with high ceilings and ample wall space so that she could see most of them at the same time while she worked on any particular one.[34]

In a method of working that over the course of her career always somehow goes one step forward and two back, Rothenberg was tackling this new image in the new studio while simultaneously finishing what would be the last of the horse paintings, *Blue Body* and *White Mountain,* at the West Broadway studio. If the latter works lack the psychological edge of her previous horse paintings, it may very well be because she had diverted her energy to the new project. As she scaled these new heads and hands up to monumental size, her version of a self empowered became far more compelling than the diminished, evanescing surrogate she was leaving behind.

She was, at the same time, in the West Broadway studio working on the first painting locating her various images in indoor, roomlike though still ambiguous spaces—a kind of place she would return to several years later in a number of paintings. In *Red Slippers,* 1981, Rothenberg places three things—a white head (with a white line through it, as if pierced by a ray of light or supported on a stick as in Balinese shadow puppets, floating the image from the top edge of the canvas to the floor implied within); to its right and behind it a blue figure sits in a black rocking chair; and downstage to the left, is a pair of red slippers on what Rothenberg calls "an empty patch," a space that is not quite floor, table, or chair. All appear to be within a darkened room, perhaps Rothenberg's own bedroom (a small boxlike room she had recently built at the back of her open loft). Compositionally, the pieces of imagery are located in space in a new way for Rothenberg as well. Juxtaposed in nonrelational scale, none of the images is a double or shadow of any other, and each is placed specifically within the composition while also appearing to float almost surrealistically in space.

New ways to locate the head image are also seen in two 1980 works. In *Jughead* Rothenberg places a profiled white head-in-the-form-of-a-jug (handle and all) into paradoxically real yet abstract space: it is inscribed as a decorative element on a large black jug (a double negative, as the image is also flopped), which is once again set into a third juglike area, this time white, taking up the central space of a black field, creating an extremely odd painting—even for Rothenberg—an abstracted still life. And in an untitled drawing, a frontal head (as in the Heads and Hands paintings) is sited within a circular band. This drawing has sometimes been called Untitled (AEIOU), 1980, perhaps as an acknowledgment that these new heads can speak or at least have the rudimentary tools to do so, as compared to the earlier heads, in which speech was obviously suppressed by various images stuffed into their mouths.

As Rothenberg remembers the transitional 1980-81 period: "It wasn't a decision. With the last two [horse] paintings, there wasn't a letdown, there was a little confusion, but it resolved itself in my just bravely jumping into this head and hand thing—not knowing if it was an image worth using or an image that people would find relatable or understandable, but I called it 'all I had to work with at the time'—I had my head and my hand. I am a painter and I realized that the human being was coming in. I couldn't deal with outright figurative—human-figure—painting at the time." Following her usual process of evoking an image onto the canvas, Rothenberg acknowledged the emergence of an undisguised though highly abstracted self-portrait, featuring the painter's two essential assets: head and hands.

She selected from the little crayon-on-canvas studies a sequence that noted the different hand positions superimposed on or juxtaposed to the fistlike head: "the fist, the splayed hand, the upside-down hand." She then renamed the content. As Rothenberg describes the evolution, "They started to look like different weathers to me. Cold ones, a hot one, a night one. So I got involved in that. And then I started thinking—I deliberately wanted a mist one. I started to play with the weather idea and then it was done." The Heads and

UNTITLED
(AEIOU)
1980
Acrylic and flashe on paper
41½ × 30″

JUGHEAD
1980
Acrylic on canvas
60 × 68″

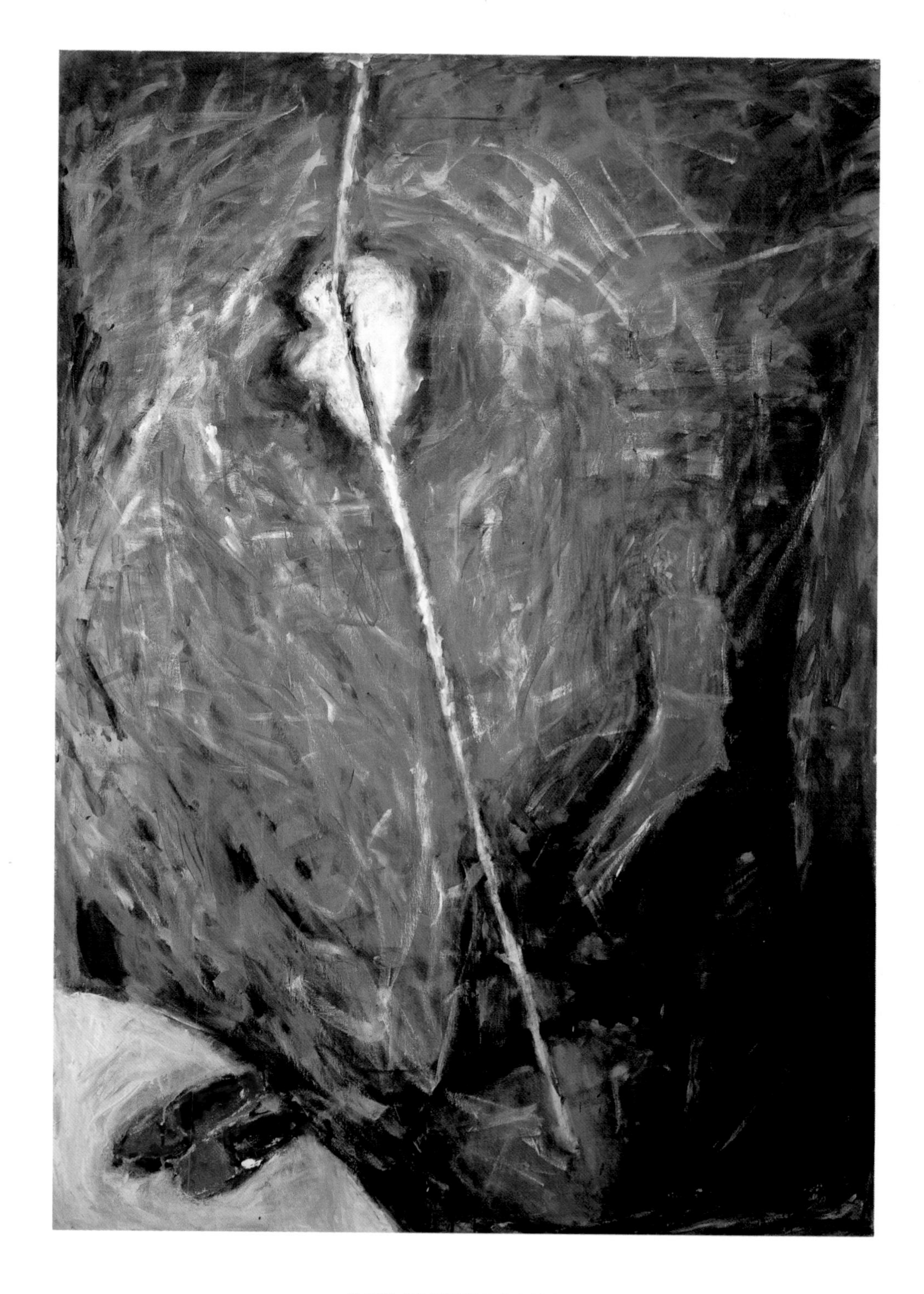

RED SLIPPERS 1980-81
Acrylic and flashe on canvas
77 × 52″

UNTITLED
1981
Charcoal on paper
28¾ × 22½″

Hands paintings were jarring. These highly simplified, outlined faces, as frontal as mug shots yet at a scale impacting the cool Pop billboard and the heated arena of Abstract Expressionist actions, were bold, bare, direct. As Peter Schjeldahl wrote, they "suggest images from the very backbrain depths. . . . No message, no storytelling, no empathy, no pathos, no mysticism, no coyness. It's all there in the paint, the dense red or black or white or blue outlines smoking in the dirty white or black grounds. (The surfaces often evoke a choking atmosphere, full of flying ash and pumice.) Thus—again, and to a new extreme of shivery force—the hint of a diabolical sense of humor, a strange, cold joy."[35]

The year Rothenberg spent formally exploring the Head and Hand images constituted her first sustained period of working successfully outside of the domestic routine of her West Broadway home/studio. Along with the ambition that goes with making a suite of works on such a large scale, these paintings convey a sense of humor, an almost childlike openness that was refreshing after the particularly somber, even excruciating images of dismembered bones and choking heads that had both preceded and helped to generate them. And these monumental heads, in turn, led her to investigate ways of handling the surface to imbue her work with climate that was both meteorological and emotional. In 1980–81, on complet-

UNTITLED
1981
Graphite on paper
28 × 17″

UNTITLED
1981
Graphite on paper
26¾ × 23″

ing the Heads and Hands paintings, Rothenberg saw that her surface handling, though not her imagery, was taking a kind of Impressionist tack just as the art world was beginning to absorb her work, somewhat uneasily, into the Neo-Expressionist arena that was gaining prominence in the United States and Europe.

The 1980 Venice Biennale summarized the diversity of the 1970s while reporting on the new focus on painting that was beginning to usher in the decade. "New Spirit in Painting," held at London's Royal Academy in the fall of 1980, trumpeted the news. Rothenberg and her work were once again considered a bridge between generations and changing styles. Her vigorous brushstroke and densely worked surfaces, as well as the Sturm und Drang of the last horse paintings, invited comparison to the stylistic imperatives and disjunctive use of image fragments of a younger generation of Expressionists, including the Americans Julian Schnabel and David Salle; the Italians Sandro Chia, Enzo Cucchi, and Francesco Clemente (all of whom, including Rothenberg, were in the Aperto section of the 1980 Venice Biennale); and to her contemporaries, the Germans Georg Baselitz and Anselm Kiefer. (Both Baselitz and Kiefer were represented in the German Pavilion of the 1980 Biennale, while Rothenberg's work was also included in the American Pavilion in a show summarizing the 1970s called "Drawings: The Pluralist Decade.")

Yet Rothenberg's works had none of the historicism or the impacted overlays of big themes drawn from the larger culture that characterized the regularly monumental canvases of much Neo-Expressionist painting. Most of the Neo-Expressionist artists were aiming for operatic syntheses, complexity, and grandeur; Rothenberg was looking to simplify—her line, her composition, her image, her subject matter. And while the Neo-Expressionists' images were drawn from various appropriations of cultural sources, Rothenberg's came from within. Further, many of the Neo-Expressionist works dealt with apocalyptic themes; in Rothenberg's, as critic Robert Storr has pointed out, "We are watching the emergence of a world, not its demoralizing retreat or its furious explosion and collapse."[36]

The 1980s were also to be the decade of Europe. While Rothenberg was working on the Heads and Hands paintings, she was visited in her studio by some of the organizers of "New Spirit in Painting."[37] She was also visited by curators from the Stedelijk Museum and the Kunsthalle Basel, both of whom offered her shows, her first solo museum exhibitions in Europe. Alexander van Grevenstein of Amsterdam's Stedelijk Museum planned with Rothenberg a show of yet-to-be-painted works for the fall of 1982. Jean Christophe Ammann selected for Basel the Heads and Hands paintings as well as other recent paintings and drawings for a show that fall (1981) to coincide with two other shows by American artists, namely Robert Moskowitz and Julian Schnabel. The installation at the Kunsthalle situated Rothenberg's work as the link between New Image and Neo-Expressionism. The route through the exhibition began with several rooms of Robert

Moskowitz's paintings, led into a series of galleries with Rothenberg's diverse expressions, and concluded with Julian Schnabel's smashed-plate paintings and other mixed-medium works that gave Neo-Expressionism its earliest forceful and controversial voice.

By the summer of 1981, however, after completing the Heads and Hands paintings, Rothenberg's work had changed profoundly once again. Left with the idea of exploring "weathers" but having no image to work with, she found herself "just noodling" and decided to switch from painting in acrylics to using oils, "just to shake things up in general."

Rothenberg remembers a suggestion made to her at the time by painter Elizabeth Murray. "She believed," says Rothenberg, "that I was already very painterly and thought I could get much more painterly excitement from using the real stuff, not the plastic paint." During the summer of 1981, Rothenberg began to paint with oil; she found her subject—boats—bobbing in the creek behind her summer home in Long Island.[38] Once again, she recalls, she was asking herself, " 'What am I going to do?' as I did with the Heads and Hands. So I decided not to think about it, just to see what working with oil was like."

She found herself newly attracted to the way the brush moved and the differences between working with acrylic and oil, which she likened to yogurt and stiff butter, respectively. With oil, "each stroke had a life to it—a certain plastic power." Using acrylics, she could work an entire surface, leaving mistakes and blobs and drips, her soupy medium allowing her to spread the paint widely and quickly. With her brush loaded with oil, the increments of paint and the width of the stroke were smaller, tighter, choppier, and, what was equally important, stayed wet longer—and it was this choppy stroke that led her to the image of the choppy water of the creek.

Susan Rothenberg with *Maggie's Split,* 1981-82, and *The Creek,* 1981-82, while in progress

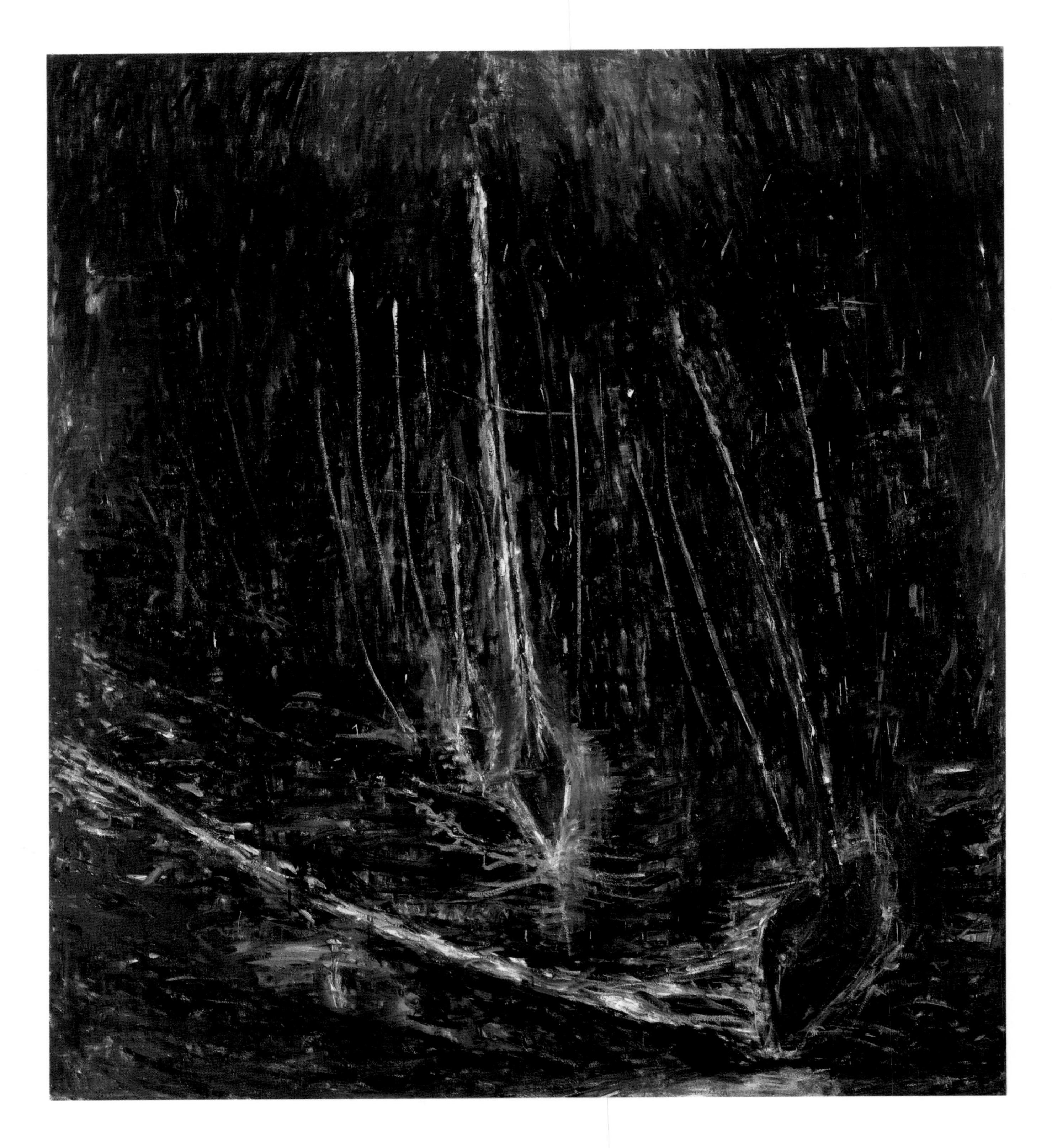

THE CREEK 1981-82
Oil on canvas
88¼ × 78″

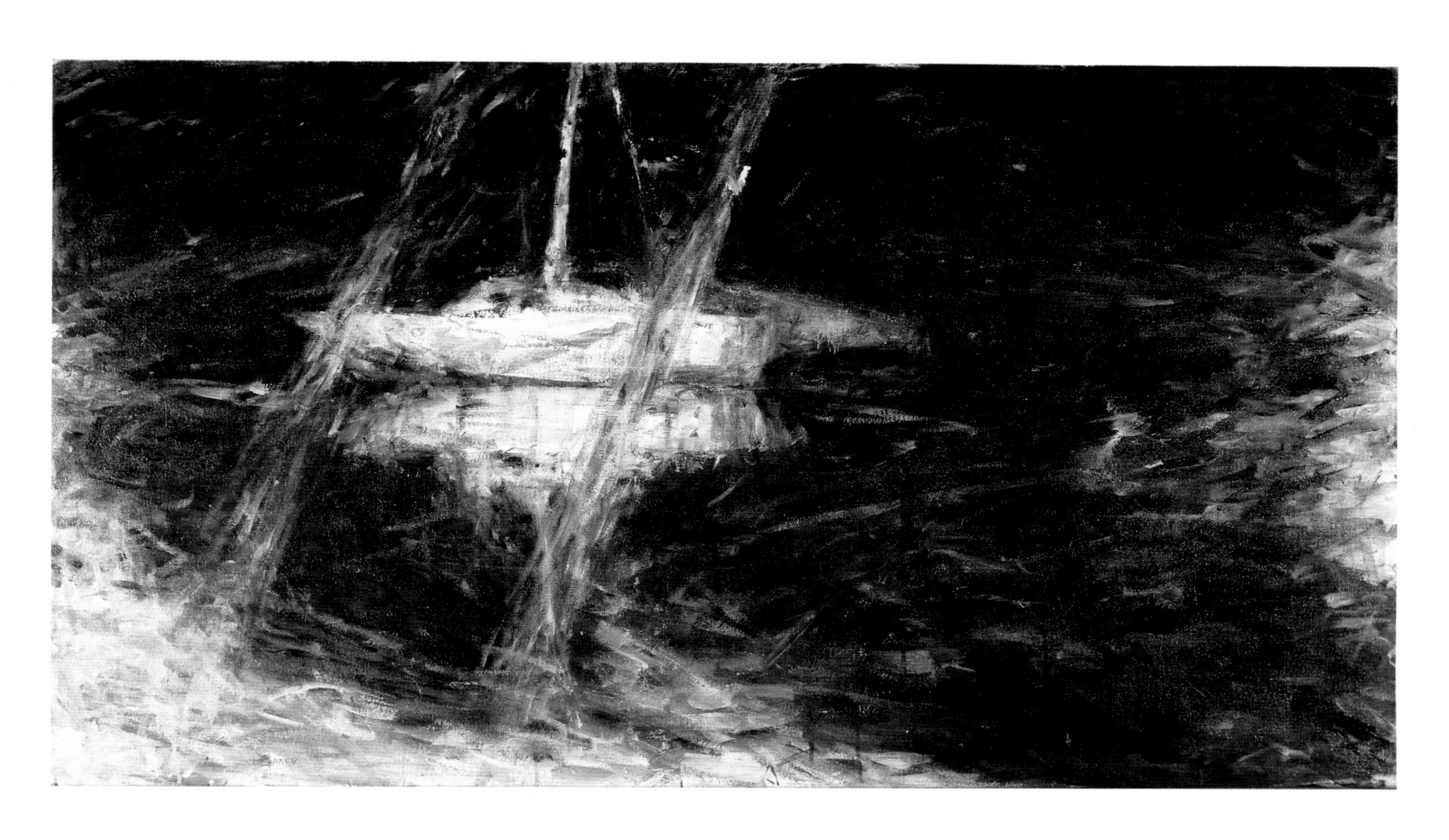

TWO RAYS 1981
Oil on canvas
30½ × 55″

"At first it was literally water, and then—if you're not delineating a different kind of space—everything became watery-looking. So even when I wasn't evoking water—which the first ones definitely were—all of them looked watery." In the course of exploring water and boats, she began to paint light and actual reflections rather than her formal devices of figures and invented shadows. Once again she restricted her palette. Working in black-and-white, Rothenberg abandoned for a time the blues and reds that had supplanted her signature sienna. The small *Two Rays* depicts a sailboat and its reflection (both white in dark black waters) with the two white rays of its title diagonally streaming down and framing both boat and reflections and dynamically locking top and bottom of canvas together without stopping the implied shifting action of the boats and their changeable reflections in the water.

Working with oil, and building her canvases of paint and the flurries of small, choppy strokes rather than almost drawing with a painterly sweep her images into their fields, Rothenberg finally was able to eliminate her minimal amount of differentiation between figure and ground by dissolving the one into the other. By the time she headed off for the opening of her Basel exhibition in the fall of 1981, the paintings she was making bore no resemblance to Neo-Expressionist work. In addition to the abstracted sort of "weathers" she had found in the Heads and Hands, here were her own impressions of light and seascape—the sights from her own home—more Monet in appearance than Munch.

During the fall of 1981 and the winter and spring of 1982, Rothenberg moved her studies of boats on water and their shadows and reflections to her West Broadway studio, where she continued to work on them from memory. (She gave up the Franklin Street studio when the five Heads and Hands paintings were completed.) At the same time she continued to find domestic images for her studies of figures in motion. She painted her nine-year-old daughter practicing cartwheels *(Maggie's Cartwheel)* and ballet exercises *(Maggie's Split)*. Rothenberg returned yet again to heads in *Three Plus One,* superimposing three bandlike heads and placing a footprint off to one side. By the spring and summer of 1982, Rothenberg again found herself stuck, without a single image that she could refigure repeatedly. By summer the impending Stedelijk show as well as domestic pressures were looming.

Rothenberg was about to move from her home on West Broadway, the site of her beginnings as an artist, the lucky place that she knew, to a new home and studio at the northern edge of TriBeCa. At the same time, she was "quitting booze and was in a tough new place," as she put it, as well as beginning to see a psychotherapist.[39] These two difficult processes encouraged her to see herself with new clarity but also elicited confusion, and the results were readily apparent in her work. Her immediate fears, however, revolved around working in a new space and readying the new paintings for the Stedelijk exhibition.

Rothenberg discussed the prospect of canceling the exhibition with her dealer, Miani Johnson, who suggested that she wait until August 1982 before deciding. With the

MAGGIE'S CARTWHEEL 1981-82
Oil on canvas
25 × 30½″

Installation
The Stedelijk Museum, Amsterdam, 1982
Left to right: *White Mountain,* 1980-81
Maggie's Cartwheel, 1981-82
Blue Oval, 1981
Big and Little Head, 1980-81 (through doorway)
Blue Body, 1980-81

BLUE OVAL 1981
Oil on canvas
19½ × 14″

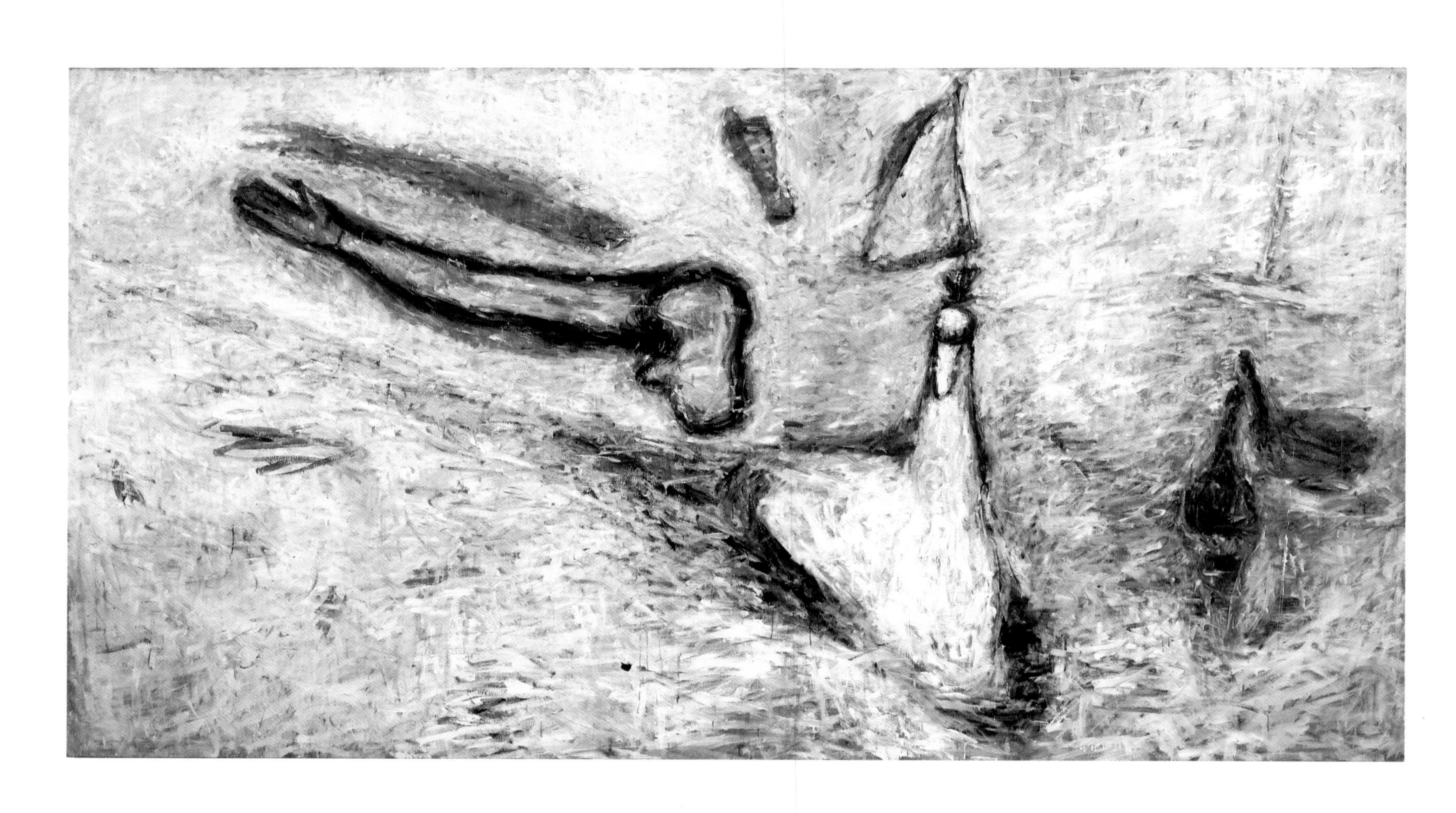

WITHALL 1982
Oil on canvas
5′5⅛″ × 10′6¾″

permission to cancel in place, Rothenberg found herself working with great momentum and a sense of ease that gave her the freedom to use anything that was available to her: "I put everything I wanted to in," she remembers. "Bits and pieces from other paintings, the real swans that were on the creek, the sailboats. The hard part was understanding that I could put a figurative—a human-figure—element in there. But Christ, it was there." (Almost immediately after completing the first sailboats, Rothenberg began to include a ghostly figure on board that echoed the shapes of the sails.)

Everything that spilled from her head and hand, including a disembodied arm and hand itself, as well as heads, full figures, swans, boats, footprints—imagistically and procedurally streams of consciousness—were explored against an agitated, watery ground with no concern for "the rules." Flatness had gone by the wayside, replaced by representational, often volumetric images and their actual reflections, and the previously suppressed figure was visible—full frame as well as in fragments. If her early attempts in oil looked impressionistic, these, with their odd juxtapositions, fragmentation, dreamlike bits and pieces, dislocations of relative scale and place, with virtually no editing of content, began to look strangely surreal. Further, Rothenberg had broken with her customary way of exploring images new to her—that is, by progressing from small to medium to large canvases—to simultaneously work in all sizes and scales from the diminutive *Baby Swan Family* (six inches square) to the fifteen-and-a-half-foot sweep of *Tenmen.* She worked in square, vertical, and horizontal formats, extreme variations for an artist who had rarely veered from a standard horizontal rectangle.

Withall is probably the tour de force of this period. Centered in its watery field is a swan with a tiny sailboat situated behind it but which actually perches on its head. To its left is a human head with an arm projecting out of it (as well as a shadow/reflection of the arm above). Between these images and slightly above is a footprint (from *Three Plus One*); to the right of the swan is the ghost of a sailboat and some other shadowy figures adrift in space. The painting not only summarizes a lexicon of images but takes them and their wildly painted surfaces to a level of compositional and narrative absurdity that makes them seem all at once ordinary and exotic, familiar yet foreign, intimate and theatrical.

But if the surreal aspect of these works signaled imagistic fragments as pieces of psyche, automatically evoked onto and into dreamlike spaces (rather than the iconic isolation of a single image within a field as in her earliest horses or the immediately preceding Heads and Hands paintings), Rothenberg also at this time made self-portrait-like works and her first and only named *Self-Portrait.* The rendering of a head with small, tablike ears has a cigarette and smoke emerging from an almost cartoon-like version of an animal head. As with the Heads and Hands series, when Rothenberg admitted her self rather than a surrogate into the work, the vision of self-image was modest, reduced to very few indicators, notations of either an animal-like presence or the fewest detached linear elements that could be imagined together to construct or identify human form. Presented is

SELF-PORTRAIT 1982
Oil on canvas
15¼ × 21″

BLUE BARS 1982
Oil on canvas
87 × 52″

UNTITLED
1982
Pencil on paper
20¼ × 23¾″

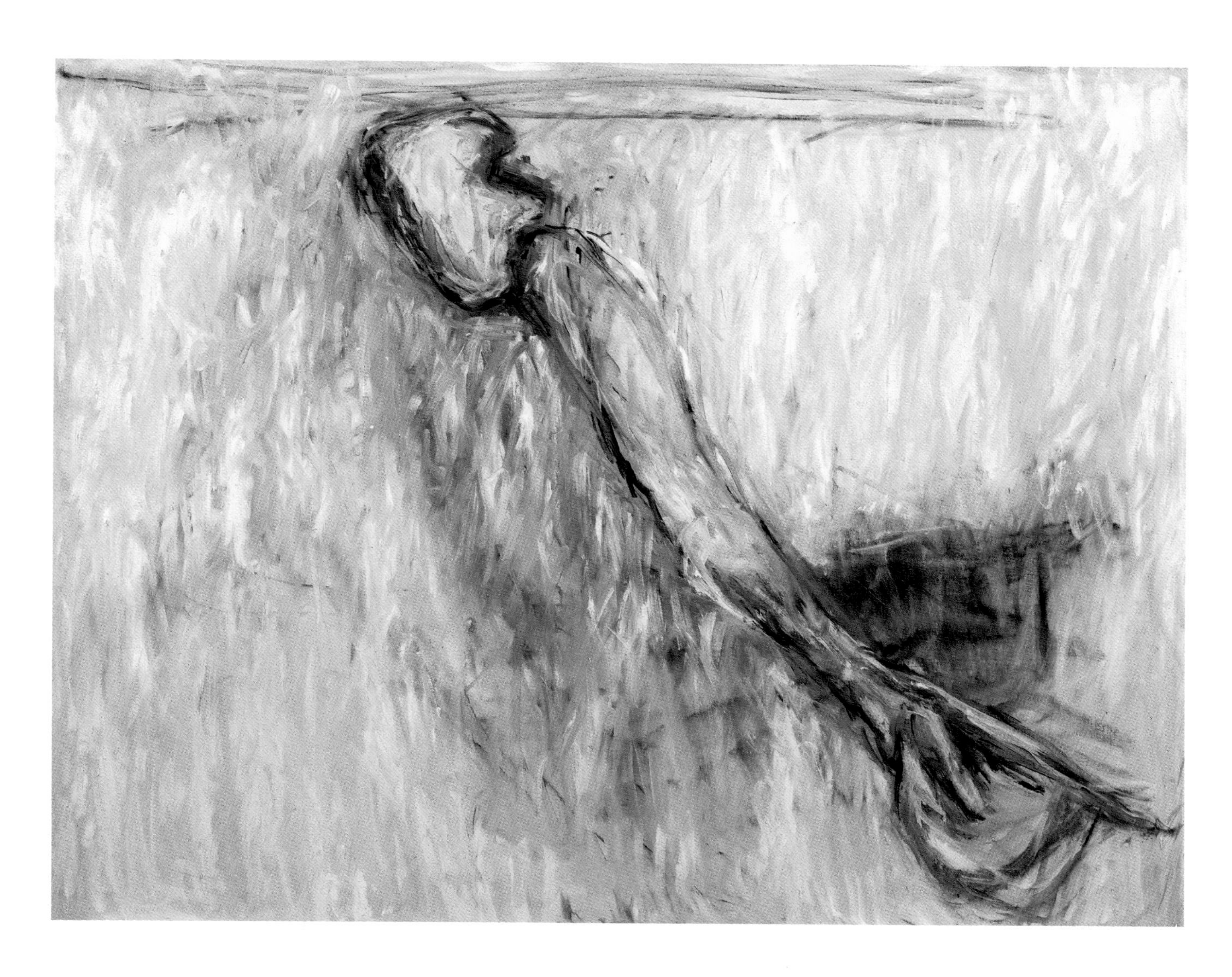

BEGGAR 1982
Oil on canvas
39½ × 50½″

a simplified set of contours, someone floating there, open and rather innocent, summarily and forthrightly stated.

Not surprisingly, given the psychological depths of these paintings, Rothenberg's emotionally charged blue turns up frequently—sometimes as body fragments, sometimes as field, sometimes as bars or lines that serve as markers of thoughts or projections of feelings. In *Little Blue Freak* a small circle of head and arms, barely inscribed at the top of the blue field, hovers above a white circle of a body (recalling *Blue Body,* one of the last two horse paintings), while in *Blue Oval* an outlined profile head sits above an oval torso fragment and a black lozenge foot/footprint; a black line zigzags through the head and down toward its exit at the right edge of the canvas. The three *Blue Bars,* noted in the title of a 1982 painting, hover in the middle zone of the canvas, floating above a head blowing smoke into a hat, as if they were Rothenberg's formal equivalent of the cartoonist's balloon in which narration, dialogue, and thoughts appear. (Her bars, though, offer an open-ended suggestion that the viewer fill in the blanks.) In *Tenmen,* which in its final state isolated one figure (and its projection, as in *Our Lord* from 1979) in the center of an attenuated horizontal field, a single blue line extends from the right edge of the canvas, piercing and barely exiting the head, like a thought, a memory of the nine other figures that had once been there but had been painted out, and which Rothenberg described as having been moving across the canvas in a kind of "pilgrimage."

The works from mid-1982 were painted in many different tones of white—from acidy yellows to warmer, lusher, gray hues. Some, like *Asian Sex* or *Beggar,* appear to have been painted with sheets of rain. If Rothenberg's paring away of excess figures in *Tenmen* as well as the almost existential isolation of a figure from a turbulent but undetailed world is reminiscent of Alberto Giacometti's sculptures, so too do her palette and brushstroke at this time bring to mind his paintings. Yet rather than reflecting the compression of Giacometti's space, Rothenberg's remains expansive. Again, the invocation of another admired artist (Rothenberg had known his works well from the Albright-Knox) was more a condensation of memories than a specific reference. As she has said, acknowledging the similarities to Giacometti, "If you're going to deal with the human figure, you're likely to bump into him."

Further, the palette as well as the imagery of these works reflected different moods and emotional states. Rothenberg could draw from feelings ranging from the height of elation to the depths of exhaustion and despair. *Patches* contains a floating body—a separate, bowed head above it, a detached spine splaying off to the right, and a telescoping three-part arm shooting down and across the left area of the canvas. "*Patches,*" Rothenberg recalls "was done with great humor and glee and no expectation of turning out a real painting. It was a flyer. I got so annoyed at trying to make things conscious to myself. I thought, Okay, you've got this painting, and threw up three black patches in a compositionally correct way. If you want to start somewhere, put some stones into this landscape, and somewhere in the back of

ASIAN SEX 1982
Oil on canvas
62 × 62″

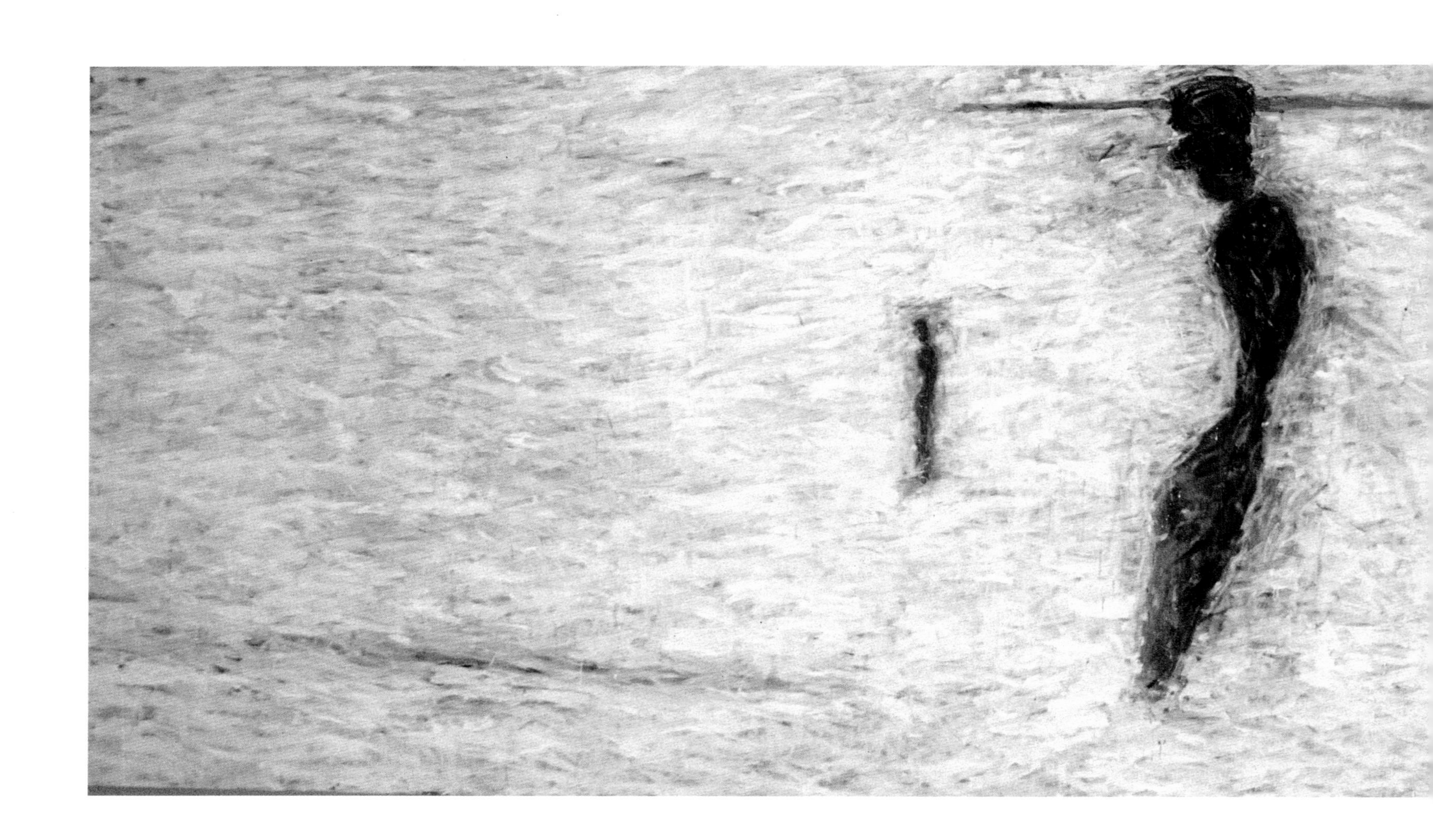

TENMEN 1982
Oil on canvas
5′1″ × 15′6¾″

Susan Rothenberg with *Patches,* 1982, at the Los Angeles County Museum of Art, 1983

Installation
Willard Gallery, New York, 1983
Left to right: *Rest,* 1981 (top)
Cocoon, 1981 (bottom)
Hourglass, 1982
Speedboat, 1981
Two Rays, 1981
Reflections, 1981
Headlights, 1982–83
Beggar, 1982

PATCHES 1982
Oil on canvas
7′3″ × 9′9″

HOURGLASS 1982
Oil on canvas
88 × 80″

THE MONK 1983
Oil on canvas
8′9″ × 5′9″

SNOWMAN 1983
Oil on canvas
79 × 86½″

my subconscious came this noseless figure and these three arms. And I don't know if this is true, but it reminded me of E. T. I did see the movie." From this jokey start came an image she would reuse many times (*The Monk,* 1983, would include the same bowed head; and *Snowman,* 1983, displays a similar pose, though its head, while appearing to bow, has actually been knocked off by a speeding snowball and is falling—the actions frozen as if in a blurred snapshot).

Beggar, 1982, also depicts a head and an outstretched arm, with hat in hand. (It relates both to *Blue Bars* and Untitled, 1982, a drawing in which Rothenberg doubles the hand and hat, as well as a leg, and begins to show sequential movement.) The image and surface handling in *Beggar* explicitly derived from Rothenberg's much bleaker attitude of the previous months. "This was a very painful, sad moment in my life," she remembers, "dealing with alcohol, dealing with Maggie, dealing with lots of things, dealing with moving to a new home. It was . . . a conscious reflection of the mood I was in." Its single sweep from head to hand, as well as its content, brings to mind Bruce Nauman's *From Hand to Mouth,* 1967, a wax-over-cloth cast fragment of the same anatomical territory. Nauman's, however, is an external commentary, a verbal punning on the plight of the artist in general (and a literal cast of someone other than himself to generalize from the one to the many), while Rothenberg's is an internal meditation on her own reaching out from an emotionally impoverished, exhausted nadir.

All of these paintings, plus the five Heads and Hands paintings, and many others, were in her Stedelijk exhibition, which opened the day before the opening of a group exhibition in Berlin entitled "Zeitgeist," which heralded Neo-Expressionism as the spirit of the decade. At the Stedelijk, Rothenberg presented a new body of work that departed from the prevailing mode and reflected an extraordinarily complex personal and painterly search. In Berlin she was represented by three of her earliest horse paintings (two of them, *Algarve* and *United States,* were from her first show seven years before at 112 Greene Street), and she found that she was the only woman in an exhibition of more than fifty artists.

Rothenberg's singular position in the Berlin exhibition generated further complications; Rothenberg was doubly isolated, first by finding herself the lone woman in the show and second by the fear that she would be "hassled or hazed" by feminist artists because she hadn't responded to indirect requests that she demonstrate against the event. Lacking information about both the show and the demonstration, she was isolated by her very inclusion.

Reluctant to be political, as she had been unwilling to espouse any theoretical positions regarding her art, she nonetheless found that her isolation and singularity had themselves become political in the changing climate of the art world. "Zeitgeist" not only proclaimed Neo-Expressionism the dominant mode in art-making but also reflected the heroics and male cast to the work and male casting of the scene. Having avoided thus far the persona of the successful artist, Rothenberg now found herself in the position of a public figure. She

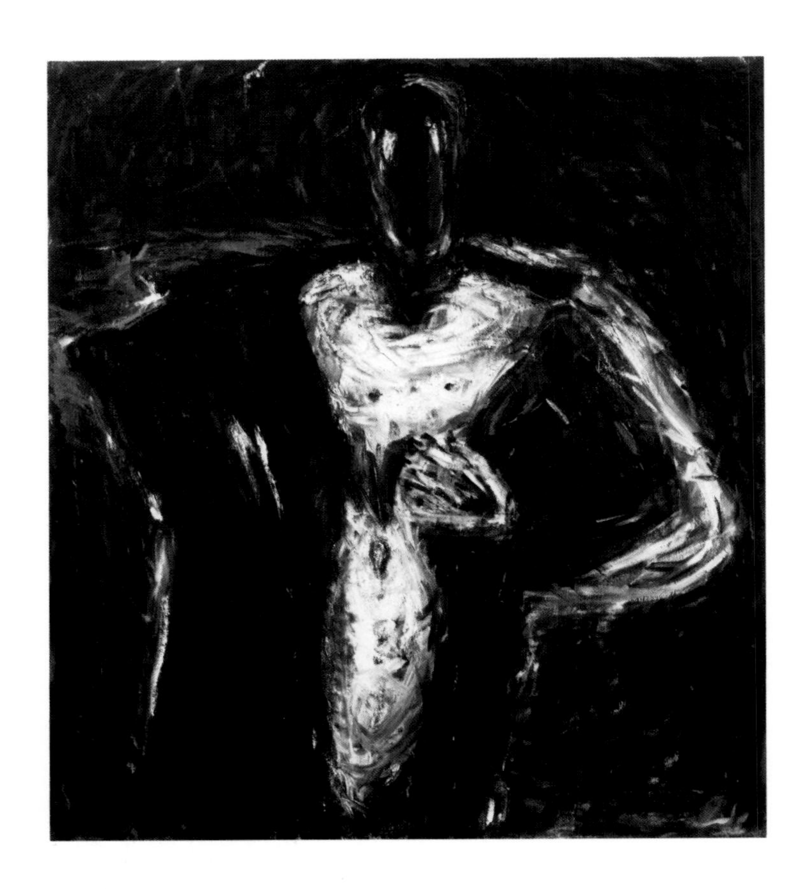

OVERCOAT
1982-83
Oil on canvas
44 × 39½″

had outgrown her "Orphan Annie" act, and she decided from that time on she would no longer participate in group shows where she was the only woman artist and that she would have to make her position clear. Identifying privately with feminist goals was no longer sufficient.

This nascent willingness to connect to a larger world, to identify with other people, would soon be reflected in her work. By 1983 she was ready to look outside herself and her immediate surroundings—to look to human beings, identifiable people, and to begin to capture more personal moments. Unlike the cultural reporting that was at the core of much Neo-Expressionist work, Rothenberg's connectedness took the form of looking to specific people, to the immediate world around her, and to her own family history to locate particular "emotional moments" rather than the more general "emotional states" her previous works had focused on.

Such moments were signs of human gesture in both the affective and motile senses of the word. As Rothenberg has said regarding her painting *Overcoat,* "It began as a figure either taking off or putting on an overcoat, either coming or going, but it very quickly unbecame that";[40] it was in fact the emblem of the end of a love affair. The figure in *The Monk,* suspended in space like a marionette, bowing its head, keyed into many of Rothenberg's thoughts at the time. As she told Lisbet Nilsen: "Sometimes the painting starts to relate very directly to either sights seen or experiences felt; other times it just goes off on a tangent

GREEN RAY 1984
Oil on canvas
7′ × 8′11″

that you really can't articulate. Some of the pictures are truly mysterious to me—which is why I so often say publicly that I don't know or don't care what they're really about. And yet I also can say that the paintings are prayers—that they have to do with whatever it is that makes you want more than what daily life affords. I think they're a lot about sublimation, about the things that don't happen in your life, that you get to *paint.* You have the freedom to make them up for yourself. Or—you can exorcise. You get to put the world together the way you want."[41]

If Rothenberg had sequentially tackled emotional and stylistic territories almost in a syncopated fashion that put her continually out of step with (though in hindsight usually ahead of) the art world, this implication of spiritualism, indeed outright humanism, was the biggest shift yet. Much Neo-Expressionist work had dealt with big ideas about humanity but had stopped short of intimate ideas about human contact and compassion.[42] In fact, by the mid-1980s, in the quickening tempo of action and reaction, the new art had swung away from the emotional bombast, impassioned surfaces, and grand themes of Neo-Expressionism to a reductive commentary on the commodification of culture, reflected in a highly polished, almost baroque Neo-Minimalism. Rothenberg continued to follow her own personal imperative, which took her into newly intimate territory.

Simultaneous with finding a new kind of metaphysical content in works like *The Monk,* Rothenberg also found a new kind of impossible physical force to capture. Her defying of gravity, actually playing with it, is seen in *The Monk* as well as in *Green Ray,* where two panda-puppet heads float beneath two puppeteer heads. The bobbing, shifting action first captured in the boat paintings would turn to outright interest in speed and motion. The first signs of this interest were seen in *Snowman,* whose veering snowball is equal in importance to the falling head it has just knocked off. In *Falling Rock,* 1983, and *Bucket of Water,* 1983-84, this idea becomes the central focus. Speed, spill, and continuous movement were beginning to replace Rothenberg's signature stop-action technique.

With *Bucket of Water* Rothenberg also began to locate specific places and relationships between people as well as offering almost a Cubist faceting of motion in progress. Looking out of her studio on Long Island one summer, she saw a neighbor who had an aviary tossing feed from a bucket, and it was the connection both to *this* person (not a generalized idea of a figure) in *this* place, and the continuous movement of the bucket that held Rothenberg's attention. Despite the realism of the scene, Rothenberg introduced an element that is both a formal, and impossible presence. A purple horizontal figure shoots across the rather empty left section of the canvas and abuts the vertical figure at the shoulder. Appearing at first to be another distended arm in the arc of point-by-point arm movements, this wraithlike form serves much the same linear and spectral purposes as the green line in *Green Ray* or the blue line in *Tenmen.*

The neighbor was the same woman who became the model for *Grandmother,* 1983-84, one of Rothenberg's most intimate paintings and the first in which she included two

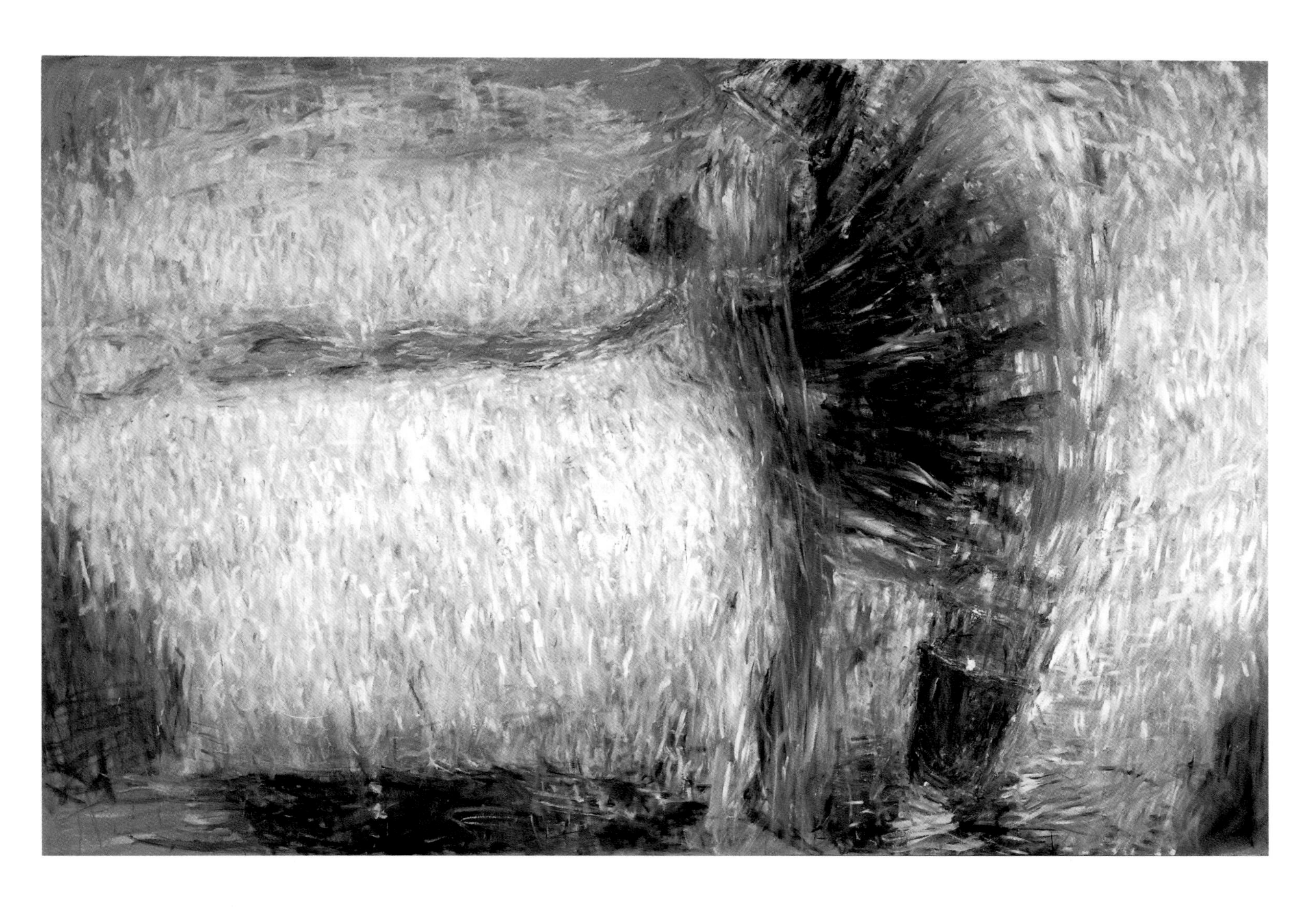

BUCKET OF WATER 1983-84
Oil on canvas
7′ × 10′7″

GRANDMOTHER 1983-84
Oil on canvas
7′5″ × 9′4½″

separate figures relating to each other (rather than fragments of figures, or figures and shadows designed to double the identity of a single figure). The grandmother is shown standing in a pool of water holding her grandchild tenderly in her arms. As Rothenberg told Grace Glueck, it was "the first time I'd done a special moment. She was standing outside my studio last summer, affectionately complaining about having to look after the kid. Yet as she held it, it drank in her love like milk. I spent a long time deciding to dare to do such a sentimental picture. But then I thought, 'Why not?'"[43]

From 1983 to 1985, Rothenberg let a whole new cast of characters into her painting: friends, family members, even the family dog, Al. Memory images of important moments and meaningful figures began to be admitted to the work. As the subject matter became familiar—for the first time Rothenberg knew a good deal about what her images were going to look like before she began to paint them on canvas—she challenged herself with a new set of painterly problems, among them, the aforementioned idea of conveying a sense of continuous movement and the question of how to handle a fuller range of colors. (Color continued to be used to punctuate her monochromatic fields rather than in any naturalistic sense. And for the most part, as in *Green Ray,* the purple of *Bucket of Water,* or the yellow in *Al with Bananas,* a single color is used.)

After having concentrated as much on pools or spills of light-filled water as on the full figures themselves in *Bucket of Water* and *Grandmother,* in 1984 Rothenberg did a drawing "with not much thought in mind other than it would be a figure partially dissolved by light. In other words, the features wouldn't necessarily have to be distinguished and whatnot." The resulting figure is as stark, formal, and abstracted as a Greek kouros; its flattened facial planes might easily be made of timeworn stone and be seen in glaring outdoor light. He is, though, a thoroughly modern man, with his dark trousers and watchful, spectacled eyes.

In observing what she had intuitively evoked onto the charcoal drawing—a process Rothenberg described as "moving my hand on the paper . . . like a Ouija board"[44]—she thought simply "that it was looking like Mondrian." That she called the figure Mondrian, when in fact he looks much like several other of her figures from the early 1980s, is typical of Rothenberg's claim to an image and subject matter. "It just reminded me of him. I had seen some photographs of him in a catalogue or survey books. It just looked like this thin, spare, severe, lonely whited-out man, and I just got into my head, That's Mondrian. If I was somebody else it might have popped into my head that it was William Burroughs or some other spare, skinny, stark man. But I had made eyeglasses on him. I just decided that it was Mondrian. And I liked the drawing a lot, so I did the painting. And then I started to play with the idea of making paintings of Mondrian [as a] kind of imaginary dialogue with him."

The Mondrian image Rothenberg found in this untitled drawing from 1984 turned out to be as psychologically charged and autobiographically compelling as the abstracted

UNTITLED
1984
Charcoal on paper
29½ × 42½″

horses of the 1970s and the Heads and Hands of 1980-81, and it soon became apparent that the Mondrian drawing introduced another iconic figure into her work—one that was so provocative as to generate an entire series within the year. The drawing also represents two firsts for Rothenberg. It was the first time she used a specific art-historical figure in her work (in fact, if we consider all of the Mondrian paintings as an entity, it was the only instance). More important is that it marked a completely new relationship of drawing to painting for Rothenberg. It was the first time a work on paper had specifically generated a painting. As she recently explained for the first time: "I used to do drawings after painting when there was not energy to paint. I used drawing in a lighter way—when I didn't feel like painting. The Mondrian drawing changed that. The drawing had magic, generative power, and the process reversed. It was the first time that I felt, This drawing needs to be a painting. It wasn't a diagram but actually generated an image. And I've continued to use drawing that way. It's still true."

Part homage, part affectionate display of rebellion toward an admired master, the Mondrian series begins with a painting based on Untitled, 1984. In *Mondrian,* 1984, the figure looks out from a nine-foot-high canvas. Both the perspective from which we look into the painting and the scale of the figure within it theatrically magnify this giant in twentieth-century art. We see Mondrian from above, as if we were perched in the flies observing an actor leaving the stage (despite the fact that by virtue of the painting's size and the scale of the figure within it we are looking up at him). A chair is behind him, and a second chair is dwarfed toward the rear in a corner. We see Mondrian, cropped at the legs, monumentally coming up into our space, like an idol, both mythical and matinee.

As she told Grace Glueck, this Mondrian painting is "privately, secretly a little bit of an homage. I really have tremendous feeling about who he must have been, both about how screwed up he probably was, and also how pure and wonderful and disciplined. . . . I'm most unlike him—it's really about the attraction of opposites—but he moves me as much as someone might who's more a kindred spirit."[45]

Although their works are stylistically overtly different—Rothenberg's representational imagery and intuitive, personal approach is the antithesis of Mondrian's cerebral geometric abstraction—their works have a kinship in at least one fundamental way. Mondrian's concept of "dynamic equilibrium," of balancing his asymmetrical geometries might well be applied to Rothenberg's own compositional method of keeping space tensely activated. She not only has played symmetry against asymmetry but from the start has been involved

UNTITLED
1984
Charcoal on paper
49 × 37″

UNTITLED
1984
Charcoal on paper
47½ × 31″

MONDRIAN 1984
Oil on canvas
9′1″ × 7′

Installation
Willard Gallery, New York, 1985
Left to right:
Red Blush, 1984-85
Elizabeth, 1984-85
INGspray, 1984-85

with balancing forces with counterforces—geometries for her early horses, bones for later ones, and shadows for her figures. A kind of perpetual motion is captured in the bobbing of boats against water, and in her works of the 1980s, the dancers, jugglers, vaulters, and spinners all depend literally on dynamic equilibrium to accomplish their tasks.

If the first Mondrian drawing and painting are awesomely heroic, the subsequent paintings in the series are playful and at times a bit perverse. In *Mondrian Dancing,* 1984-85, Rothenberg gives him a female partner and impacts both his and her own love of dancing as well as inevitably signaling Mondrian's masterwork *Broadway Boogie Woogie.* For *INGspray,* 1984-85, she mischievously puts the urbane gentleman who supposedly hated the color green outdoors in a field, inclining his face up as if sunbathing and giving his mouth a slight curl implying a wryly self-satisfied smile. (The title is also child's play—pig Latin for spring.)

In *A Golden Moment,* 1985, Rothenberg locates Mondrian's signature primaries and rigorous geometries in miniature, laid out on a table before him like paint chips or playing cards. The overall composition of a card-playing figure seated at a table under the glare of an overhead light is much like Rothenberg's portrait of her father of the previous year, *L. R.,* which literally depicts a golden moment in the family's history. Unlike the mood of quiet, rather amused contemplation in the Mondrian painting, the ambience, as well as the light of *L. R.* is strained and taut. Rothenberg's father is shown settling a business dispute by drawing cards. "Whoever pulled the ace had the choice of buying the other members out or selling out themselves. It was a very tense moment. It seemed like a wild way to get out of it—it had become an impossible power struggle for these five men. And it was my

MONDRIAN DANCING 1984-85
Oil on canvas
78¼ × 91″

A GOLDEN MOMENT 1985
Oil on canvas
54 × 48″

L. R.
1984
Oil on canvas
47 × 36″

PILLOW
1984
Oil on canvas
46½ × 54½″

dad's way of dealing with it." Rothenberg's father lost the draw, but his loss was paradoxical, radically altering his own sense of worth, in two ways. He lost his job, his professional identity, yet earned a million dollars in the moment. The idea that success turned on luck stuck with Rothenberg, as well as what that moment must have looked and felt like.[46]

Out of fairness, Rothenberg tried to make a portrait of her mother that would similarly isolate a single critical moment, but the only image that stuck with her for *Pillow,* 1984, was of her mother's illnesses, a consistently recurring moment of being bedridden. The figure is also seen in chiaroscuro; the only light illuminating the canvas emanates from the pillow that supports and envelops her and, oddly, from the soles of her feet, which are depicted parallel to the picture plane.[47] There is also a portrait of *Papa Cohen,* 1985, her grandfather; of her dog, *Al with Bananas,* 1984; of *Elizabeth,* 1984–1985, Elizabeth Murray; and of Rothenberg with Maggie (page 125).

In 1985 Rothenberg also made two works—*Biker* and *Holding the Floor*—that furthered her investigations of speed and motion. The strong impact of *Biker* and the apparent speed and continuous motion of the bike as it races forward—though with only the sparest notations indicating the rider's head floating above and disconnected from its torso, a disembodied hand also reaching toward the head, and the wheels of the bike spinning through water and spraying it into the air—recall the earlier horses charging as if to break

BIKER 1985
Oil on canvas
74¼ × 69″

Installation
Willard Gallery, New York, 1985
Left to right:
Bucket of Water, 1983-84
Biker, 1985
Trumpeter, 1984-85

UNTITLED
1984
Charcoal on paper
18¼ × 24½″

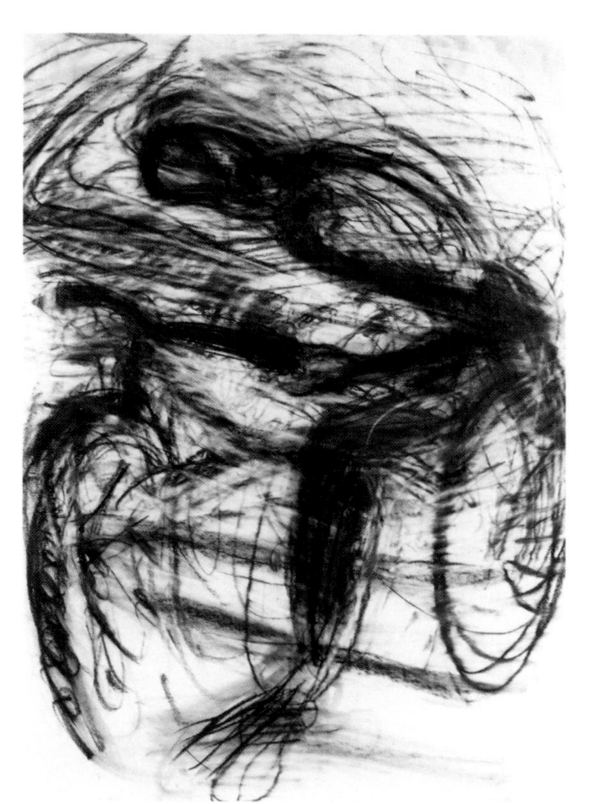

BIKER
1985
Charcoal on paper
43 × 31″

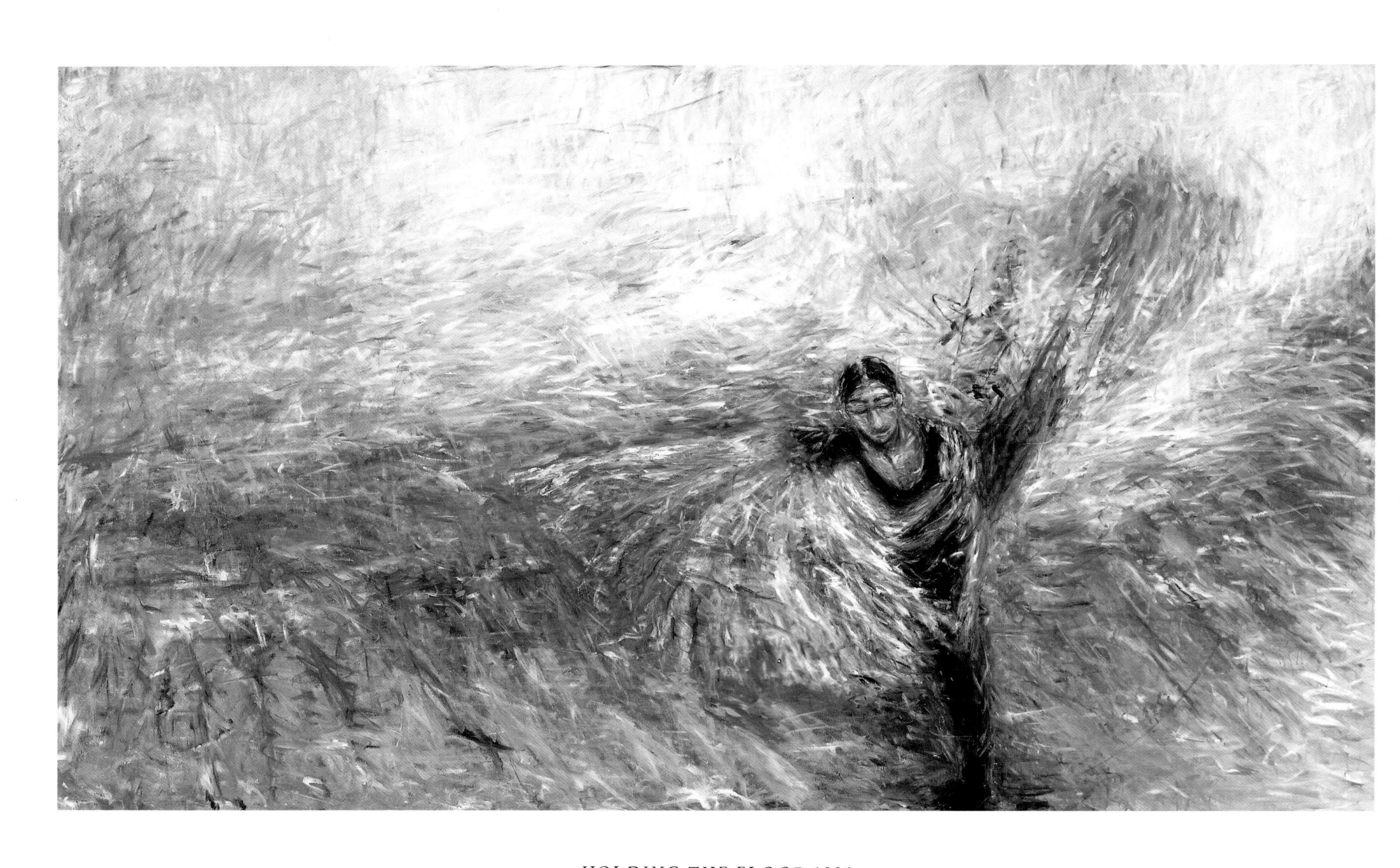

HOLDING THE FLOOR 1985
Oil on canvas
7′3″ × 12′3 1/16″

directly out of the picture plane, as well as the spills of *Bucket of Water.* The painting also evidences Rothenberg's most successful use of color; using what she calls only a "puff" of red and blue with black and white, she applied the paint so freely that it alone supplies the momentum. The related black-and-white Biker drawings are even more dynamic.

The painting has an ease with color—an elegance in its essential construction of the image of color that Rothenberg has yet to equal—as well as a contradictory tension of both centripetal and centrifugal forces in operation. In other respects, the painting is one of Rothenberg's "oddballs"; during a period of making particular, recognizable people, this one is an anonymous figure, and is also symbolically ambiguous.[48] In addition, the abstracted figure is constructed more of negative space than positive—the empty places between head and torso, head and hand, and torso and bicycle create the figure and its posture even though those spaces are as airy as the sky above—while the other figures from the same period are the most full bodied, almost modeled with blended colors, of any Rothenberg has ever made.

In *Holding the Floor* a dancer is firmly grounded on one leg, a fixed arabesque countered by the sweeping gesture of one arm. As is the case with all of Rothenberg's paintings whose subjects are in some way portraits, the sitter never sits for the painting and in fact rarely knows that he or she is the ostensible subject until being told by Rothenberg, seeing the painting itself, reading its title, or seeing other published references. I myself was the subject of such a surprise with *Holding the Floor.* Even more curious than seeing a bit of a likeness embedded into one of Rothenberg's more generic figures and faces was to read Rothenberg's take on the painting: "*Holding the Floor* is about an imagined moment in a real person's fantasy based on fact."[49] Rothenberg's ability to generate more complicated truths and an eerie sort of hyperreality based on the simple observation of the difference between studying dance and the dream of being a dancer—this adolescent girl's dilemma, which is as much Rothenberg's moment as any girl's—is like a jazz musician's riffs expanding on the meaning and resonance of a few notes. Rothenberg's further description of the painting is wonderfully telling of what painting means to her: "Its complexities involve perceptual and psychological memories based on real and imagined experiences. The results are a way of discovering what I know and what I don't, what I didn't know and I knew and what I want to learn—which are things that seem close to unpaintable, which is why I love painting, which is not quite like the donkey and the carrot, but close."[50]

Rothenberg interrupted her study of continuous motion—the spinning wheels of *Biker* would turn up again as would dancers—to return to a static, anonymous single figure that, though not a Mondrian, shares more than a passing resemblance to him. She worked on *Half and Half,* 1985-87 (page 148), during the time that spanned her separation from Willard Gallery, which had represented her for ten years. Rothenberg almost surgically took the figure apart, breaking it at the waist and deploying torso and legs side by side in a brushy, ambiguous (though probably indoor) field. The arrangement, with the head and torso

G. T.
1977
Acrylic on canvas
87 × 70″

downstage from the legs and with the former almost moving out of the canvas (compositionally reminiscent of *Mondrian*), suggests that one part of the figure is moving ahead and one part is being left behind, the one fragment of a self trailing another into an undefined new territory. While the treatment of the figure is reminiscent of her own bisecting of the horse image in the mid-1970s (which nevertheless remained whole despite its minimal divide), the painting seems to mirror Rothenberg's own situation at the time: she was between things—on her own, with no gallery, and between subjects for her art as well.

Rothenberg painted one last single figure dissolving into and ascending from the watery space around it. *Red Man,* 1985-86, is an affectionate good-bye to a former boyfriend as well as to the isolated figures and intimate moments she had been using as subjects for her paintings for the preceding years. The first secret portrait, however, was done almost ten years before. *G. T.,* 1977, of George Trakas, was painted during one of their many times apart. Both *G. T.* and *Red Man* are both doubly memory images—painted from memory and as mementos to hold onto important presences even as they were absent.

Rothenberg went back to the sweeping, spinning, continuous movements she had captured in *Biker* and *Holding the Floor,* and for the first time she approached a painterly

RED MAN 1985-86
Oil on canvas
9′4″ × 7′10″

UNTITLED
1986
Acrylic, charcoal, flashe, graphite, and oil stick on paper
5 × 12′

issue as an "absolute theoretical kind of challenge." The idea of concentrating on movement was a deliberate attempt to do what she previously "didn't want to do at all," Rothenberg recalls, "[to] really try and see how much movement I'm capable of making. It was taking on a whole piece of territory that didn't feel very personal, but it seemed like, Let's sweep out this whole corner that I've never explored before and move in here for a while."

The spinners, dancers, vaulters, and jugglers made between 1986 and 1988 attempt to keep a sense of continuous motion rather than arresting it with geometries as she had done in the early horses and with the bone shapes she used to control, actually stop, the movements in the later, more animated ones. The motion in the dancers is also different from that depicted in either *Bucket of Water* or *Holding the Floor.* These two paintings focused on one continuous, steady movement (almost in the step-by-step manner of Duchamp's *Nude Descending a Staircase*) by but one part of the body—the arms—while the overall figure, as a counterpoint, remained static. With these new works, Rothenberg concentrated on the rush, the sense of air being whipped around bodies, the multiple dervish-like turns, the constancy of repetitive actions, giving a new spin to both Action Painting as well as Futurist explorations of time and motion.[51]

Each of the dancers is spinning so fast that it becomes a blur of light, sending off sparks or kicking up dust as it moves. And each of the paintings features a single or several figures twirling across a floor—coequal now with the height of the canvas, their feet at the bottom edge, the full bodies suspended from top to bottom through the invisible plumb line that a dancer maintains by spotting, keeping eyes level with and focused on a single point ahead, continually siting along the horizontal line, and whipping the head around, to stay both

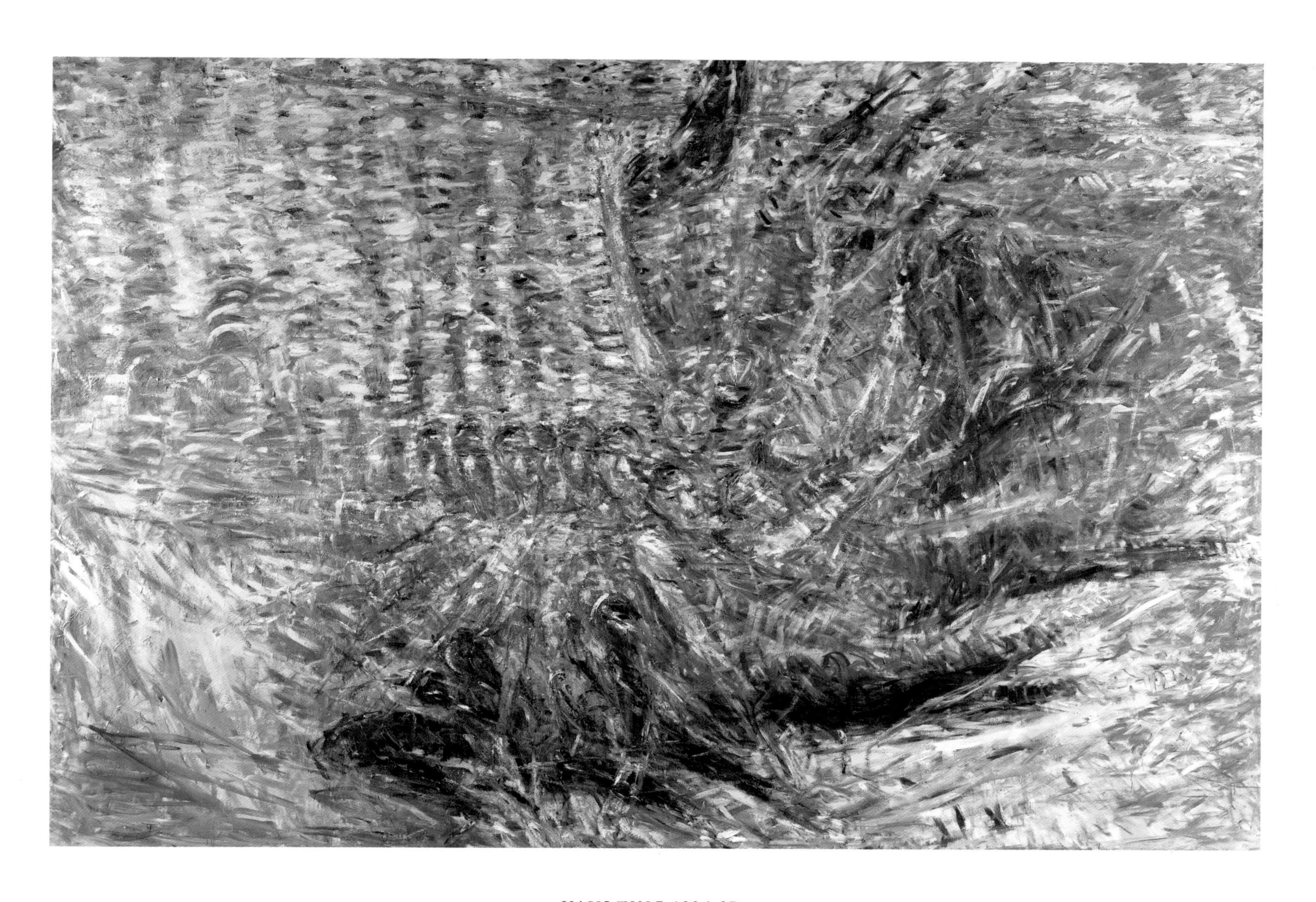

VAULTING 1986-87
Oil on canvas
7′6″ × 11′

UNTITLED
1987
Charcoal, oil, and graphite on paper
43¾ × 30″

UNTITLED
1987
Graphite on paper
22⅜ × 31″

GYRO 1986–87
Oil on canvas
8′2″ × 9′3½″

HEAD ROLL 1987
Oil on canvas
$36\frac{3}{4} \times 64\frac{1}{2}''$

UNTITLED
1987
Charcoal and pencil on paper
11⅞ × 8⅛″

UNTITLED
1986
Charcoal and pencil on paper
21 × 30″

vertical and on course without becoming dizzy. The movement depicted in each painting is a constant flow from left to right across the field, and it is the perpetual blur of movement, rather than any individualized figure, that keeps the momentum going and the canvas dynamic and compositionally taut.

These are anonymous figures once again, and confusing ones. While their path is clear, the paint handling is frenetic and somewhat shaky. Heavily worked, in stark contrast to the lightness and speed of the movements depicted, the canvases are dense, impacted, loaded with paint and an intermixing of a variety of strange colors—acidy greens, sharp oranges, and an almost Schiaparelli pink—all embedded in and mixed with a variety of white flurrying strokes. (Curiously, as Rothenberg's surfaces became as impacted and problematically clotted as they have ever been, her parallel drawings to these works are as open, linear, and airy as any she has done. Her hand is as quick and as light as the dancers' movements.) The ambiguity concerning the number of figures in each painting is puzzling even to Rothenberg: "I think they do reflect my state of being. I wanted them to be chaotic. I wasn't even clear in some of them if I meant it to be one body spinning across a canvas or a multiple repetition of bodies. In some paintings, I knew what I was looking for. In some I didn't. And the paint handling was very different. It was very jumpy, incremental. But that started with *Holding the Floor.* It was an Impressionist-looking surface. Very snowy."

Unlike Rothenberg's other works, the paintings completed during 1986 and 1987 are autobiographical mainly to the extent that they contain references to earlier works. The balls tossed by her jugglers recall *Rubber Balls*; *Night Ride* triples and darkens the image of *Biker;* the spinners and dancers derive from *Holding the Floor.* The latter also seems to go back to the suspended images of *The Monk, Green Ray, Red Slippers,* and *Smoker,* as well as the prescient dancer form in an untitled 1981 drawing (page 92). And while Rothenberg had herself studied dance as a child and in college and had performed with Joan Jonas, these paintings seem more about the dance than the dancer. The formal self-quotation (as well as her use of a specific literary source as inspiration for the jugglers),[52] rather than a renewed search for new, more personally charged images, seems related to Rothenberg's own circumstances at the time. She was herself in the process of juggling—choosing a new gallery and being caught up in the social spin of being courted by many diverse new dealers, as well as directly by collectors—and she seems to have kept herself at a distance from all that was going on even as she was participating. It was a confusing period and, in some ways, also exhilarating—personally isolating while professionally reconnecting—and a period that continued for the good part of a year, until she finally had chosen a new dealer, Angela Westwater of Sperone Westwater, New York (and her Rome-based partner, Gian Enzo Sperone).

Rothenberg's first show at Sperone Westwater was held in October 1987. She had worked through the spinners, jugglers, vaulters, and bikers, all of which were on view, and was resettled in a sense. The two odd paintings in the show were *Half and Half,* begun two

NIGHT RIDE 1987
Oil on canvas
7′9″ × 9′2¼″

HALF AND HALF 1985-87
Oil on canvas
60 × 85″

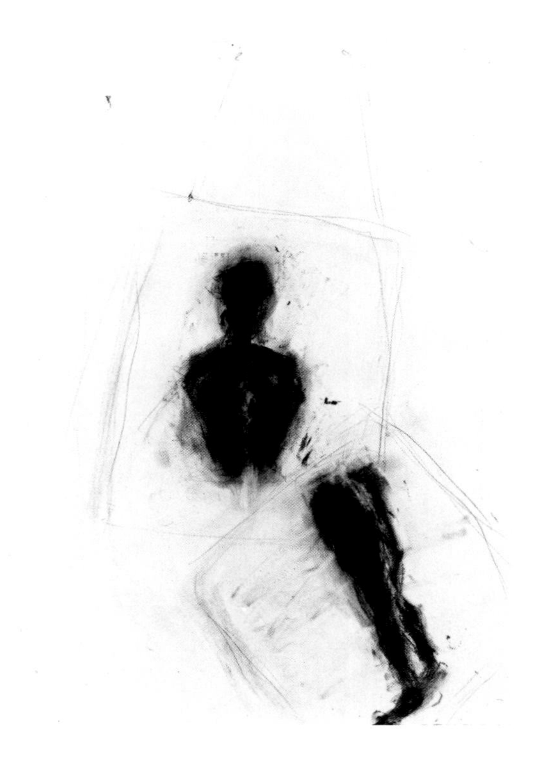

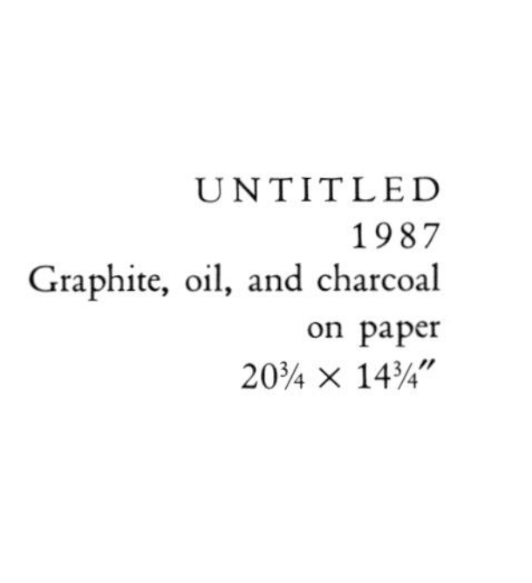

UNTITLED
1987
Graphite, oil, and charcoal
on paper
20¾ × 14¾″

UNTITLED
1986
Pencil and charcoal on paper
22 × 30″

years before, and the newest, *The Blue Chair.* The subject of the latter is a figure seated in and surrounded by a blue chair (which is mottled with white and yellow strokes, giving it a green cast), both seen from the back. The chair itself is one taken from her previous TriBeCa studio to her new one, and one in which she spent much time reading. The likelihood of this image being the artist herself is greater than at any time before. (The furniture, her own, is one clue.) Rothenberg thinks it is another Mondrian, again recomplicating the transformations and identifications, the ambiguity of the moment captured.

The Blue Chair's composition is so sure, the figure so tranquilly contained and painted with such ease that one feels comfortable in saying that the identities of self and other are fused. As Michael Brenson observed about this painting, "Although we do not see the face and are given no details, this is the only painting in which we feel the weight of an actual person and situation. If this show is a series, then this figure, in the proverbial Matissian armchair, watching the expressionistic action in the other paintings, is the anchor."[53] With its figure looking away, the painting evidences a more internalized focus and, even more specifically, a looking toward the unknown—which was always Rothenberg's more comfortable, if extremely uneasy and querulous, place. The overall configuration also seems to be predictive of both the forms and tone of the buddha paintings she was soon to make. As Rothenberg says about *The Blue Chair* and its containment, comfort, and composure, "I was definitely wanting a quiet, more static space."

Rothenberg made but three paintings on canvas in 1988, two of which were Buddhas. She herself is not certain where these images came from, although in retrospect she suspects that they hark back to some previous memory. In a recent interview she asked whether she

THE BLUE CHAIR 1987
Oil on canvas
78 × 71¼″

JUGGLER #3 1987-88
Oil on canvas
77 × 68″

had done Buddhas before and was reminded that she hadn't but had only recently talked for the first time of the stone Buddha she told all "her little problems to as a child" at the Albright-Knox; and, though she had not yet visited China, the prospect that she soon would was probably also on her mind. (The way she used negative space to build these traditionally solid forms—perversely opening up their middles with voids where rounded bellies belong—also brings to mind Rothenberg's description of the method of working with negative space she learned from Alan Atwood, the "Buddhist kind of guy" who was a drawing teacher at Cornell.) These are some of Rothenberg's most quietly ambiguous images—more puzzling and harder to pin down than many others. Cool and calm, though adding back something of the emblematic necessity that the dancers lacked, they do not feel anonymous, but neither do they share the visceral presence of her more overtly personal works.

All of the 1988 paintings use her Giotto blue color and return to the abstracted partial fragments of bodies—the pieces of corporeal space as well as consciousness—that she had tackled in the early 1980s. *Folded Buddha* and *Buddha with Bamboo* (pages 159-60) both show a figure looped around to define itself and peculiarly empty where fullness might be expected, a treatment reminiscent of the torso section of *Half and Half,* as well as an untitled 1981 drawing (page 93). Though still explicitly genderless and almost generically outlined figures once again (they are barely recognizable states rather than the full-bodied though blurred figures they followed), these images also begin to suggest a female form. In *Buddha with Bamboo,* the transformation of the rounded solidity of a Buddha shape to an open hourglass configuration is partially responsible for this quality. The bizarre treatment of the feet in *Folded Buddha* harks back to those of Rothenberg's mother in *Pillow*. *Blue Woman with Frog,* explicitly female, juxtaposes a human head and a primitive animal body of the sort the artist had abandoned almost ten years before, both located in a deeper, muddier version of her earlier red/sienna field.

Rothenberg returned to the dancers for a single project that took up most of 1988. It was her first commission—a series of six wood-panel paintings for the dining room at PaineWebber's headquarters in Manhattan. She had been interested in executing a mural project for several years, partly to escape the isolation of the studio, to work on site in a public place and engage the public in a more direct way.[54] Though the PaineWebber commission was in a more private public space than she had hoped for, the challenge of working with what turned out to be a problematic site interested her.[55]

Rothenberg turned to her advantage the difficult site in good part by her misremembering the actual spaces for which she was to make the paintings. The site encompassed six piers, each extending three feet into the room between wide expanses of plate-glass windows. What she imagined as a sweeping two-dimensional surface, for which she could parquet each wood panel into the narrow space flush with the glass, was actually a more syncopated, punctuated surface of glass to column-like separators.

1–6
1988
Oil on wood (six panels), each 10′6¾″ × 3′10⅛″

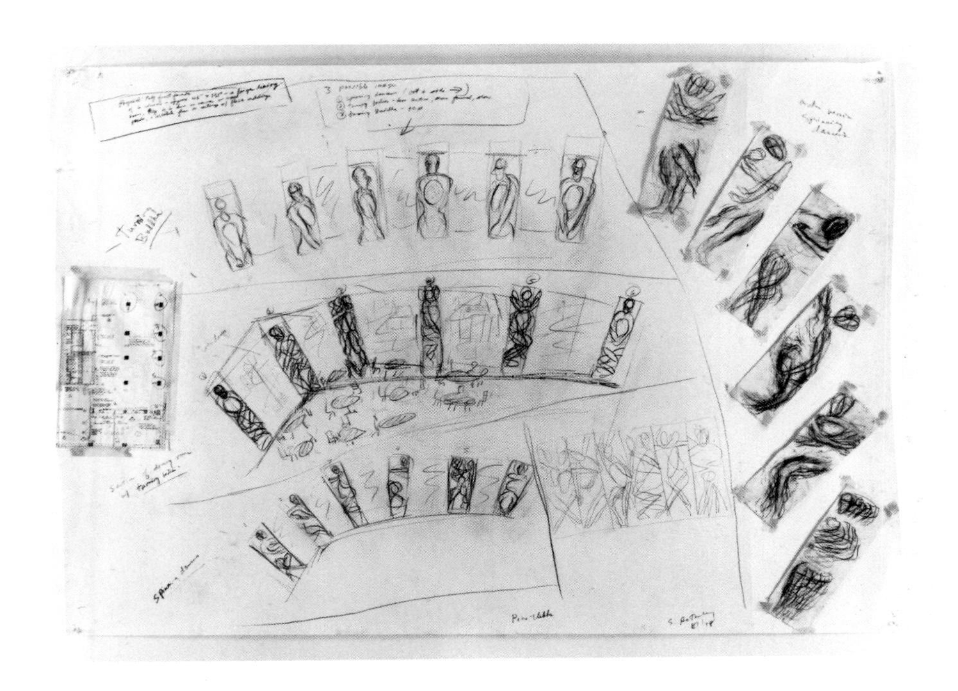

DIAGRAM FOR PAINEWEBBER COMMISSION
1987
Pencil and collage on paper,
42½ × 60¼″

INSTALLATION OF 1/6
1988
at PaineWebber Group, Inc., New York

UNTITLED
1988
Liquid graphite and charcoal on paper
42½ × 41½″

FOLDED BUDDHA 1987–88
Oil on canvas
7′7¼″ × 9′3¼″

BUDDHA WITH BAMBOO 1988
Oil on canvas
4′8″ × 9′5¼″

Rothenberg located one dancer per column. Each appears to step forward into the room (extending the forward projection of the column itself) as it simultaneously gestures laterally to the next. Movement is signaled from one to another, shooting across the gap of negative window space—revealing changing cloud formations, weathers and city views—the way electrical energy jumps nerve synapses. (The moments between the gestures have the same kind of synchronized desynchronization of Joan Jonas's *Jones Beach Piece,* in which Rothenberg performed.)

Tightly fitting each dancer into an elongated vertical panel—each measuring ten-and-a-half by almost four feet—Rothenberg perversely did not compress them but actually opened up the internal space (as she did in *Biker* and her Buddha paintings), allowing air into and actually defining the bodies. The way she cropped the figures also had the same effect—the diagonal thrusts of arm and leg seem to extend beyond each edge, heightening the sense of movement rather than stopping it. And each figure is highly differentiated in its movement as well as in the way it is painted and in its color. One is in a deep plié, about to leap; another is perfectly aligned to begin a spin; yet another is leaning into the next viscerally logical step, off kilter but in correct balance.

With this six-part work, which she titled *1-6,* Rothenberg synthesized some of her earliest ambitions and, not incidentally, saved the entire spinner series, the study of continuous movement, from being a rather academic search. As she told Hayden Herrera in 1982, referring to the full figures and fragments she had allowed herself to paint when she took to oils: "My paintings are still really visceral. It comes back to trying to invent new forms to stand in for the body since I don't want to make a realist painting. I wanted to get that body down in paint, free it from its anatomical confines. I'm very aware of my body in space—shoulders, frontal positions. I have a body language that is difficult to explain. A lot of my work is about body orientation, both in the making of the work and in the sensing of the space, comparing it to my own physical orientation."[56]

In addition to inventing new forms to reinvent the body, Rothenberg also achieved her earliest ambition of dissolving figure and ground into sky and air (there is little distinction between figure and ground within a panel; further, each panel seems to function as a figure, with bracketing windows serving as ground). She also appears to have accomplished an impossible fantasy, one that she had for the earlier spinner paintings and which she discussed with Amei Wallach in a 1986 interview: "I have a feeling [the figures] are a kind of body metaphor for human limitations and also reach. There's nowhere else you can see so clearly what the human body can't do. It can't fly. It can't."[57] Between the windows of this commission, Rothenberg's dancers appear ready to do just that.

UNTITLED
1989
Charcoal, graphite, and chalk on paper
49⅞ × 38⅛″

AFTER COMPLETING THE COMMISSION FOR PAINEWEBBER IN THE fall of 1988, Rothenberg found herself repeating a familiar refrain. She was at a loss for an image, "stuck once again." The spinners and dancers had been worked through, and Rothenberg found herself not only without an image that would carry her but also in another kind of vortex. She and the artist Bruce Nauman were involved in a cross-country courtship between New Mexico and New York, with flying stops to Florida to see an ailing father and help her mother nurse him. Rothenberg found herself not only without an image but with neither a place nor the time to work. What she was doing was connecting to both a new family and reconnecting to her own family in a new way. In February 1989 Rothenberg and Nauman married and began to plan a new home and studios in New Mexico.[58]

When she began to paint again, she started with portraits, trying some of her seventeen-year-old daughter, Maggie, which did not work out, and others of Nauman, which soon transformed into studies of an impossible body posture, a "U-turn" form where legs descend from the torso but bend back up behind the figure, a strange combination of the mythical and observed, an invented merman floating in a deep blue field. As Rothenberg told writer Dodie Kazanjian, "I wanted to do something with the body in a much slower

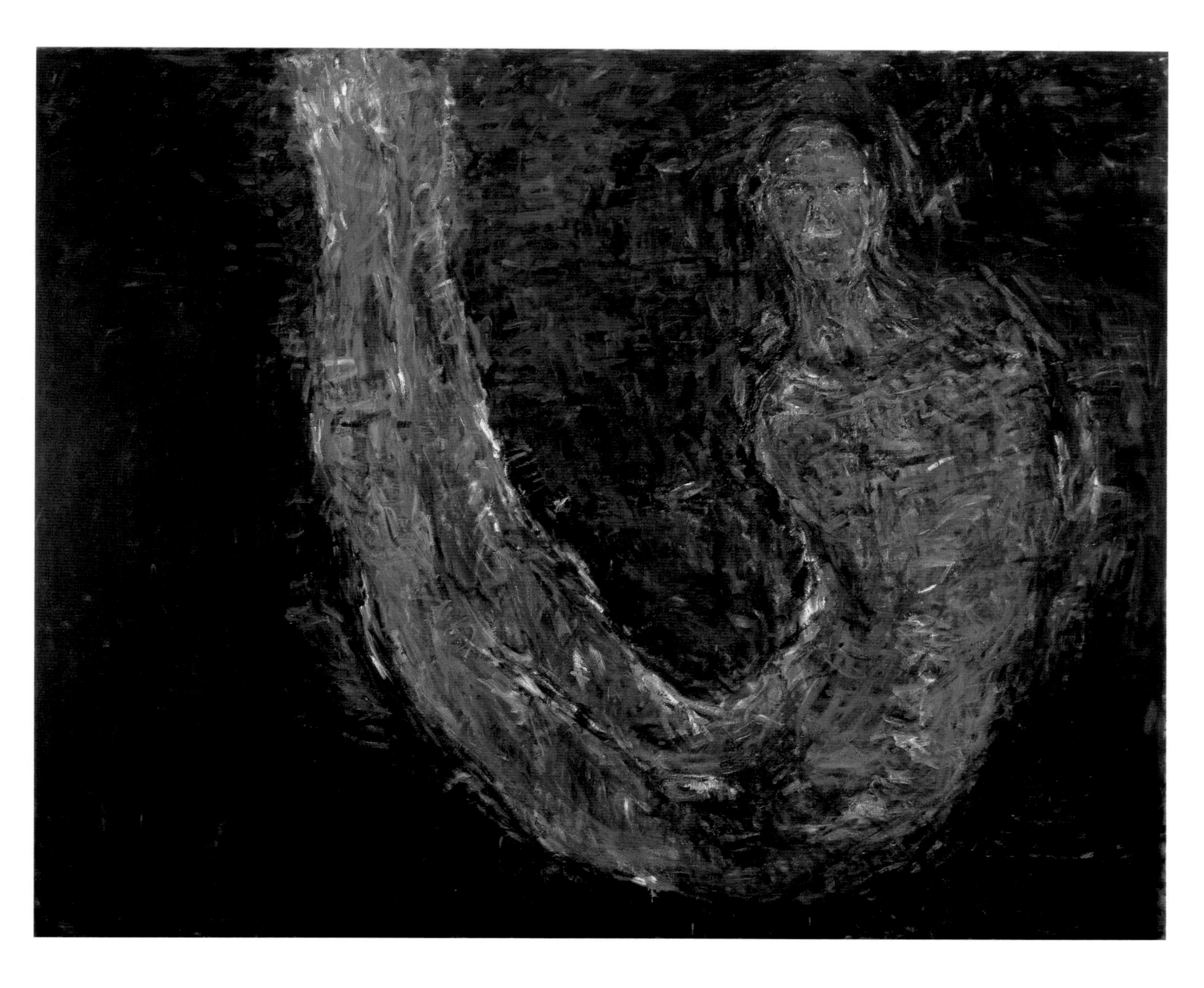

BLUE U-TURN 1989
Oil on canvas
7′7″ × 9′4″

FISH SCULPTURE
1987
Cast from wax and shell maquette and molded in aluminum-powder-filled epoxy resin, mounted by the artist on granite block sculpture
3 × 2 × 12¼″
granite block
5 × 3 × 8½″

way, twist it or fold it or do something with it. I don't have the words for it. Not for myself or for you."[59] Rothenberg—as well as Nauman—had been completely turned around by the quick turn of personal events, and in her typical fashion she drew on her experience, literalizing it and emotionally evoking it, using her Giotto blue. In *Blue U-Turn,* 1989, the image appears to be part animal, part human; it is water bound, and its movement recalls her only sculpture—a slithering fish whose scales are made of seashells she had gathered on Long Island.[60]

In paintings such as *Orange Break,* in which a "U-turn" body breaks apart and appears to be turning head over heels, head between thighs, the bend of the turning body becomes a literal spin of undisguised sexuality, of body parts coupling and changing. The color in these new works calls on Rothenberg's familiar blue and her sienna of the 1970s horses. *Bone Heads* reuses the isolated bone shape of the early 1980s merged with the sienna of the horses but now is the sexual connection itself. A crazy range of pinks and oranges that has something in common with the strange palette of the spinners turns up; this time the palette is the result of a welcoming present from Nauman, who had stocked her temporary studio in Pecos, New Mexico, by shopping at the local art-supply store, tossing paint tubes into his basket as if he were selecting Easter candies. The wildness of the canvases, the overtly sexual imagery, the spinning images (*Pinwheel* is the name of one) are buoyant, giddy, somewhat mixed up, yet extremely forthright statements of all that was in her life at the time.

ORANGE BREAK 1989-90
Oil on canvas
79¾ × 95″

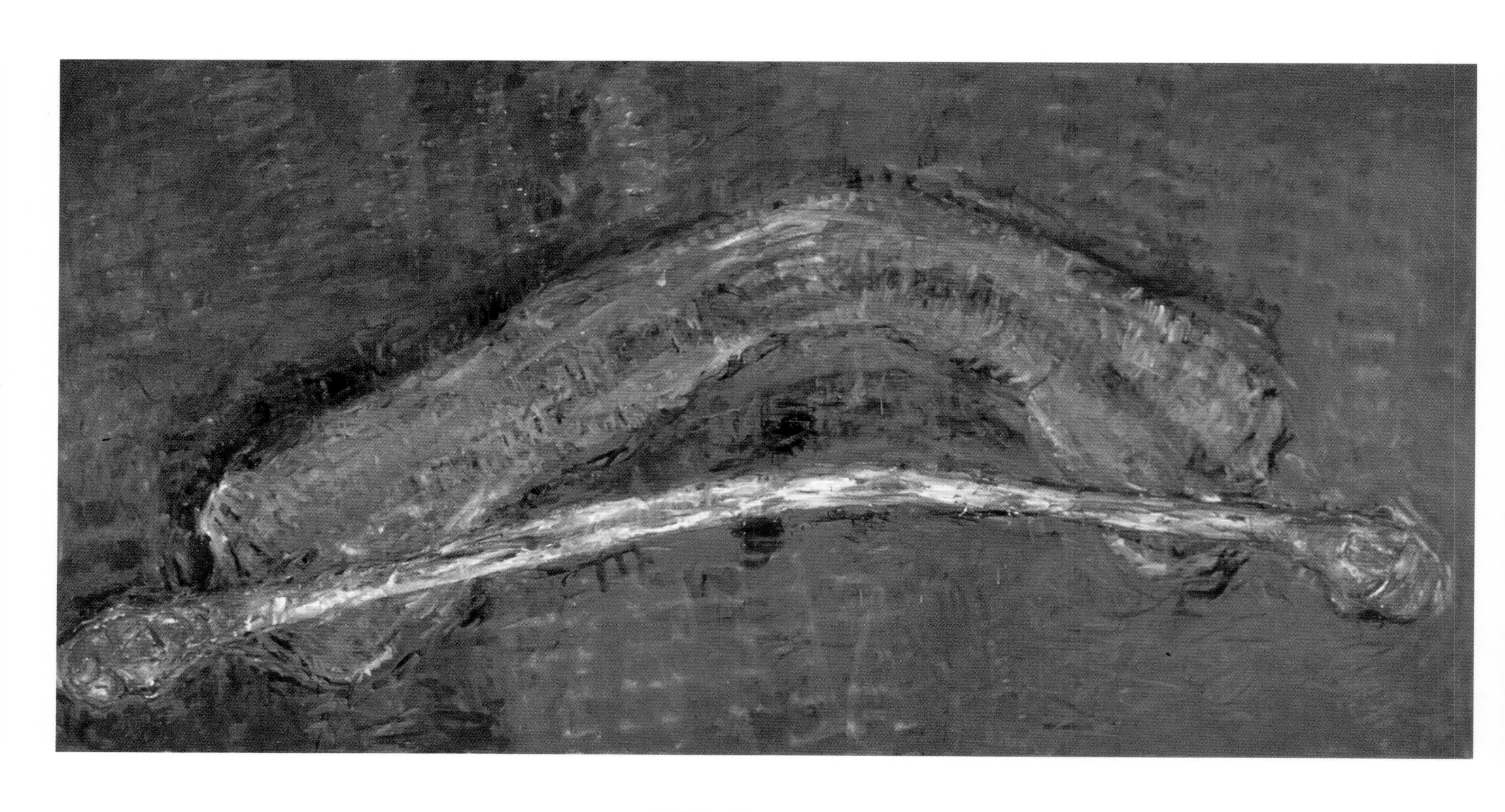

BONE HEADS 1989–90
Oil on canvas
6′5″ × 12′8″

Susan Rothenberg in her studio with *Bone Heads,* 1989–90, in progress. The artist later said, "It never worked with the heads arcing up, so I flipped it and repainted it."

BLUEBIRD WINGS
1989
Oil on canvas
65 × 43″

Although she was still a commuter from her base in New York, by the fall of 1989 Rothenberg began to feel somewhat settled in New Mexico, and she found that the U-turn images had also left her. In their place were some new images, one of which was a return in part to an old one. Into a single painting she found herself putting a piece of a bluebird wing, an isolated horse head, and a cedar tree, all located in the reds and siennas of a New Mexico landscape, painted from memory though derived from the specific site on which the couple was building a new home and studios. (The painting, *Bluebird Wings,* 1989, no longer contains the tree; it was painted out as the work was completed.)[61] The central image—the horse head—was, however, no longer the emblematic horse of the mid-1970s, nor was it the isolated, symbolically surrealistic fragment of the late 1970s and early 1980s; rather, it derived from observing a real subject in a real place, and the painting was a connection to and a way of locating herself in the new landscape.

Rothenberg was, for the first time, spending time with horses. Nauman had moved his quarter horses from his home in Pecos to their new 600-acre spread in Galisteo even before the construction crews had begun their work. She was learning to ride—on her own horse, a Spanish Barb called Cica, a gift from Nauman. The young woman who had painted horses "with no particular connection to them" was once again painting horses but with a very particular, muscular connection this time. Comparing what she now knows to what she thought she knew, Rothenberg recently said: "I used to think of them as flat, quiet images. Now I know they're all muscle and gristle and each one's different. They step on your foot—it hurts."

Two more horse paintings quickly followed. *Three Heads* and *Heads at a Tank* were, as Rothenberg says, "quiet paintings again after having some, you know, strugglers." In spite of her newfound knowledge of what horses are like, or perhaps because of the particular moments she chose for her observations, these new horses are quiet, seductive images, so completely transforming the horse head and neck into serpentine form as to be equivalently abstraction or representation. (Or perhaps, even, animal and vegetable; they have been likened both to dinosaurs and asparagus.) In *Three Heads* the three entwining necks on a grayed green field are as abstractly formal as any image Rothenberg has ever painted—but for their title, they might well be unnameable as anything other than an intimate play of graceful form in purely abstract space. Reusing the image of the extended necks in *Heads at a Tank,* Rothenberg imbues the horses leaning down into a pool of water (as well as their black reflections in the white, moonlike trough) with a dense Ryder-like mystery as well as a surprising and moody realism. The same image serves as both the purest abstraction Rothenberg has yet made and also her most realistic, intimist work.

Having spent the decade of the 1970s married, working in her first New York studio, and witnessing the birth of her daughter as well as her first success as a painter, and the 1980s single, seeing her daughter through a turbulent adolescence as well as herself and her own work through an equally tumultuous period, Rothenberg begins the 1990s with a new family and a new studio in New Mexico, once again making camp there until her new home is completed, while her almost eighteen-year-old daughter heads off for her first year of college. What Rothenberg takes with her and uses in the awesomely isolated setting of her New Mexico studio will be in good part what allowed her to maintain her individuality within the heated complexities of the New York art world: a fiercely self-critical attitude toward her work and an independence from the expectations of others; a willingness to look forthrightly at anything that might be available to her as both subjects and styles for her painting, to draw from within as well as from the sights before her; and a brave commitment to telling truths as she sees them, whether in her paintings or in her words.

She will also take along a dog-eared, spiral-bound notebook whose modesty belies its contents. It is the record Rothenberg began to keep of her paintings when her first works left her studio to be shown at Willard Gallery in 1975. In the fifteen-odd years since Rothenberg first began to use it—a period that marked the professionalization of the avant-garde, often accompanied by such corporate fittings as administrative assistants and

THREE HEADS 1990
Oil on canvas
40 × 64″

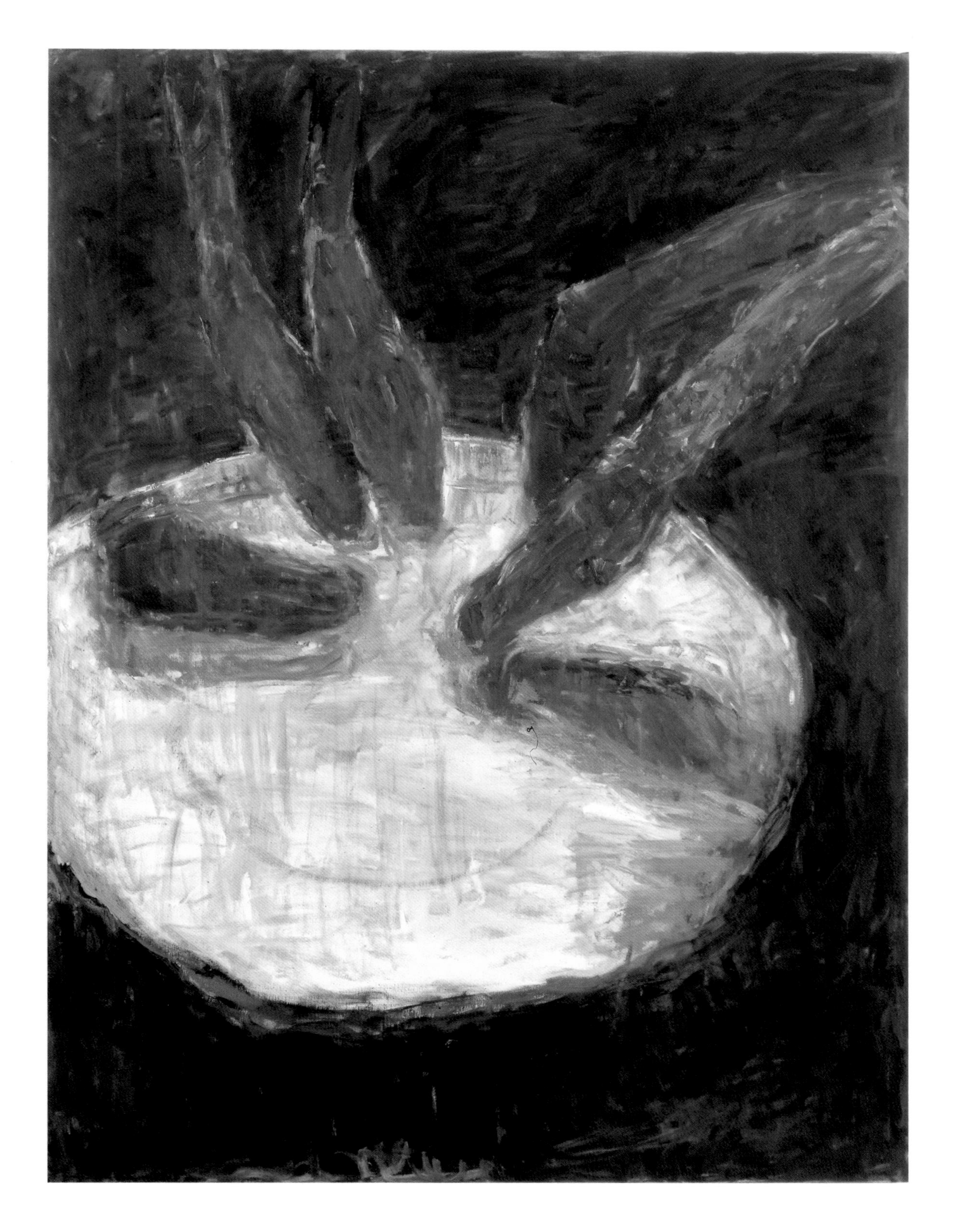

HEADS AT A TANK 1990
Oil on canvas
66½ × 49½″

computer inventories—Rothenberg has entered each work as it is completed by hand, usually in pencil. There are still pages to be filled.

But what she has left behind is as likely to turn up in her new works as what she finds in New Mexico—and in herself there. Any of the images she once thought completely digested might readily reappear. The horses already have. And as she has done many times when an image has departed, as the U-turn bodies did in 1990, Rothenberg talks of doing portraits and landscapes. She now speaks of doing a portrait of "Avi, the waiter," whom she has known for ten years, "like a Goya, with his white starched shirt, black hair, and Aztec face." She talks of looking to the red earth of New Mexico, which, perversely, she might paint "green." She also speculates about the possibility of using the clay found on their land: perhaps once again making clay pigments and using that "correct" earth color from which she built her first authoritative paintings; perhaps using the clay for sculpture—returning to a thwarted ambition of her college years.

Immediately ahead, though, are a fragment of a particular image in a particular place—an intimate moment—and a bit of the impossible. As Rothenberg describes her next project: "I'd like to do one giant horse painting. Sometimes the horses come in to drink at night—and it's all gray. And they whooooosssh, they suck water—they don't gobble and drink it. They just put their noses in; you almost can't hear it. And it becomes very quiet, very still around this moonlighty water. I'd like to do one huge painting of the sound. I don't understand how to do that. Yet."

Susan Rothenberg, 1989

NOTES

1. Susan Rothenberg in Grace Glueck, "Susan Rothenberg: New Outlook for a Visionary Artist," *New York Times Magazine,* 22 July 1984, 22.
2. Susan Rothenberg in Suzanne Muchnic, "Emotional States of Susan Rothenberg," *Los Angeles Times,* 6 September 1983, sec. 4, p. 6.
3. Susan Rothenberg in Peter Blum, "A Biographical Note" in *Susan Rothenberg* (Basel: Kunsthalle, 1981), unpaginated.
4. Lisbet Nilsen, "Susan Rothenberg: Every Brushstroke Is a Surprise," *Art News* (February 1984): 50.
5. Unless otherwise noted all Rothenberg quotations are from several taped and follow-up interviews with the artist conducted specifically for this book by the author in 1989 and 1990, and from film and audiotape interviews, also conducted by the author, in 1986 and 1987 for the film *Four Artists: Robert Ryman, Eva Hesse, Bruce Nauman, Susan Rothenberg* (New York: Michael Blackwood Productions, 1988).
6. Nilsen, "Susan Rothenberg: Every Brushstroke Is a Surprise," 50.
7. The Albright-Knox Art Gallery (organized originally as The Buffalo Fine Arts Academy in 1862) was the fourth public museum founded in the United States, and was perhaps singular in its early ambition and approach to exhibiting and acquiring modern art. Beginning in 1926, under the leadership of A. Conger Goodyear (subsequently a founder of the Museum of Modern Art, New York, in 1929, and its first president), a "Fellows for Life" Fund, supported by members' annual one-hundred-dollar contributions, was established to encourage the acquisition of new work. In 1939, with the support of Seymour Knox and others, its "Room for Contemporary Art" and a purchasing fund were established to further encourage the acquisition of experimental work. See Steven Nash et al., *The Albright-Knox Art Gallery: Paintings and Sculpture from Antiquity to 1942* (New York and Buffalo: Rizzoli International Publications, in association with the Albright-Knox Art Gallery, 1979), and The Buffalo Fine Arts Academy, *Contemporary Art: 1942-72. Collection of the Albright-Knox Art Gallery* (New York: Praeger Publishers, 1972).
8. Ruth Harris was the teacher.
9. Rothenberg's college dance teacher was Peggy Atherton; the childhood teacher was Seenie Rothier.
10. All four had considerable success as young artists in the New York art world, and though their works were very different from each other's, all dealt with ideas of a built environment, a reinvented world. The three sculptors—Singer, Saret, and Matta (who in the 1970s changed his name to Matta-Clark)—often drew on natural materials or preexisting architectural sources; Evans created his civilizations in the form of watercolor postage stamps of nations he had also invented. Matta died of cancer at the age of thirty-five in 1978; Evans died in 1977 at thirty-two in a fire in his studio in Amsterdam.
11. Listening to Rothenberg's description of these student sculptures (no photos exist) and of her teacher's intensely personal reaction, it is tempting to speculate on the psychosexual threat of these "toothy" clocks in classic Surrealist terms. But these student experiments, bad or good, were about rather simplistic formal problems and borrowings, rather than explorations of content, Surrealist provocations, or other matters. As Rothenberg has said about these sculptures, "If there was anything serious—those clocks were about hating alarms and rules of time."
12. As David Bourdon notes in *Andy Warhol* (New York: Harry N. Abrams, 1990), 225, the Dom was a dance hall for hire in the Polski Dom Narodny [National Polish Home at 23 St. Marks Place], which Warhol sublet for the month of April 1966: "Warhol took out a half-page ad in the April 7, 1966, *Village Voice:* 'Do you want to dance and blow your mind with / THE EXPLODING PLASTIC INEVITABLE / live / Andy Warhol / The Velvet Underground / and / Nico.' The ad also listed Ingrid Superstar, Mary Woronov (a dark-haired actress who performed stylized S & M-type dances on stage, light works by Daniel Williams, color slides by Jackie Cassen, and movies (*Vinyl, Sleep, Eat, Kiss, Empire, Whips, Faces, Harlot, Hedy, Couch,* and *Banana*). For two dollars on weeknights (fifty cents more on Fridays and Saturdays) anyone could gain access to Warhol and his company of underground zanies."
13. Rothenberg remembers Poons's ellipses as being "one of the few series of paintings that I would truly wish to have. I was devastated when he started pouring and glopping. I still am. I think he did some of the best paintings there are."
14. As Rothenberg told Grace Glueck ("Susan Rothenberg: New Outlook for a Visionary Artist," 20): "The whole year of 1968 is lost to me. I don't remember where I was, nor do my parents or friends."
15. Rothenberg saw shows by Neil Jenney and Susan Hall at 98

Greene Street Loft, an early alternative space founded by collectors Holly and Horace Solomon and directed by poet Ted Greenwald. The space showcased theater events, poetry readings, photography, Conceptual and Narrative art projects, as well as site-specific installations.

16. Rothenberg's titles, like the paintings themselves, often go through several changes. Her first titles, recorded in her notebook, are almost shorthand notes to herself recording essentials of a painting. *Black and White,* for example, whose black horse is depicted on a white field, became *North Wall* when it was exhibited on the eponymous wall at Willard Gallery.

    Though her drawings are for the most part untitled, very few of Rothenberg's paintings are. In 1990, for purposes of clarity, she gave titles to those Heads and Hands paintings of 1980-81 that had been untitled: they are now called *Red Head* and *Black Head,* which formerly had been called Untitled (Night Head). She also changed Untitled (Red Head), 1978, to *Red Head (Head within Head),* and gave titles to three previously untitled student works of c. 1967-68: *Rubber Balls, Screen Door,* and *Nine Sheep,* as well as to *First Horse,* 1974.

17. She worked as a receptionist for Blue River Handprints for about a year and clerked in the newspaper store below her West Broadway loft.

18. The alternative spaces 112 Greene Street and The Clocktower were founded by Jeffrey Lew and Alanna Heiss, respectively. Their programming was determined as much by the artists, dancers, and musicians who worked in these places as by the administrators who kept the spaces going. Food, at Prince and Wooster streets, was one of SoHo's first restaurants. It was founded by Tina Girouard, Caroline Goodden, and Gordon Matta (Rothenberg's Cornell colleague, the link among all the alternative spaces) and employed many artists in addition to serving as the local commissary.

19. Richard Armstrong, "Between Gesture and Geometry," in *The New Sculpture 1965-75: Hesse, Smithson, Tuttle, Nauman, Serra, Le Va, Saret, Sonnier, Benglis, Shapiro,* edited by Richard Armstrong and Richard Marshall (New York: Whitney Museum of American Art, 1990), 16.

    Rothenberg saw the Anti-Illusion exhibition and she knew many of the artists. Her friends in the show actually fell into two camps: The Chatham Square gang, including Sonnier and Serra (and also Mary Heilman, Tina Girouard, and Dickie Landry, who were not in the show), was more Rauschenbergian—performance oriented and gregarious—while Duff and Jenney were part of the more Johnsian group living in a building on Suffolk Street (where sculptor Robert Lobe, who was in the show, and painter Eddie Shostak also lived). This group's work shared a restrained formality, a more painterly touch, an emphasis on craftsmanship, as well as a kind of self-conscious if inscrutable reference to contemporary theory and objects.

20. Rothenberg in Nilsen, "Susan Rothenberg: Every Brushstroke Is a Surprise," 50.

21. Ned Rifkin, *Robert Moskowitz* (Washington, D.C., and New York: The Hirshhorn Museum and Sculpture Garden, Smithsonian Institution, and Thames & Hudson, 1989), 29 and footnotes 23, 48. Rifkin quotes Shapiro on the horse and rider of his untitled 1973 sculpture: "When I made [it], it seemed embarrassing. . . . I used paint to camouflage the piece, to deny it." Rifkin concludes, "Both works are reluctant self-portraits, disclosing a touching vulnerability in an uncannily similar manner."

    Moskowitz, like Rothenberg, cites Robert Richenberg, with whom he studied at Pratt in 1953, as an influential and encouraging teacher (Rifkin, p. 13).

22. Using one's own body as the field or site of artworks that were subsequently photographed, filmed, or videotaped was a formal strategy of much work called Body Art, Narrative Art, Conceptual Art, or Performance Art at the time. Charles Simonds filmed himself emerging from earthy clay, building his tiny villages using the same material on his own body's terrain; Hannah Wilke photographed herself with chewing-gum "scars" affixed to her body; and Bruce Nauman in performance, video, film, and photographs tested certain ordinary but isolated body postures.

23. Hilton Kramer, "Paintings by Susan Rothenberg at the Willard Gallery," *New York Times,* 24 April 1976, 17.

24. As Rothenberg remembers, "I thought, well, this is some mechanism of publicity and people are like lemmings and do what critics tell them to. Because critics were really shat upon downtown for the most part. I guess they liked Robert Pincus-Witten and some critics who sat down and drank with the artists."

    Though she received encouragement from Matta and Serra, Rothenberg remembers other artists saying they did not really understand the work and "In fact, I think politically or sociologically it was thought to be pretty uncool to be showing in an old-fashioned gallery."

    Willard Gallery was not only uptown (located at Madison Avenue and Seventy-second Street) but also exhibited older artists, such as Mark Tobey and Morris Graves, with whom the gallery had been identified since its founding in the late 1930s by Marian Willard, along with young artists such as Rothenberg, John Duff, Ed Baynard, Lois Lane, and Judy Shea, whom Miani Johnson, Willard's daughter, began to show when she joined the gallery in 1970. Willard, which had been one of the first galleries to focus on contemporary American art, closed in 1987.

25. Kramer, "Paintings by Susan Rothenberg," 17.

26. Carter Ratcliff, "Art Stars for the Eighties," *Saturday Review,* February 1981, 13.
27. It is possible that with *Four Color Horse,* her first break from the monochrome palette, Rothenberg was exploring her own history as well. She introduced color into her work the way Szabo had taught, with a sequential use of primaries, though she had, in her own way, muddied them all. In later paintings, both the primaries and a master of handling them, Piet Mondrian, also became her subject and content.
28. The artists in "New Image Painting" were Nicholas Africano, Jennifer Bartlett, Denise Green, Michael Hurson, Neil Jenney, Lois Lane, Robert Moskowitz, Susan Rothenberg, David True, and Joe Zucker.

    The idea of conflating abstraction and representation was evident in sculpture by Joel Shapiro and Bryan Hunt, though the Whitney exhibition restricted itself to painting. Both were included in two previous shows on this new direction in art-making: "Hunt, Jenney, Lane, Rothenberg, Shapiro," at Vassar College Art Gallery (1978) and "Abstract Images," at Willard Gallery (1977).
29. As Rothenberg later told critic Roberta Smith: "We were all very separate islands in a sea of sculpture. . . . We weren't a movement, we were a bunch of individuals who were introducing images. It seemed very strange to me that we could all be brought together and called something." See Roberta Smith, "A Painting Landmark in Retrospect," *New York Times,* 1 August 1987, sec. 2, p. 29.

    "New Image" as a term would be attached to both Rothenberg's and Jenney's work longer than to that of any of the others. The differences in their attitudes toward imagery, subject matter, and formal concerns are informative. As Jenney stated in his catalogue text, "I was more concerned with approaching the viewer with relationships—for instance, a crying girl and a broken vase, birds and jets, or forest and lumber. . . . I'm interested in objects existing and relating to other objects. I wanted the objects to be stated emphatically with no psychological implications." See Richard Marshall, *New Image Painting* (New York: Whitney Museum of American Art, 1978), 38. The psychological weight of Rothenberg's images was as pressing as the equivalence of figure and ground. Her iconoclastic approach was accurately noted in her catalogue statement: "I am an image maker who is also an image breaker—trying for a little more." She went on, as usual, to discuss the "geometries, the center line," and other divisions as being "the main fascinators" (Marshall, *New Image Painting,* 56).
30. Untitled, 1977, lithograph printed in three colors from three plates on Rives BFK Linen paper with a collé, all extensively hand colored by the artist with mixed mediums. Edition: Eighteen plus one artist's proof and three hors-de-commerce proofs. Each impression is unique. Each print is so thoroughly reworked by the artist that the very notion of reproduction in printmaking is subverted in favor of the improvisatory nature of Rothenberg's drawing. See Jeremy Lewison, "Form and Expression in Susan Rothenberg's Prints," in Rachel Robertson Maxwell, *Susan Rothenberg, The Prints: A Catalogue Raisonné* (Philadelphia: Peter Maxwell, 1987), 9.
31. Eliza Rathbone discusses the "self-reflective" content of the 1978-79 fragmented horses and cites in a footnote Rothenberg's comments to Peter Schjeldahl (in *Vanity Fair,* August 1983, 85): "I was beginning to realize the horses were self-portraits." See Eliza Rathbone, *Susan Rothenberg* (Washington, D.C.: The Phillips Collection, 1985): 10, 28, footnote 3.
32. In a footnote explicating Freud's reference, Strachey quotes a letter from Freud to Fliess, wherein: "Freud describes the famous principle of Itzig, the Sunday horseman: 'Itzig, where are you riding to?'—'Don't ask *me!* Ask the *horse!*'" See Sigmund Freud, *Interpretation of Dreams,* ed. and trans. James Strachey (New York: Avon Books, 1965), 265, footnote 1.
33. As Rothenberg has said, "*Blue Body* and *White Mountain,* which were just about the energy of a form, had very little to do in any way physiologically with the horse structure. Just the head was in one [with] a huge circle representing the body; and a horse head was in the other, and those were the last horse paintings."
34. Rothenberg sublet a studio from artist Bruce Robbins on Franklin Street in TriBeCa.
35. Peter Schjeldahl, "Bravery in Action," *Village Voice,* 29 April 1981, 81.
36. Robert Storr, "Spooks and Floats," *Art in America* (May 1983): 158.
37. "New Spirit in Painting" was organized by Norman Rosenthal, Christos Joachimides, and Nicholas Serota. The latter two visited Rothenberg. "New Spirit in Painting" did not include a single woman artist, a fact widely noted in reviews of the show. Joachimides and Rosenthal also organized "Zeitgeist," in Berlin in 1982, for which Rothenberg's works were selected and where she was the only woman artist in the exhibition.
38. Rothenberg had been spending summers on Long Island since 1976, at first renting houses on the North Fork, later on the South. She bought a home in Sag Harbor, where she built the first studio to her own specifications, in 1985.
39. Rothenberg would abandon both AA and therapy for a time; she did a four-year program of psychoanalysis at the end of the 1980s.
40. Rothenberg in Nilsen, "Susan Rothenberg: Every Brushstroke Is a Surprise," 47. Rothenberg's quote was referring to *Overcoat.*

41. Ibid., 47-48.
42. The subject had always been a part of Joseph Beuys's work, but was so highly masked and symbolized, as well as interwoven with political and didactic ambition, as to make the works seem like archetypal cultural artifacts rather than self-revelations—an approach that one could say was more Jungian than Freudian. Jonathan Borofsky dealt with the same allusions, but his route was more generalized—as in his banners illustrating the themes "Art Is for the Spirit," and "All Is One." That both Beuys and Borofsky presented these subjects in theatrical installations, making their works, by definition, vanguard, kept sentiment within detached conceptual bounds. Closest in their personally probing spirit and devastatingly bleak or giddy views of the human condition were Philip Guston's paintings of the 1970s. (Curiously, the lima bean–shaped head of Rothenberg's disembodied figures is very close to the form used by both Guston and Borofsky.)
43. Rothenberg in Glueck, "Susan Rothenberg: New Outlook for a Visionary Artist," 46.
44. Ibid., 16.
45. Ibid.
46. Rothenberg's Mondrian is an amalgam of artist, authority figure, father, and self. In *Between the Lines,* a 1983-84 lithograph and woodcut (Universal Limited Art Editions), Rothenberg pays homage to Mondrian and identifies with him in several ways. She puts him before a lower Manhattan skyline, her own neighborhood; collages a yellow rectangle between the eyes of his double, an androgynously female figure; and signs the print with a red finger mark. In discussing the print with Jeremy Lewison, she described imagining Mondrian as "a serious man but not very able to deal with people." See Jeremy Lewison, in Maxwell, p. 9.
47. Rothenberg told Grace Glueck ("Susan Rothenberg: New Outlook for a Visionary Artist," 27): "I know it was supposed to be my mother, because the pillow was there right away. Yet it's not the shape of her body, nor her face. So I begin to think it's not her, it's me. I don't know quite who it is."
48. In The Museum of Modern Art collection records for the painting, Rothenberg answers "no" to the question, "Was a specific model or scene used?" but "probably" to "Has the subject any special personal, topical or symbolic significance?" (Dated December 1, 1987; see copy in Ephemera file, Rothenberg, Museum of Modern Art, New York.)
49. Susan Rothenberg in Richard Marshall, *50 New York Artists: A Critical Selection of Painters and Sculptors Working in New York* (San Francisco: Chronicle Books, 1986), 94.
50. Ibid.
51. Robert Hughes notes Balla and talks also of "the familiar cultural pathos, distantly related to Picasso's circus folks but less sentimental," in his discussion of Rothenberg's "manipulators of the fleeting instant." Robert Hughes, "Spectral Light, Anxious Dancers," *Time,* 9 November 1987, 109. In addition to the modern tradition of using such imagery, from Degas and Picasso to Léger and Calder, Rothenberg's spinners, jugglers, and vaulters also bring to mind an ancient one, the entertainments in Etruscan tomb painting: the dancers, and particularly the wrestlers turning in midair. In these Etruscan paintings, horses and their shadows are painted in sienna as well as blue, the latter serving to abstract the animals' naturalism. See Massimo Pallottino, *Etruscan Painting* (Geneva: Skira, 1952).
52. The jugglers specifically derive from a literary source. As Rothenberg told Valerie Gladstone, the idea came from a passage in Vladimir Nabokov's *Laughter in the Dark:* "I don't usually do this, take inspiration from a book—actually I thrive on junky novels—but listen to this line: 'the shadow of many-colored balls flying in a curve, the ghost of a juggler on a shimmering curtain . . .' Isn't it wonderful? I can imagine a whole series of juggler paintings. If I do some shimmering balls . . . and I always like to paint arms and heads." See Valerie Gladstone, "Art in a Spin—Susan Rothenberg," *Elle,* October 1987, 108.
53. Michael Brenson, "Art: A New Direction for Susan Rothenberg," *New York Times,* 23 October 1987, C34.
54. Rothenberg had explored the possibility of doing a mural in a New York City public library, visiting sites in the Bronx, Manhattan, and Staten Island, but this had not materialized.
55. Rothenberg remembers, "I was getting annoyed at the art world, and I wanted to do something in the city for a different bunch of people. And I thought I wanted to be present there, to be available to people in a way that would break the old ivory-tower, stuck-in-the studio way of working—you know, be more in the world. And I had originally thought that I would paint on site, but that proved to be impossible at PaineWebber. People were eating there. So I realized I had to do the work in my studio in Sag Harbor."

    Rothenberg originally submitted two choices to PaineWebber. As she describes them, "One was the six spinners; the other was a set of twenty Buddhas—most of them with a big white oval cutout in the middle. They were less volatile and lively than the spinners and PaineWebber chose the action ones."
56. Susan Rothenberg in Hayden Herrera, "Expressionism Today: An Artists' Symposium," *Art in America* (December 1982), 139.
57. Amei Wallach, "Picture of a Painter in Motion," *Newsday,* 24 August 1986, part 2, p. 4.
58. Rothenberg and Nauman married in a ceremony at City

Hall, Staten Island, New York. They had first met in 1969 in New York, met again in 1979 when Rothenberg made her first trip to New Mexico, and over the course of twenty years had run into each other from time to time at various openings. They met again at a dinner in the fall of 1988 at Angela Westwater's, when their longtime acquaintance changed quickly into something much more.

59. Dodie Kazanjian, "New Image," *Vogue,* May 1990, 320. In fact, the year before, Rothenberg had twisted the figure in *Folded Buddha.*

60. *Fish Sculpture.* 1987. Cast from wax-and-shell maquette molded in aluminum powder-filled epoxy resin and mounted on a granite block; sculpture, 3½ × 2 × 12¼″; base, 5 × 5 × 8½″. Published by Universal Limited Art Editions; edition of eleven, with five artist's proofs. The mold for the maquette was destroyed. This sculpture was first made as a contribution to a "Save the Whales" benefit at a Sag Harbor gallery. The artists were asked to make their works from materials found on local beaches. It was subsequently cast as an edition.

61. Rothenberg's paintings often undergo many transformations as they are completed. She usually continues to paint on a canvas as it is hung for a gallery exhibition, giving it what she calls "final hits." At times, she has reworked a painting years after it was made. One of her few portrait commissions, of Miani Johnson (c. 1979), a gift for Johnson from her husband, was borrowed back around 1981 for a bit of fixing and was returned with a new hairdo, costume, and palette. (This painting is also unusual in that instead of using geometric or bone shapes to achieve a dynamic balance of figure and field, Rothenberg attached a velvet swag to the painting itself.) *Three Trees,* 1983-84/87, also was borrowed back from its owner (who had newly acquired it), achieving its final form in 1987.

LIST OF ILLUSTRATIONS

Note: The titles and dates given here supersede those in all previously published listings. Dimensions of works have been verified whenever possible and are given in inches (up to 99) or feet and inches, height preceding width. Numbers preceding entries refer to page numbers.

14 *Rubber Balls.* c. 1967–68. Aluminum and oil-based house paint on canvas, c. 8 × 5′. Destroyed by the artist after damage in storage

16 *Screen Door.* c. 1967–68. Mixed mediums, including collaged air-conditioner filter, on canvas, 72 × 60″. Destroyed by the artist after damage in storage

16 *Nine Sheep.* c. 1967–68. Oil-based house paint on Masonite, c. 4 × 4′. Destroyed by the artist after damage in storage

21 *(W)holes and Parts #4.* September 1971. Paper, glue, and aluminum paint, 48 × 54″. Destroyed

22 *Multiple Splice.* May 1972. Woven canvas, laths, aluminum paint, and graphite, 48 × 72″. Destroyed

25 Susan Rothenberg (in hoop) performing in Joan Jonas's *Jones Beach Piece,* 1970. Photograph Richard Landry

25 Susan Rothenberg (leaning back on glass) in Joan Jonas's *Mirror Piece,* 1970. Photograph © 1970 Peter Moore

27 *First Horse.* 1974. Tempera, matte, flashe, pencil, and gesso on unstretched canvas, 26 × 28″. Private Collection

28 *Foxes on a Hill.* 1972. Acrylic on canvas, 53 × 77½″. Private Collection

30 Untitled. 1974. Acrylic and tempera on canvas, 36 × 45″. Private Collection

31 *Triphammer Bridge.* 1974. Acrylic on canvas, 5′7″ × 9′7″. Collection Edward R. Broida Trust

32 *Mukuhara.* 1974. Acrylic, tempera, and pencil on canvas, 54 × 64″. Collection Hannelore B. Schulhof, New York

34 *Mary I.* 1974. Acrylic and tempera on canvas, 46 × 78″. Private Collection

34 *Mary II.* 1974. Acrylic and tempera on canvas, 46 × 78″. Private Collection

34 *Mary III.* 1974. Acrylic and tempera on canvas, 44 × 66½″. Private Collection

35 Test photographs, Susan Rothenberg, 1974

37 *Stable.* 1974. Acrylic and tempera on canvas, 5′8″ × 10′. Private Collection

38 *White Robe.* 1974. Acrylic and tempera on canvas, 64 × 86″. Private Collection

39 *Double Masked Heads.* 1974. Acrylic and tempera on canvas, 65 × 78½″. The Eli and Edythe L. Broad Collection

41 *Layering.* 1975. Acrylic and tempera on canvas, 66½ × 82½″. The Helman Collection, New York

42 *Flanders.* 1976. Acrylic and flashe on canvas, 65¾″ × 98¾″. Private Collection

43 *Algarve.* 1975. Acrylic and tempera on canvas, 9′6″ × 9′3″. Collection Edward R. Broida Trust

44 *United States.* 1975. Acrylic and tempera on canvas, 9′6″ × 15′9″. Saatchi Collection, London

45–46 *Siena Dos Equis.* 1975. Acrylic and tempera on canvas, 9′6″ × 22′10″. Private Collection

48 Untitled. 1976. Acrylic and tempera on paper, 39¼ × 50″. Collection Ann and Joel Ehrenkranz

48 Untitled. 1976. Acrylic and pencil on paper, 38½ × 50″. Private Collection

50 *Four Color Horse.* 1976. Acrylic and flashe on canvas, 5′7″ × 9′4″. Private Collection

51 *Axes.* 1976. Synthetic polymer paint and gesso on canvas, 5′4⅝″ × 8′8⅞″. Collection The Museum of Modern Art, New York. Purchased with the aid of funds from the National Endowment for the Arts

52 Installation, Willard Gallery, New York, 1977. *Left to right: Double Measure,* 1977; *Axes,* 1976; *Scat,* 1977; Untitled #44, 1977

53 *Butterfly.* 1976. Acrylic and matte medium on canvas, 69½ × 83″. Collection Maggie Trakas

54 Susan Rothenberg with *From Buffalo,* 1976–77, in progress. Photograph Andy Grundberg

54 *From Buffalo.* 1976–77. Acrylic on canvas, 61 × 77½″. Collection David Wirtz

55 *I x I.* 1977. Acrylic and flashe on canvas, 6′5¼″ × 8′8″. Hirshhorn Museum and Sculpture Garden, Smithsonian Institution. Joseph M. Hirshhorn Purchase Fund, 1990

56 *Double Measure.* 1977. Acrylic and tempera on canvas, 6′4″ × 10′. Collection Miani Johnson/Willard Gallery, New York

57 Susan Rothenberg signing her first print, Untitled, 1977, a lithograph printed in three colors from three plates on Rives BFK Linen paper with a collé, all extensively hand colored by the artist with mixed mediums; image 9¾ × 15½″, paper 12 × 15½″. Printed by Chris Erickson at Derrière L'Étoile Studios, published by the artist. Photograph Andy Grundberg

59 *Red Head (Head within Head).* 1978. Acrylic on canvas, 76 × 60″. Collection Edward R. Broida Trust

60 *Blue Frontal.* 1978. Acrylic, flashe, and tempera on canvas, 77 × 88½″. Private Collection

61 *Study (Throw-up Head).* 1978. Acrylic on canvas, 17½ × 17″. Private Collection

61 *Stick in Throat.* 1978. Acrylic on canvas, 7½ × 7½″. Private Collection

61 *Hands and Shadows.* 1978-79. Acrylic and flashe on canvas, 48 × 58″. Collection Mr. and Mrs. Steven Ames

63 *Squeeze.* 1978-79. Acrylic and flashe on canvas, 92 × 87″. Collection Frances and John Bowes

64 *Somebody Else's Hand.* 1979. Acrylic and flashe on canvas, 21 × 36″. Saatchi Collection, London

64 Untitled. 1978. Acrylic on paper, 50 × 38½″. Collection Miani Johnson/Willard Gallery, New York

64 Untitled. 1978. Acrylic and flashe on paper, 14 × 22¼″. Collection of Laila and Thurston Twigg-Smith

65 *Kelpie.* 1978. Acrylic and flashe on canvas, 6′5″ × 9′1″. Collection Gerald S. Elliott

66 *Mr. Bear.* 1978. Acrylic and flashe on canvas, 95 × 75″. Museum Moderner Kunst Wien, Leihgabe Sammlung Ludwig, Aachen

67 Installation, Willard Gallery, New York, 1979. *Left to right: Pontiac,* 1979; *For the Light,* 1978-79; *Outline,* 1978-79; *Tattoo,* 1979

68 Untitled. 1979. Acrylic and flashe on paper, 36½ × 36⅝″. Des Moines Art Center. Purchased with funds from the Gardner and Florence Call Cowles Foundation, 1979.10

69 *For the Light.* 1978-79. Acrylic and flashe on canvas, 8′9″ × 7′3″. Collection of the Whitney Museum of American Art. Purchase, with funds from Peggy and Richard Danziger. 79.23

70 *Outline.* 1978-79. Acrylic and flashe on canvas, 73 × 50″. Private Collection

71 Untitled. 1978-79. Acrylic and pencil on paper, 20 × 20″. Collection Walker Arts Center, Minneapolis. Art Center Acquisitions Fund

72 *Pontiac.* 1979. Acrylic and flashe on canvas, 88 × 61″. Collection Miani Johnson/Willard Gallery, New York

73 *Smoker.* 1978-79. Acrylic and flashe on canvas, 62¼ × 45″. Collection Edward R. Broida Trust

75 *Tattoo.* 1979. Acrylic and flashe on canvas, 5′7″ × 8′7″. Collection Walker Art Center, Minneapolis. Purchased with the aid of funds from Mr. and Mrs. Edward R. Ruben, Mr. and Mrs. Julius E. Davis, The Art Center Acquisition Fund, and the National Endowment for the Arts, 1979

76 *The Hulk.* 1979. Acrylic and flashe on canvas, 6′5¾″ × 8′8″. Collection The Museum of Contemporary Art, Los Angeles: The Barry Lowen Collection

77 Rothenberg with Untitled, 1979, in progress. Photograph Francis Bota

77 Untitled. 1979. Acrylic and flashe on paper, 50 × 38″. Collection Miani Johnson/Willard Gallery, New York

78 *Our Lord.* 1979. Acrylic and flashe on canvas, 69 × 36″. Private Collection

79 *Blue Body.* 1980-81. Acrylic and flashe on canvas, 9′ × 6′3″. The Eli and Edythe L. Broad Collection

79 *White Mountain.* 1980-81. Acrylic and flashe on canvas, 8′9″ × 6′3″. Collection Courtney and Steven Ross

80 *Wishbone.* 1979. Acrylic and flashe on canvas, 8′6″ × 6′4″. Collection Mr. and Mrs. Harry W. Anderson

81 *Tuning Fork.* 1980. Acrylic and flashe on canvas, 83 × 79″. Collection Emily Fisher Landau, New York

82 Studies for Heads and Hands. c. 1980. Crayon on canvas, dimensions *(clockwise from top left)*: 14½ × 12¼″, 12½ × 11¼″, 11½ × 7½″, 11½ × 14½″, 11½ × 14½″, 10½ × 12¼″, 11¼ × 7″. Private Collection

83 *Grey Head.* 1980-81. Acrylic and flashe on canvas, 9′2″ × 9′6″. Collection Mr. and Mrs. Bagley Wright

84 *Blue Head.* 1980-81. Acrylic and flashe on canvas, 9′6″ × 9′6″. Collection Virginia Museum of Fine Arts, Richmond. Gift of the Sydney and Frances Lewis Foundation

85 *Big and Little Head.* 1980-81. Acrylic and flashe on canvas, 9′3″ × 9′6″. Collection Miani Johnson/Willard Gallery, New York

86 *Red Head.* 1980-81. Acrylic and flashe on canvas, 8′11″ × 8′11½″. Private Collection

87 *Black Head.* 1980-81. Acrylic and flashe on canvas, 8′8″ × 9′6″. Collection Munson-Williams-Proctor Institute Museum of Art, Utica, New York

90 Untitled (AEIOU). 1980. Acrylic and flashe on paper, 41½ × 30″. Collection Jules and Barbara Farber, Amsterdam

90 *Jughead.* 1980. Acrylic on canvas, 60 × 68″. Private Collection

91 *Red Slippers.* 1980-81. Acrylic and flashe on canvas, 77 × 52″. Collection Mr. and Mrs. Ira Milstein

92 Untitled. 1981. Charcoal on paper, 28¾ × 22½″. Courtesy Alan Shayne

93 Untitled. 1981. Graphite on paper, 28 × 17″. Collection Regina K. Fadiman

93 Untitled. 1981. Graphite on paper, 26¾ × 23″. Collection Miani Johnson/Willard Gallery, New York

95 Susan Rothenberg with *Maggie's Split,* 1981-82, and *The Creek,* 1981-82, in progress. Photograph Helaine Messer

96 *The Creek.* 1981-82. Oil on canvas, 88¼ × 78″. Collection The Stedelijk Museum, Amsterdam

97 *Two Rays.* 1981. Oil on canvas, 30½ × 55″. Collection Douglas S. Cramer, Los Angeles

99 *Maggie's Cartwheel.* 1981-82. Oil on canvas, 25 × 30½″. Collection Ellen and Ellis Kern

100 Installation, The Stedelijk Museum, Amsterdam, 1982. *Left to right: White Mountain,* 1980–81; *Maggie's Cartwheel,* 1981–82; *Blue Oval,* 1981; *Big and Little Head,* 1980–81 (through doorway); *Blue Body,* 1980–81

101 *Blue Oval.* 1981. Oil on canvas, 19½ × 14″. Collection Mr. and Mrs. Jay Bennett

102 *Withall.* 1982. Oil on canvas, 5′5⅛″ × 10′6¾″. Collection The Stedelijk Museum, Amsterdam

104 *Self-Portrait.* 1982. Oil on canvas, 15¼ × 21″. Private Collection

105 *Blue Bars.* 1982. Oil on canvas, 87 × 52″. Collection Miani Johnson/Willard Gallery, New York

106 Untitled. 1982. Pencil on paper, 20¼ × 23¾″. Collection Paul J. T. Sinclaire, New York City

107 *Beggar.* 1982. Oil on canvas, 39½ × 50½″. Collection Maggie Trakas

109 *Asian Sex.* 1982. Oil on canvas, 62 × 62″. Collection Bette and Herman Ziegler

110–11 *Tenmen.* 1982. Oil on canvas, 5′1″ × 15′6¾″. Collection The Carnegie Museum of Art, Pittsburgh; Museum Purchase: Gift of Mr. and Mrs. Anthony J. A. Bryan and A. W. Mellon Acquisition Endowment Fund, 1983

112 Susan Rothenberg with *Patches,* 1982, and *(at far left) Snowman,* 1983, at the Los Angeles County Museum of Art, 1983. Photograph Gary Freedman, *Los Angeles Times*

112 Installation, Willard Gallery, New York, 1983. *Left to right: Rest,* 1981 (top); *Cocoon,* 1981 (bottom); *Hourglass,* 1982; *Speedboat,* 1981; *Two Rays,* 1981; *Reflections,* 1981; *Headlights,* 1982–83; *Beggar,* 1982

113 *Patches.* 1982. Oil on canvas, 7′3″ × 9′9″. Saatchi Collection, London

114 *Hourglass.* 1982. Oil on canvas, 88 × 80″. Dallas Museum of Art. Anonymous Gift

115 *The Monk.* 1983. Oil on canvas, 8′9″ × 5′9″. Private Collection

116 *Snowman.* 1983. Oil on canvas, 79 × 86½″. Collection Los Angeles County Museum of Art

118 *Overcoat.* 1982–83. Oil on canvas, 44 × 39½″. Private Collection

119 *Green Ray.* 1984. Oil on canvas, 7′ × 8′11″. Collection Edward R. Broida Trust

121 *Bucket of Water.* 1983–84. Oil on canvas, 7′ × 10′7″. Collection Miani Johnson/Willard Gallery, New York

122 *Grandmother.* 1983–84. Oil on canvas, 7′5″ × 9′4½″. F. Roos Collection, Switzerland

124 Untitled. 1984. Charcoal on paper, 29½ × 42½″. Collection Jeanne and Richard Leavitt

125 Untitled. 1984. Charcoal on paper, 49 × 37″. Private Collection

126 Untitled. 1984. Charcoal on paper, 47½ × 31″. Private Collection

127 *Mondrian.* 1984. Oil on canvas, 9′1″ × 7′. Private Collection

128 Installation, Willard Gallery, New York, 1985. *Left to right: Red Blush,* 1984–85; *Elizabeth,* 1984–85; *INGspray,* 1984–85

129 *Mondrian Dancing.* 1984–85. Oil on canvas, 78¼ × 91″. The Saint Louis Art Museum. Purchased with funds given by the Shoenberg Foundation

130 *A Golden Moment.* 1985. Oil on canvas, 54 × 48″. The Eli and Edythe L. Broad Collection

131 *L. R.* 1984. Oil on canvas, 47 × 36″. Private Collection

132 *Pillow.* 1984. Oil on canvas, 46½ × 54½″. Courtesy Alan Shayne

133 *Biker.* 1985. Oil on canvas, 74¼ × 69″. Fractional gift of PaineWebber Group, Inc., New York, to The Museum of Modern Art, New York

134 Installation, Willard Gallery, New York, 1985. *Left to right: Bucket of Water,* 1983–84; *Biker,* 1985; *Trumpeter,* 1984–85

135 Untitled. 1984. Charcoal on paper, 18¼ × 24½″. Private Collection

135 *Biker.* 1985. Charcoal on paper, 43 × 31″. Collection Eric Fischl

136 *Holding the Floor.* 1985. Oil on canvas, 7′3″ × 12′3⁵⁄₁₆″. Collection of the Whitney Museum of American Art, New York. Purchase, with funds from the Painting and Sculpture Committee. 86.40

138 *G. T.* 1977. Acrylic on canvas, 87 × 70″. Private Collection

139 *Red Man.* 1985–86. Oil on canvas, 9′4″ × 7′10″. Courtesy Mr. and Mrs. Richard C. Hedreen

140 Untitled. 1986. Acrylic, charcoal, flashe, graphite, and oil stick on paper, 5 × 12′. Collection Robert F. Fogelman

141 *Vaulting.* 1986–87. Oil on canvas, 7′6″ × 11′. The Cleveland Museum of Art. Leonard C. Hanna, Jr., Fund. 88.12

142 Untitled. 1987. Charcoal, oil, and graphite on paper, 43¾ × 30″. Courtesy Meryl and Robert Meltzer

142 Untitled. 1987. Graphite on paper, 22⅜ × 31″. Collection Charles Lund

143 *Gyro.* 1986–87. Oil on canvas, 8′2″ × 9′3½″. Private Collection

144 *Head Roll.* 1987. Oil on canvas, 36¾ × 64½″. Collection Judy and Harvey Gushner, Bryn Mawr, Pennsylvania

145 Untitled. 1987. Charcoal and pencil on paper, 11⅞ × 8⅛″. Courtesy Sperone Westwater, New York

145 Untitled. 1986. Charcoal and pencil on paper, 21 × 30″. Barbara Krakow Gallery, Boston, Massachusetts

147 *Night Ride.* 1987. Oil on canvas, 7′9″ × 9′2¼″. Collection Walker Art Center, Minneapolis. Walker Special Purchase Fund, 1987

148 *Half and Half.* 1985–87. Oil on canvas, 60 × 85″. Private Collection

149 Untitled. 1987. Graphite, oil, and charcoal on paper, 20¾ × 14¾″. Collection Joëlle and Paul Killian

150 Untitled. 1986. Pencil and charcoal on paper, 22 × 30″. Collection Lee and Lawrence Ramer, Los Angeles

151 *The Blue Chair.* 1987. Oil on canvas, 78 × 71¼″. Collection Emily Fisher Landau

152 *Juggler #3.* 1987–88. Oil on canvas, 77 × 68″. Collection Mr. and Mrs. Philip Berman, Allentown, Pennsylvania

154–56 *1–6.* 1988. Oil on wood (six panels), each 10′6¾″ × 3′10⅛″. PaineWebber Group, Inc., New York

157 Diagram for PaineWebber commission, 1987. Pencil and collage on paper, 42½ × 60¼″. Collection Paine-Webber Group, Inc., New York

157 Installation of *1–6,* 1988, at PaineWebber Group, Inc., New York

158 Untitled. 1988. Liquid graphite and charcoal on paper, 42½ × 41½″. Collection Gian Enzo Sperone, Rome, Italy

159 *Folded Buddha.* 1987–88. Oil on canvas, 7′7¼″ × 9′3¼″. Courtesy Meryl and Robert Meltzer

160 *Buddha with Bamboo.* 1988. Oil on canvas, 4′8″ × 9′5¼″. The Oliver-Hoffmann Collection

162 Untitled. 1989. Charcoal, graphite, and chalk on paper, 49⅞ × 38⅛″. Courtesy Steve Martin

163 *Blue U-Turn.* 1989. Oil on canvas, 7′7″ × 9′4″. F. Roos Collection, Switzerland

164 *Fish Sculpture.* 1987. Cast from wax and shell maquette and molded in aluminum-powder-filled epoxy resin, mounted by the artist on granite block, sculpture 3 × 2 × 12¼″; granite block 5 × 3 × 8½″. Edition of 11, with 5 artist's proofs. Published by Universal Limited Art Editions, Inc., New York

165 *Orange Break.* 1989–90. Oil on canvas, 79¾ × 95″. Private Collection

166 *Bone Heads.* 1989–90. Oil on canvas, 6′5″ × 12′8″. The Eli and Edythe L. Broad Collection

167 Susan Rothenberg in her studio with *Bone Heads,* 1989–90, in progress. Photograph Brigette Lacombe

168 *Bluebird Wings.* 1989. Oil on canvas, 65 × 43″. Private Collection

170 *Three Heads.* 1990. Oil on canvas, 40 × 64″. Private Collection

171 *Heads at a Tank.* 1990. Oil on canvas, 66½ × 49½″. Collection Locksley Shea Gallery

172 Susan Rothenberg, 1989. Photograph Brigette Lacombe

CHRONOLOGY

1945	Born in Buffalo, New York, January 20.
1962	Enters Fine Arts School, Cornell University, in September, with intention to become a sculpture major.
1964	Studies sculpture at State University of New York, Buffalo, New York, during summer.
1965	Flunks sculpture course at Cornell. Quits school in February.
	Lives in Hydra, Greece, for five months.
	Returns to Cornell in September. Refused admission to sculpture department. Becomes painting major.
1966	Engages in independent study program in New York City for spring semester.
1967	Graduates with B.F.A. degree from Cornell University.
	Spends summer in Formentera, Spain.
	Studies at Corcoran School of Art, George Washington University, Washington, D.C., from September to November. After leaving school, continues to live in Washington, D.C.
1969	Settles in New York City.
	Studies dance with Deborah Hay and Joan Jonas.
1970	Works as assistant to Nancy Graves and Joan Jonas.
	Performs in Joan Jonas's *Jones Beach Piece, Mirror Piece,* and *Underneath.*
1971	Marries George Trakas.
1972	Daughter, Maggie, born November.
1974	Paints *First Horse.*
	Exhibits *Triphammer Bridge* in "New Talent" at A. M. Sachs Gallery, New York, first painting included in gallery show.
1975	First solo exhibition, "Three Large Paintings" at 112 Greene Street, New York.
1976	First solo show at Willard Gallery, New York.
	Included in "New Acquisitions" at The Museum of Modern Art, New York.
	Receives Creative Artists Public Service (CAPS) grant.
1977	Makes first prints, lithographs, at Derrière l'Étoile Studios, New York. Published by the artist.
	Teaches at California Institute for the Arts, Valencia.
1978–79	Included in "New Image Painting" at Whitney Museum of American Art, New York.
1979	Included in Whitney Biennial.
	Included in "American Painting: The Eighties" at Grey Gallery and Study Center, New York University, New York. Show travels to Houston and Paris.
	Receives grant from National Endowment for the Arts.
	Divorced from George Trakas.
	Travels to New Mexico.
1980	Appears in Aperto section of Venice Biennale.
	Included in "Drawings: The Pluralist Decade" at the American Pavilion, Venice Biennale. Show travels to Philadelphia, Copenhagen, Hovikodden (Norway), Madrid, and Lisbon.
	Receives Guggenheim Fellowship.
1980–81	Does Heads and Hands paintings.

1981 Switches from acrylic to oil paint (summer).
Solo exhibition at Kunsthalle Basel, Switzerland, simultaneous with solo exhibitions of Robert Moskowitz and Julian Schnabel. Shows travel together to Frankfurt and to Humlebaek, Denmark, into 1982.

1982 Solo exhibition at Stedelijk Museum, Amsterdam.
Exhibited in "Zeitgeist" at Martin-Gropius-Bau, Berlin.

1983 Included in Whitney Biennial.
Receives American Academy and Institute of Arts and Letters award.
Solo exhibition at Los Angeles County Museum, California. Show travels to San Francisco, Pittsburgh, Boston, Aspen, Detroit, London, and Richmond (Virginia).

1984 Does first Mondrian drawing and paintings.
Included in "An International Survey of Recent Painting and Sculpture" at Museum of Modern Art, New York.
Receives Charles Flint Kellogg Award in Arts and Letters, Bard College.

1985 Included in Whitney Biennial.
Included in "1985 Carnegie International," at Museum of Art, Carnegie Institute, Pittsburgh, Pennsylvania.
Awarded Grand Prix at the Sixteenth International Biennial of Graphic Art, Yugoslavia.
Solo exhibition at Phillips Collection, Washington, D.C. Show travels to Portland, Oregon, into 1986.

1986 Begins "spinners" and "vaulters," paintings of figures in continuous motion.

1987 Makes first sculpture, *Fish Sculpture,* which was later cast as an edition by Universal Limited Art Editions, New York.
First solo show at Sperone Westwater, New York.

1988 Travels in China.
Included in "1988 Carnegie International" at Museum of Art, Carnegie Institute.
Executes first commission, *1-6,* for the PaineWebber Group, Inc., New York.
Publication of *Susan Rothenberg, The Prints: A Catalogue Raisonné* by Rachel Robertson Maxwell.

1989 Marries Bruce Nauman.
Learns to ride a horse.
Begins to use horse imagery again.

1990 Moves to New Mexico.
Elected member of American Academy and Institute of Arts and Letters.
Solo exhibition at Rooseum—Center for Contemporary Art, Malmö, Sweden.

SELECTED EXHIBITION HISTORY

Solo Exhibitions

1975 "Three Large Paintings," 112 Greene Street, New York, October 25-November 15.

1976 "Susan Rothenberg," Willard Gallery, New York, April 10-May 8.

"Susan Rothenberg," Sable-Castelli, Toronto, April 10-24.

1977 "Susan Rothenberg," Willard Gallery, New York, April 2-May 5.

1978 "Susan Rothenberg, Matrix/Berkeley 3," University Art Museum, University of California, Berkeley, January 20-April 20. Catalogue.

"Susan Rothenberg," Greenberg Gallery, Saint Louis, Missouri, May 1-31.

"Susan Rothenberg, Recent Work," Walker Art Center, Minneapolis, Minnesota, May 20-July 2.

1979 "Susan Rothenberg," Willard Gallery, New York, March 24-April 19.

1980 "Susan Rothenberg: Recent Paintings," Mayor Gallery, London, February 2-March 15; Galerie Rudolph Zwirner, Cologne, April 25-May 24.

1981 "Susan Rothenberg: Five Heads," Willard Gallery, New York, April 10-May 16.

1981-82 "Susan Rothenberg," Kunsthalle Basel, Switzerland, October 3-November 15. Catalogue. With simultaneous solo exhibitions "Robert Moskowitz" and "Julian Schnabel." Shows traveled together to Frankfurter Kunstverein, Frankfurt, December 7-January 31, 1982; Louisiana Museum, Humlebaek, Denmark, March 13-May 2.

"Susan Rothenberg," Akron Art Museum, Ohio, November 21-January 10, 1982.

1982 "Susan Rothenberg: Recent Paintings," Stedelijk Museum, Amsterdam, October 14-November 29. Catalogue.

1983 "Susan Rothenberg," Willard Gallery, New York, March 19-April 23.

1983-85 "Susan Rothenberg," Los Angeles County Museum of Art, California, September 1-October 16; San Francisco Museum of Art, California, November 10-December 25; Museum of Art, Carnegie Institute, Pittsburgh, January 18-March 18, 1984; Institute of Contemporary Art, Boston, April 10-June 3; Aspen Center for the Visual Arts, Colorado, July 5-August 19; The Detroit Institute of Arts, Michigan, September 9-October 21; The Tate Gallery, London, November 21-January 20, 1985; The Virginia Museum of Fine Arts, Richmond, February 26-March 27. Catalogue.

1984 "Susan Rothenberg Prints, 1977-1984," Barbara Krakow Gallery, Boston, March 10-29. Catalogue.

"Currents: Susan Rothenberg," ICA, Boston, April.

"Susan Rothenberg Prints, 1977-1984," Davison Art Center Gallery, Wesleyan University, Middletown, Connecticut, October 31-December 6.

1985 "Centric 13: Susan Rothenberg—Works on Paper," University Art Museum, California State Center, Long Beach, March 12-April 21; Des Moines Art Center, Iowa, June 21-July 28. Catalogue.

"Susan Rothenberg," Willard Gallery, New York, April 18-May 18.

"Susan Rothenberg, Prints," Des Moines Art Center, Iowa, September-October.

"Susan Rothenberg, Prints," A. P. Giannini Gallery, San Francisco, October 17-December 10.

1985-86	"Susan Rothenberg, New Prints," Gemini G.E.L., Los Angeles, September-October.
	"Susan Rothenberg: Recent Paintings and Prints," Phillips Collection, Washington, D.C., September 21-November 17; Portland Center for the Visual Arts, Oregon, December 19-February 9. Catalogue.
1987	"Susan Rothenberg: The Horse Paintings," Larry Gagosian Gallery, New York, January 14-February 20. Catalogue.
	"Susan Rothenberg," Sperone Westwater, New York, October 17-November 14. Catalogue.
1987-88	"Heads, Hands, Horses: Susan Rothenberg Prints," University of Iowa Museum of Art, Iowa City, November 21-January 3, 1988. Catalogue.
1988	"Drawing Now: Susan Rothenberg," The Baltimore Museum of Art, Maryland, February 23-April 4.
	"Susan Rothenberg," Galleria Gian Enzo Sperone, Rome, June 20-September.
1990	"Susan Rothenberg, Sperone Westwater, New York, April 28-May 26. Catalogue.
	"Susan Rothenberg," Rooseum—Center for Contemporary Art, Malmö, Sweden, June 30-August 17. Catalogue.

Group Exhibitions

1974	"New Talent," A. M. Sachs Gallery, New York, June 4-27.
1975	"Gallery Group," Willard Gallery, New York, June 7-27.
1976	"Selections," Willard Gallery, New York, February 7-March 4.
	"New Acquisitions," The Museum of Modern Art, New York, May 26-August 16.
	"New Work/New York," Fine Arts Gallery, California State University, Los Angeles, October 4-28.
	"Animals," Holly Solomon Gallery, New York, November 13-December 11.
1977	"Abstract Images," Willard Gallery, New York, January 4-February 3.
	"Painting 1975-76-77," Sarah Lawrence College, Bronxville, New York, April 2-20; American Foundation for the Arts, Miami, Florida, April-July; Contemporary Arts Center, Cincinnati, August 11-September 18. Catalogue.
	"A Painting Show," P.S. 1, Institute for Art and Urban Resources, Long Island City, New York, May 1-31.
	"Extraordinary Women," The Museum of Modern Art, New York, July 22-September 29.
	"American Drawn and Matched," The Museum of Modern Art, New York, September 20-December 4. Catalogue.
	"New York: The State of the Art," New York State Museum, Albany, October 8-November 28. Catalogue.
	"Susan Rothenberg/Judith Ornstein," Willard Gallery, New York, November 29-December 24.
1977-78	"Critics Choice," Lowe Art Gallery, Syracuse University, New York, November 9-December 11; Munson-Williams-Proctor Institute, Utica, New York, January 3-29, 1978. Catalogue.
1978	"Seven Artists: Contemporary Drawings," Cleveland Museum of Art, Ohio, February 28-April 30.
	"The Minimal Image," Protech-McIntosh Gallery, Washington, D.C., March 7-April 5.
	"Hunt, Jenney, Lane, Rothenberg, Shapiro," Vassar College Art Gallery, Poughkeepsie, New York, April 9-June 4. Catalogue.

1978-79 "New Image Painting," Whitney Museum of American Art, New York, December 5-January 28. Catalogue.

1978-80 "American Painting of the 1970s," Albright-Knox Art Gallery, New York, December 8-January 14, 1979; Newport Harbor Art Museum, Newport Beach, California, February 3-March 18; The Oakland Museum, California, April 10-May 20; Cincinnati Art Museum, Ohio, July 6-August 26; Art Museum of South Texas, Corpus Christi, September 9-October 21; Krannert Art Museum, University of Illinois, Champaign, November 11-January 2, 1980. Catalogue.

1979 "1979 Biennial Exhibition," Whitney Museum of American Art, New York, February 11-April 8. Catalogue.

"Visionary Images," The Renaissance Society of the University of Chicago, Chicago, May 6-June 16. Catalogue.

"A Decade in Review: Selections from the 1970s," Whitney Museum of American Art, New York, June 19-September 2.

"The New American Painting I," Janie C. Lee Gallery, Houston, October.

1979-80 "American Painting: The Eighties," Grey Gallery and Study Center, New York University, New York, September 5-October 13; Contemporary Arts Museum, Houston, October 28-December 30; The American Center, Paris, April-May 1980. Catalogue.

1980 "Tendences actuelles de l'art americain," Daniel Templon, Paris, January 12-February 7.

"Pictures in New York Today," Padiglione d'Arte Contemporanea di Milano, Milan, March 20-April 20.

"Lois Lane, Susan Rothenberg," Clarke-Benton Gallery, Santa Fe, New Mexico, March 30-April 30.

"La Biennale di Venezia, 1980," Aperto section, International Pavilion, Venice, June 1-September 30.

"Painting and Sculpture Today, 1980," Indianapolis Museum of Art, Indiana, June 24-August 17. Catalogue.

1980-81 "Drawings: the Pluralist Decade," U.S. Pavilion, 39th Venice Biennale, Venice, June 1-September 30; Institute of Contemporary Art, University of Philadelphia, October 4-November 9; Museum of Contemporary Art, Chicago, May 29-June 26. Catalogue.

"Group Exhibition," Audrey Stohl Gallery, Memphis, Tennessee, December 5-January 14, 1981.

1981 "Selected by Donald Sultan," Texas Gallery, Houston, January 6-24.

"Lane, Obuck, Rothenberg, Sultan, Torreano," Young-Hoffman Gallery, Chicago, March 20-April 18.

"Contemporary Drawings: In Search of an Image," University Art Museum, Santa Barbara, California, April 1-May 1. Catalogue.

"Menagerie," Goddard-Riverside Community Center, New York, April-May.

"A New Bestiary: Animal Imagery in Contemporary Art," Institute of Contemporary Art of the Virginia Museum of Fine Arts, Richmond, June 1-August 16.

"The Image in American Painting and Sculpture, 1950-1980," Akron Art Museum, Ohio, September 12-November 8.

1981-82 "Animals in American Art, 1880-1980," Nassau County Museum of Fine Arts, Roslyn, New York, October 4-January 17, 1982. Catalogue.

1982 "4th Biennale of Sydney, Australia," April 7-May 23. Catalogue.

"Focus on the Figure: Twenty Years," Whitney Museum of American Art, New York, April 15-June 13. Catalogue.

"74th American Exhibition," The Art Institute of Chicago, June 12-August 1. Catalogue.
"Block Prints," Whitney Museum of American Art, New York, September 9-November 7.
"Group Exhibition of American Paintings," Akira Ikeda Gallery, Tokyo, October 4-30.
"The Expressionist Image," Sidney Janis Gallery, New York, October 9-30.
"Zeitgeist," Martin-Gropius-Bau, Berlin, October 15-December 19. Catalogue.
"White-and-Black Drawings," Willard Gallery, New York, December 1-23.

1982-83 "Figures of Mystery," Queens Museum, New York, November 26-January 23, 1983. Catalogue.
"Myth," Bonlow Gallery, New York, November 30-January 8, 1983.
"New Figuration in America," Milwaukee Art Museum, Wisconsin, December 3-January 23, 1983. Catalogue.

1983 "A Painting Exhibition," Paula Cooper Gallery, New York, January 18-February 23.
"Drawing Conclusions: A Survey of American Drawings, 1958-1983," Daniel Weinberg Gallery, Los Angeles, January 20-February 26.
"1983 National Drawing Invitational," Sarah Spurgeon Fine Arts Gallery, Central Washington University, Ellensburg, January 24-February 18.
"Prints from Blocks, Gauguin to Now," The Museum of Modern Art, New York, March 6-May 15. Catalogue.
"1983 Biennial Exhibition," Whitney Museum of American Art, New York, March 15-May 29. Catalogue.
"The Horse Show," Robert Freidus Gallery, New York, May 17-June 18.
"Minimalism to Expressionism: Painting and Sculpture Since 1965 from the Permanent Collection," Whitney Museum of American Art, New York, June 2-December 4.
"New York Painting Today," Three Rivers Arts Festival, Sponsored by the Carnegie Institute, Pittsburgh, June 8-26. Catalogue.
"47th Annual Mid-Year Exhibition," Butler Institute of American Art, Youngstown, Ohio, June 26-August 28. Catalogue.
"Selected Drawings," Jersey City Museum of Art, New Jersey, September 14-October 15.
"Ars 83 Helsinki," Ateneumin Taidemuseo, Helsinki, October 14-December 11. Catalogue.
American Academy and Institute of Arts and Letters, New York, November 14-December 18.

1983-84 "Back to the USA," Kunstmuseum, Lucerne, May 9-July 31; Rheinisches Landesmuseum, Bonn, October 27-January 15, 1984; Würtenbergischer Kunstverein, Stuttgart, April-June. Catalogue.
"Tendencias en Nueva York," Palacio de Velázquez, Parue del Retiro, Madrid, October 11-December 4; Fundacio Joan Miró, Parc de Montjuic, Barcelona, December 21-January 29, 1984. Catalogue.

1983-85 "Rothmans Presents: American Accents," The Gallery/Stratford, Ontario, June 6-August 7; College Park, Toronto, August 18-September 17; Musée du Québec, Québec City, September 22-October 26; Art Gallery of Nova Scotia, Halifax, January 5-February 6, 1984; Art Gallery of Windsor, Ontario, February 23-March 25; Edmonton Art Gallery, Alberta, April 5-May 13; Vancouver Art Gallery, British Columbia, July 5-August 26; Glenbow Museum, Calgary, Alberta, September 13-October 30; Musée d'Art Contemporain, Montreal, November 29-January 30, 1985. Catalogue.

1984 "Issues in Contemporary Prints, 1974-1983," Fogg Art Museum, Harvard University, Cambridge, Massachusetts, February 3-March 20.

"Parasol and Simca: Two Presses/Two Processes," Center Art Gallery, Bucknell University, Lewisburg, Pennsylvania, February 3-April 4; Sardoni Art Gallery, Wilkes College, Wilkes-Barre, Pennsylvania, April 15-May 16.

"Contemporary Drawing as Idea: Concepts, Records, Projects," Sarah Lawrence Gallery, Bronxville, New York, February 7-March 11.

"A Celebration of Women Artists, Part II: The Recent Generation," Sidney Janis Gallery, New York, February 11-March 3. Catalogue.

"Pressures of the Hand: Expressionist Impulses in Recent American Art," Brainard Art Gallery, State University College, Potsdam, New York, March 10-April 15.

"Visions of Childhood: A Contemporary Iconography," Whitney Museum of American Art, New York, Downtown Branch, March 28-May 11.

"The Meditative Surface," Renaissance Society of the University of Chicago, April 1-May 16.

"An International Survey of Recent Painting and Sculpture," The Museum of Modern Art, New York, May 17-August 19. Catalogue.

"Artists Choose Artists," CDS Gallery, June.

"Selected Drawings by Eleven Artists," Willard Gallery, New York, September 5-October 6.

"Susan Rothenberg/Bruce Metcalf," DBR Gallery, Cleveland, Ohio, September 18-October 6.

"Image and Impressions: Painters Who Print," Walker Art Center, Minneapolis, Minnesota, September 23-November 26. Catalogue.

"Painting Now," The Kitakyūshū Municipal Museum, Kitakyūshū, Japan, October 6-28.

1984-85 "Content: A Contemporary Focus, 1979-1984," Hirshhorn Museum and Sculpture Garden, Washington, D.C., October 4-January 6, 1985. Catalogue.

1985 "New Acquisitions: Prints and Photographs," New York Public Library, New York, February 1-May 16.

"1985 Biennial Exhibition," Whitney Museum of American Art, New York, March 13-June 2. Catalogue.

"States of War: New European and American Paintings," Seattle Art Museum, Washington, April 18-June 23. Catalogue.

"Horses in 20th-Century Art," Nicola Jacobs Gallery, London, June 26-August 31. Catalogue.

"American Paintings 1975-1985: Selections from the Aaron and Phyllis Katz Collection," The Aspen Art Museum, Colorado, July 6-August 25.

"An Exhibition of Small Paintings and Sculptures," Larry Gagosian Gallery, Los Angeles, September 24-October 16.

"Aids Benefit Exhibition: A Selection of Works on Paper," Daniel Weinberg, Los Angeles, November 9-30.

"37th Annual Purchase Exhibition," American Academy and Institute of Arts and Letters, New York, November 18-December 15.

"16th International Biennial of Graphic Art," Yugoslavia. Recipient Grand Prix.

1985-86 "1985 Carnegie International," Museum of Art, Carnegie Institute, Pittsburgh, November 9-January 5, 1986. Catalogue.

"Vom Zeichnen: Aspekte der Zeichnung 1960-1985," Frankfurter Kunstverein, Frankfurt, November 19-January 1, 1986; Kasseler Kunstverein, Kassel, January 15-February 2; Museum Moderner Kunst, Vienna, March 13-April 27. Catalogue.

"Works on Paper," Galerie Barbara Farber, Amsterdam, November 30-January 18, 1986.

1986 "The Art of Drawing," Barbara Mathes Gallery, New York, February 7-April 5.

"Three Printmakers," Whitney Museum of American Art, New York, February 12-April 27. Catalogue.

"Matière première," Le Centre d'Action Culturelle Pablo Neruda, Corbeil-Essones, France, February 20-March 17.

"75th Anniversary of 'The American Exhibition,'" The Art Institute of Chicago, March 8-April 27. Catalogue.

"50th Anniversary Exhibition," Willard Gallery, New York, May 15-June 27.

"50th National Mid-Year Exhibition," Butler Institute of American Art, Youngstown, Ohio, June 29-August 24.

"Prospect 86," Frankfurter Kunstverein, Frankfurt, September 9-October 11. Catalogue.

"Prospect 86," Schirn Kunsthalle, Frankfurt, September 9-November 11.

"Black and White: Loaned to American Express Co." A Project of the Associate Council, Art Advisory Service, The Museum of Modern Art, New York, Fall / Winter.

"Drawings," Willard Gallery, New York, December 6-24.

1986-87 "Works by American Women, 1976-1986," First Bank of Minneapolis, Minnesota, October 15-January 15, 1987.

"Boston Collects: Contemporary Painting and Sculpture," Museum of Fine Arts, Boston, October 22-February 1, 1987. Catalogue.

"Drawings," Barbara Krakow Gallery, Boston, November 29-January 7, 1987.

"From Icon to Symbol: American Art 1973-1979," Blum Helman Warehouse, New York, November 29-January 10.

1986-90 "Focus on the Image, Selections from the Rivendell Collection," Phoenix Art Museum, Arizona, October 5, 1986-February 7, 1987; Museum of Art, University of Oklahoma, Norman, April 25-August 30; Munson-Williams-Proctor Institute Museum of Art, Utica, New York, September 27-March 20, 1988; University of South Florida Art Galleries, Tampa, April 17-September 10; Lakeview Museum of Art and Sciences, Illinois, October 1-January 2, 1989; University Art Museum, California State University, Long Beach, January 30-May 28; Laguna Gloria Art Museum, Austin, Texas, June 25-January 2, 1990. Catalogue.

1986-91 "International Art Show for the End of World Hunger," International Monetary Fund Visitor's Center, Washington, D.C., October 14-November 12, 1986; Minnesota Museum of Art, Saint Paul, September 13-November 15, 1987; Heinie-Onstad Museum, Oslo, Norway, December 3-January 17, 1988; Stavanger Kulturhus, Norway, January 24-February 7; Göteborgs Konstmuseum, Göteborg, Sweden, February 20-April 4; Kölnischer Kunstverein, Cologne, April 22-May 29; Musée des Arts Africains et Océaniens, Paris, June 8-July 20; Barbican Art Gallery, London, August 3-October 2; Círculo de Bellas Artes, Madrid, January 17-February 24; Arti et Armiticiae, Amsterdam, March 17-April 23; Salas Nacionales de Exposición, Buenos Aires, May 30-June 22; Museu de Arte de São Paulo, Brazil, July 6-28; Sala Mendoza, Caracas, August 10-September 17; Scottsdale Center for the Arts, Arizona, November 17-January 14, 1990; Museo de Arte Contemporáneo de Puerto Rico, San Juan, January 26-March 23; Schneider Museum of Art, Ashland, Oregon, April 5-May 25; Setagaya Art Museum, Tokyo, July 7-August 5; El Museo del Barrio, New York, January 24-March 15, 1991.

1987 "Prints," Willard Gallery, New York, February 5-March 7.

"The Presence of Nature—Some American Paintings," Barbara Krakow Gallery, Boston, October 10-November 4.

1987-88 "The Monumental Image," University Art Gallery, Sonoma State University, California, March 12-April 17; University Art Gallery, California State University, San Bernadino, May 7-June 4; University Art Gallery, California Polytechnic State University, San Luis Obispo, September 21-October 23; Nevada Institute for Contemporary Art, University of Nevada, Las Vegas, November 15-December 20; University Art Gallery, California State University, Northridge, February 15-March 18, 1988; University Art Gallery, California State University-Stanislaus, Turlock, April 6-May 8. Catalogue.

"Lead," Hirschl & Adler Modern, New York, December 3-January 16, 1988. Catalogue.

"Individuals: A Selected History of Contemporary Art, 1945-1986," The Museum of Contemporary Art, Los Angeles, December 10-January 10. Catalogue.

1988 "The M. Anwar Kamal Collection of Art—Printmaking: Late Nineteenth and Twentieth Century," The Cummer Gallery of Art, Jacksonville, Florida, March 10-April 3, 1988.

"Gordon Matta-Clark and Friends," Galerie Lelong, New York, March 11-April 16.

"Artist Series Project," New York City Ballet, New York, April 26-May 15, 1988.

"1988—The World of Art Today," The Milwaukee Art Museum, Wisconsin, May 6-August 28, 1988. Catalogue.

"Works on Paper," John Berggruen Gallery, San Francisco, September 8-October 8. Catalogue.

1988-89 "Jennifer Bartlett, Elizabeth Murray, Eric Fischl, Susan Rothenberg," Saatchi Collection, London. November 1988-April 1989. Catalogue.

"1988 Carnegie International," Museum of Art, Carnegie Institute, Pittsburgh, November 5, 1988-January 22, 1989. Catalogue.

1990 "Exhibition of Work by Newly Elected Members and Recipients of Awards," American Academy and Institute of Arts and Letters, New York, May 16-June 10.

"Art in Europe and America: The 1960s and 1970s," Wexner Center for the Visual Arts, The Ohio State University, Columbus, May 23-August 5.

"Artists for Amnesty," Blum Helman Gallery and Germans Van Eck Gallery, New York, June 6-16.

SELECTED BIBLIOGRAPHY

Note: Books, exhibition catalogues, and films are given first in each year in alphabetical order, by author, followed by reviews and articles in chronological order.

1974 Herrera, Hayden. "Reviews: New Talent Festival." *Art News* (September 1974): 99-100.

1975 Tannenbaum, Judith. "Art Reviews: Group Show." *Arts Magazine* (October 1975): 16.

1976 Kramer, Hilton. "Paintings by Susan Rothenberg at the Willard Gallery." *New York Times,* 24 April 1976, 17.

Seiberling, Dorothy. "Dutch Treat." *New York Magazine* (3 May 1976): 72-73.

Tannenbaum, Judith. "Art Reviews: Susan Rothenberg." *Arts Magazine* (June 1976): 25.

Herrera, Hayden. "Susan Rothenberg at Willard." *Art in America* (September-October 1976): 108.

Beals, Kathie. "Newberger Show Has Bit for All." *Gannett Westchester Newspaper,* 3 September 1976, D5.

Ballatore, Sandy. "New Work from New York." *ArtWeek* (16 October 1976): 1.

Seldis, Henry J. "East Coast Meets West in 'New Work/New York.'" *Los Angeles Times,* 24 October 1976, 72.

Ballatore, Sandy. "Magazine Show." *Artforum* (December 1976): 18.

1977 Herrera, Hayden. In *Critics' Choices,* exhibition catalogue. Syracuse, N.Y.: Lowe Art Gallery, Syracuse University, 1977.

Lieberman, William S. *American Drawn and Matched,* exhibition catalogue. New York: Museum of Modern Art, 1977.

New York: The State of the Art, exhibition catalogue. Albany, N.Y.: New York State Museum, 1977.

Painting 1975-76-77, exhibition catalogue. Bronxville, N.Y.: Sarah Lawrence College, 1977.

Bourdon, David. "Voice Choices." *Village Voice,* 2 May 1977, 86.

Kramer, Hilton. "Art: New Finds at the Modern." *New York Times,* 17 June 1977, C20.

"The Younger Generation: A Cross Section." *Art in America* (September-October 1977): 86-91.

1978 Cathcart, Linda L. *American Painting of the 1970s,* exhibition catalogue. Buffalo, N.Y.: Albright-Knox Art Gallery, 1978.

Marshall, Richard. *New Image Painting,* exhibition catalogue. New York: Whitney Museum of American Art, 1978.

Morrin, Peter. ed. *Hunt, Jenney, Lane, Rothenberg, Shapiro,* exhibition catalogue. Poughkeepsie, N.Y.: Vassar College Art Gallery, 1978.

Rosenthal, Mark. *Matrix/Berkeley 3: Susan Rothenberg,* exhibition catalogue. Berkeley, Calif.: University Art Museum, 1978.

Brody, Jaqueline. "Prints and Photographs Published." *Print Collector's Newsletter* (January-February 1978): 183.

Burnside, Madeline. "New York Reviews." *Art News* (February 1978): 138.

Rosenthal, Mark. "From Primary Structures to Primary Images." *Arts Magazine* (October 1978): 106-7.

Senie, Harriet. "Is Painting Struggling with Itself." *New York Post,* 30 December 1978, 17.

1979 *1979 Biennial Exhibition.* New York: Whitney Museum of American Art, 1979.

Ratcliff, Carter. *Visionary Images: Emblematic Figuration,* exhibition catalogue. Chicago: Renaissance Society of the University of Chicago, 1979.

Rose, Barbara. *American Painting: The Eighties, A Critical Interpretation,* exhibition catalogue. New York: Grey Art Gallery and Study Center, New York University, 1979.

———. "Art for '79 Eyes." *Vogue,* January 1979, 137, 184.

Kramer, Hilton. "Art: Variety of Styles at Whitney Biennial." *New York Times,* 16 February 1979, C17.

Smith, Roberta. "Portfolio: A Celebration of Women Artists." *Ambiance,* March 1979, 84ff.

———. "The Abstract Image." *Art in America* (March-April 1979): 102-5.

Kramer, Hilton. "New Paintings at the Willard Gallery." *New York Times,* 13 April 1979, C24.

Gibson, Eric. "New York: Susan Rothenberg," *Art International* (Summer 1979): 76.

Schjeldahl, Peter. Review. *Artforum* (Summer 1979): 63.

Fuller, Peter. "The Failure of American Painting." *Village Voice,* 3 September 1979, 45, 47.

Kramer, Hilton. "Neo-Modernists—A Sense of Deja-Vu." *New York Times,* 23 September 1979, D31.

Rickey, Carrie. "American Painting: The Eighties." *Village Voice,* 24 September 1979, 85.

Smith, Roberta. "American Painting: The Eighties." *Art in America* (October 1979): 122-23.

Lawson, Thomas. "Painting in New York: An Illustrated Guide." *Flash Art,* October-November 1979, 31, 33.

1980 Bassett, Hilary D., Judith A. McKenzie, and Robert A. Yassin. *Painting and Sculpture Today, 1980,* exhibition catalogue. Indianapolis, Indiana: Indianapolis Museum of Art, 1980.

Glueck, Grace. "How Do Its Artists See the Whitney?" *New York Times,* 9 January 1980, C17.

Hill, Andrea. "Susan Rothenberg at Mayor," *Artscribe #22,* April 1980, 55-56.

Birolli, Di Zino. "Dammi il tempo di guardare." *Horor pleni,* April-May, 1980.

Rickey, Carrie. "All Roads Lead to the Venice Biennale," *Village Voice,* 9 June 1980, 71.

Nadelman, Cynthia. "New Editions." *Art News* (September 1980): 49.

Tompkins, Calvin. "Boom," *New Yorker,* 22 December 1980, 78-80.

1981 Blum, Peter. *Moskowitz/Rothenberg/Schnabel,* exhibition catalogue. Basel, Basler Kunstverein, 1981.

Contemporary Drawings: In Search of an Image, exhibition catalogue. Santa Barbara, Calif.: University Art Museum, 1981.

Rooney, Judith. *A Guide to the Collection of the Museum of Fine Arts, Houston, Texas.* Houston: Museum of Fine Arts, 1981.

Schjeldahl, Peter. *The Brute: New Poems.* Illustrations by Susan Rothenberg. Los Angeles: Little Caesar Press, 1981.

Stigliano, Phyllis, and Janice Parenta. *Animals in American Art 1880-1980,* exhibition catalogue. Roslyn, N.Y.: Nassau County Museum of Fine Arts, 1981.

Susan Rothenberg, exhibition catalogue. Foreword by Jean-Christophe Ammann; essay by Peter Blum. Basel: Kunsthalle Basel, 1981.

Ratcliff, Carter. "Art Stars for the Eighties." *Saturday Review,* February 1981, 12-20.

Schulz, Franz. Review. *Sunday Chicago Sun-Times,* 15 April, 1981.

Schjeldahl, Peter. "Bravery in Action." *Village Voice,* 29 April-5 May 1981, 81.

Foster, Hal. Review. *Artforum* (June 1981): 90.

Ratcliff, Carter. Review. *Art in America* (Summer 1981): 126-27.
Collings, Matthew. "Nothing Deep." *Artscribe #30,* August 1981, 26-29.
Kramer, Hilton. "An Audacious Inaugural Exhibition." *New York Times,* 20 September 1981, 33, 34.
Danoff, Michael. "Susan Rothenberg." *Akron Art Museum Newsletter,* 21 November 1981, 42-43.
———. "Susan Rothenberg." *Dialogue,* November-December 1981, 42-43.

1982 Bowman, Russell, and Peter Schjeldahl. *New Figuration in America,* exhibition catalogue. Milwaukee, Wisc.: Milwaukee Art Museum, 1982.
de Wilde, Edy, and Alexander von Grevenstein. *Susan Rothenberg.* Amsterdam: Stedelijk Museum, 1982.
Haskell, Barbara. *Focus on the Figure: Twenty Years,* exhibition catalogue. New York: Whitney Museum of American Art, 1982.
Lubowsky, Susan. *Figures of Mystery,* exhibition catalogue. New York: Queens Museum, 1982.
74th American Exhibition. Chicago: Art Institute of Chicago, 1982.
Vision in Disbelief, exhibition catalogue. Sydney, Australia: 4th Biennale of Sydney, 1982.
———. "Susan Rothenberg." *Louisiana Revy,* (Humlebaek, Denmark) (January 1982): 34-37.
Hunter, Sam. "Post-Modernist Paintings." *Portfolio,* January-February 1982, 46.
Zwelleger, Harry. "Amerikanische Kunst der Achtziger Jahre," *Das Kunstwerk,* February 1982, 25.
Curiger, Bice. "Robert Moskowitz, Susan Rothenberg, Julian Schnabel." *Flash Art International* (February-March 1982): 60.
Rose, Barbara. "Ugly? The Good, the Bad, and the Ugly: Neo-Expressionism Challenges Abstract Art." *Vogue,* March 1982, 370-75.
Phillips, Deborah C. "Looking for Relief? Woodcuts Are Back." *Art News* (April 1982): 92-96.
Rothenberg, Susan, and Mary Heilmann. *Bomb* (April 1982): 32-33.
Hughes, Robert. "Lost Among the Figures." *Time,* 31 May 1982, 64ff.
Schjeldahl, Peter. "King Curator." *Village Voice,* 20 July 1982, 73.
Castle, Ted. "A Bouquet of Mistakes." *Flash Art International* (Summer 1982): 54-55.
Rickey, Carrie. "Why Women Don't Express Themselves." *Village Voice,* 2 November 1982, 7.
Herrera, Hayden. "Expressionism Today: An Artists' Symposium." *Art in America* (December 1982): 65-139.
Russell, John. "A Big Berlin Show That Misses the Mark." *New York Times,* 5 December 1982, H33.
"Zeitgeist." *Kunstforum* (Cologne), December 1982, 81.

1983 *Ars 83 Helsinki,* exhibition catalogue. Essays by Matti Ranki, Pauli Paaermaa, Leena Peltola, Yrjänä Levanto, Mats B., J. O. Mallander, and Barbara J. London. Helsinki: Ateneumin Taidemuseo, 1983.
Castleman, Riva. *Prints from Blocks: Gauguin to Now,* exhibition catalogue. New York: Museum of Modern Art, 1983.
Joachimides, Christos M., and Norman Rosenthal. *Zeitgeist,* exhibition catalogue. New York: George Braziller, 1983.
47th National Mid-Year Exhibition. Youngstown, Ohio: Butler Institute of American Art, 1983.

Geldzahler, Henry. *Rothmans Presents: American Accents,* exhibition catalogue. Toronto: Rothmans of Pall Mall, Canada, 1983.

Giménez, Carmen. *Tendencias en Nueva York,* exhibition catalogue. Madrid: Palacio de Velázquez, 1983.

Honnef, Klaus, and Gabriele Honnef-Harling. *Back to the USA,* exhibition catalogue. Cologne: Rheinland-Verlag, 1983.

Kuspit, Donald B. *New York Painting Today,* exhibition catalogue. Pittsburgh, Pa.: Three Rivers Arts Festival, 1983.

1983 Biennial Exhibition. New York: Whitney Museum of American Art, 1983.

Tuchman, Maurice. *Susan Rothenberg,* exhibition catalogue. Los Angeles: Los Angeles County Museum of Art, 1983.

Glueck, Grace. "Art: 'Figures of Mystery' Shows Work by Ten." *New York Times,* 7 January 1983, C20.

Russell, John. "Art: 9-Painting Show That's Best of the Season." *New York Times,* 28 January 1983, C23.

Raynor, Vivien. Review. *New York Times,* 1 April 1983, C22.

Levin, Kim. "Art." *Village Voice,* 12 April 1983, centerfold.

Storr, Robert. "Spooks and Floats." *Art in America* (May 1983): 153-59.

Titterington, Chris. Review. *Artscribe #41,* June 1983, 61-65.

Westfall, Stephen. "Arts Reviews: Susan Rothenberg." *Arts Magazine* (June 1983): 42.

Glueck, Grace. "The Horse Show," *New York Times,* 17 June 1983, C21.

Kwinter, Sanford. Review. *Flash Art International* (Summer 1983): 62.

Russell, John. "It's Not Women's Art, It's Good Art." *New York Times,* 24 July 1983, sec. 2, pp. 1, 25.

Schjeldahl, Peter. "Putting Painting Back on Its Feet." *Vanity Fair,* August 1983.

Liebmann, Lisa. "Susan Rothenberg." *Artforum* (September 1983): 69.

Muchnic, Suzanne. "Emotional States of Susan Rothenberg." *Los Angeles Times,* 6 September 1983, sec. 6, pp. 1, 6.

Knight, Christopher. "The Painter Who Put Painting Back on Its Feet." *Los Angeles Herald Examiner,* 7 September 1983, B1-2.

Hicks, Emily. "Susan Rothenberg: Seeking Authenticity." *Artweek* (September 24, 1983): 1, 16.

Albright, Thomas. "The New Image of Rothenberg." *San Francisco Chronicle,* 19 November 1983, 38.

1984 *A Celebration of American Women Artists, Part II: The Recent Generation,* exhibition catalogue. New York: Sidney Janis Gallery, 1984.

Fox, Howard N., Miranda McClintic, and Phyllis Rosenzwieg. *Content: A Contemporary Focus 1974-1984,* exhibition catalogue. Washington, D.C., Hirshhorn Museum and Sculpture Garden, 1984.

Goldwater, Marge. *Images and Impressions: Painters Who Print,* exhibition catalogue. Minneapolis, Minn.: Walker Art Center, 1984.

McShine, Kynaston. *An International Survey of Recent Painting and Sculpture,* exhibition catalogue. New York: Museum of Modern Art, 1984.

Rosenthal, Mark. "Jennifer Bartlett . . . Susan Rothenberg, et al." *Art of Our Time: The Saatchi Collection,* vol. 4. New York: Rizzoli, 1985.

Susan Rothenberg Prints, 1977-1984, exhibition catalogue. Boston: Barbara Krakow Gallery, 1984.

Storr, Robert. "Fantômes et Flottaisons." *Artpress* (January 1984): 9-11. Reprinted from *Art in America,* May 1983.

Nilson, Lisbet. "Susan Rothenberg: Every Brushstroke Is a Surprise," *Art News* (February 1984): 46-54.
Brenson, Michael. "Today's Landscapes Grapple with America." *New York Times,* 5 February 1984, sec. 2, p. 29.
Herrera, Hayden. "In a Class by Herself." *Connoisseur* (April 1984): 112-17.
Kelley, J. "American Art Since 1970: A Shaky Transition." *Artweek* (April 7, 1984): 1.
Temin, Christine. "Rothenberg's New Works Seen at ICA." *Boston Globe,* 13 April 1984, 80.
Glueck, Grace. "Susan Rothenberg: New Outlook for a Visionary Artist." *New York Times Magazine,* 22 July 1984, cover and pp. 16ff.
Bourdon, David. "The Go-Betweens." *Vogue,* September 1984, 98.
———. "Primitive Mysteries, New Images." *Vogue,* September 1984, 103.
Russell, John. "Drawings by Eleven Artists." *New York Times,* 7 September 1984, C16.
Larson, Kay. "The Cooked and the Raw." *New York Magazine,* 24 September 1984, 103.
Ackley, Clifford. "I Don't Really Think of Myself as a Printmaker: Susan Rothenberg." *Print Collector's Newsletter,* September-October 1984, 128-29.
Carducci, Vincent A. "Susan Rothenberg." *New Art Examiner,* December 1984, 68.
Heartney, Eleanor. "Images and Impressions at the Walker Art Center: Belief in the Possibility of Authenticity." *Arts Magazine* (December 1984): 118-21.

1985 Brandt, Frederick R. *Lewis—Late 20th Century: Selections from the Sydney and Frances Lewis Collection in the Virginia Museum of Fine Arts.* Richmond: Virginia Museum of Fine Arts, 1985.
Brown, David. *Horses in Twentieth-Century Art,* exhibition catalogue. London: Nicola Jacobs Gallery, 1985.
Felshin, Nina, and Thomas McEvilley. *Focus on the Image: Selections from the Rivendell Collection,* exhibition catalogue. New York: ITA Corp., 1985.
Glenn, Constance W. *Centric 13: Susan Rothenberg,* exhibition catalogue. Long Beach, Calif., University Art Museum, California State University, 1985.
Guenther, Bruce. *States of War: New European and American Painting,* exhibition catalogue. Seattle, Wash.: Seattle Art Museum, 1985.
1985 Biennial Exhibition. New York: Whitney Museum of American Art, 1985.
1985 Carnegie International, exhibition catalogue. Pittsburgh: Carnegie Institute of Art, 1985.
Rathbone, Eliza. *Susan Rothenberg,* exhibition catalogue. Washington, D.C.: Phillips Collection, 1985.
Susan Rothenberg/1982-1985, exhibition catalogue. Richmond: Virginia Museum of Fine Arts, 1985.
Burr, James. "Around the Galleries: Paint for Paint's Sake." *Apollo,* January 1985, 64.
Shone, Richard. "London: Twentieth-Century Exhibitions." *Burlington Magazine,* March 1985, 178.
Moritz, Charles, ed. "Susan Rothenberg." *Current Biography* (March 1985): 26-30.
Petzal, Monica. "Susan Rothenberg." *Art Monthly,* March 1985, 15-17.
Proctor, Roy. "10 Rothenberg Paintings at the Virginia Museum." *Richmond News Leader,* 9 March 1985.
Russell, John. "Art: Whitney Presents Its Biennial Exhibition." *New York Times,* 22 March 1985, C23.
Zaya, Octavio. "Susan Rothenberg: De la superficie a la profundidad." *Hartisimo* (Spring 1985).
Wilson, William. "A Sizeable Minority Breaks Out." *Los Angeles Times,* 1 April 1985, sec. 6, p. 1.

Brenson, Michael. "Susan Rothenberg." *New York Times,* 26 April 1985, C23.

Hughes, Robert. "Careerism and Hype Amidst the Image Haze." *Time,* 17 June 1985, 78-83.

Bauer, Catherina. "Koncentration och sammanhang." *Svenska Dagbladet,* 11 July 1985.

Richard, Paul. "Susan Rothenberg and the New York Palette." *Washington Post,* 21 September 1985, C1-2.

Kessler, Pamela. "Susan Rothenberg: Gathering Ghosts." *Washington Post Weekend,* 27 September 1985, N41.

Allen, Jane Adams. "Susan Rothenberg's New Images." *Washington Times,* 29 September 1985.

Cohen, Ronny. "The Medium Isn't the Message. *Art News* (October 1985): 74-81.

Grimes, Nancy. "Susan Rothenberg." *Art News* (October 1985): 127.

Iovine, Julie V. "Query." *Connoisseur* (October 1985): 186.

McEvilley, Thomas. "Susan Rothenberg." *Artforum* (October 1985): 122.

Flam, Jack. "Art: Bravura Brushwork." *Wall Street Journal,* 7 October 1985, 20.

1986 Godfrey, Tony. *The New Image: Painting in the 1980s.* New York: Abbeville Press, 1986.

Individuals: A Selected History of Contemporary Art, exhibition catalogue. Essays by Kate Linker, Donald Kuspit, Hal Foster, Ronald J. Onorato, Germano Celant, Achille Bonito Oliva, John C. Welchman, and Thomas Lawson. Los Angeles: Los Angeles County Museum of Art, 1986.

Marshall, Richard. *50 New York Artists: A Critical Selection of Painters and Sculptors Working in New York.* San Francisco: Chronicle Books, 1986.

"New Acquisitions." *Bulletin of the Whitney Museum of American Art* (1986/87): 6, 65.

Sims, Patterson, and Suzanne Stroh. *Downe, 1976-1986: Ten Years of Collecting Contemporary Art* (Selections from the Edward R. Downe, Jr., Collection), exhibition catalogue. Wellesley, Mass.: Wellesley College Museum, 1986

Stebbins, Theodore E., Jr., and Judith Hoos Fox. *Boston Collects,* exhibition catalogue. Boston: Museum of Fine Arts, 1986.

Weiermair, Peter. *Prospekt 86,* exhibition catalogue. Frankfurt: Frankfurter Kunstverein, 1986.

———. *Vom Zeichnen: Aspekte der Zeichnung 1960-1985,* exhibition catalogue. Frankfurt: Frankfurter, Kuntsverein, 1986.

Wallach, Amei. "Picture of a Painter in Motion." *Newsday,* 24 August 1986, sec. 2, cover and pp. 4-5.

Moorman, Margaret. "New Editions: Review of New Prints." *Art News* (October 1986): 102-4.

"Prints and Photographs Published—Susan Rothenberg." *The Print Collector's Newsletter* (November-December 1986): 182.

Tuchman, Phyllis. "70s Imagery Tells How We Got to Where We Are Today." *Newsday,* 14 December 1986, sec. 2, p. 19.

1987 Conklin, Jo-Ann. *Heads, Hands, Horses: Susan Rothenberg Prints,* exhibition catalogue. Iowa City, Iowa: University of Iowa Museum of Art, 1987.

Dunham, Judith. curator. *The Monumental Image,* exhibition catalogue. Sonoma, Calif.: Sonoma State University, 1986.

Maxwell, Rachel Robertson. *Susan Rothenberg, The Prints: A Catalogue Raisonné.* Philadelphia: Peter Maxwell, 1987.

Susan Rothenberg, The Horse Paintings: 1974-1980, exhibition catalogue. New York: Larry Gagosian Gallery, 1987.

Susan Rothenberg: Paintings, exhibition catalogue. New York: Sperone Westwater, 1987.

Brenson, Michael. "Rothenberg Horses at the Gagosian Gallery." *New York Times,* 23 January 1987, C23.

Oliva, Achille Bonito. "Spostamenti allegorici dell'arte," *Tema celeste* (January-March 1987): 28-35.

Cottingham, Laura. "Women Artists: A Question of Difference." *Art and Auction* (March 1987): 122-27.

Schwabsky, Barry. "Susan Rothenberg." *Arts Magazine* (April 1987): 107.

Yau, John. "Susan Rothenberg: Gagosian Gallery." *Artforum* (April 1987): 122-23.

Wolff, Theodore F. "The power and influence in today's art world. . . ." *Christian Science Monitor,* 20 April 1987, 26-27.

Bell, Jane. "Susan Rothenberg: Gagosian." *Art News* (May 1987): 147.

Gimmelson, Deborah. "Works on Paper." *Art and Auction* (May 1987): 162-68.

Taylor, Paul. "Changing in Midstream." *Manhattan Inc.,* May 1987, 178.

Heartney, Eleanor. "How Wide Is the Gender Gap?" *Art News* (Summer 1987): 139-45.

Smith, Roberta. "A Painting Landmark in Retrospect." *New York Times,* 2 August 1987, sec. 2, pp. 1, 29.

Newhall, Edith. Galleries. *New York Magazine* (21 September 1987): 74.

Gladstone, Valerie. "Art in a Spin—Susan Rothenberg." *Elle* (American ed.) (October 1987): 108-10.

Letters to the Editor (under "The Gender Gap"). *Art News* (October 1987): 90.

Brenson, Michael. "Art: A New Direction for Susan Rothenberg." *New York Times,* 23 October 1987, C34.

Danto, Ginger. "What Becomes an Artist Most." *Art News* (November 1987): 149-53.

Hess, Elizabeth. "Energetic Works by Rothenberg at Westwater." *New York Observer* (2 November 1987): 17.

Hughes, Robert. "Spectral Light, Anxious Dancers." *Time* (9 November 1987): 109.

Larson, Kay. Review. *New York Magazine* (9 November 1987): 122-23.

Voice Choice. *Village Voice,* 10 November 1987, 48.

Cameron, Dan. "Opening Salvos, Part One." *Arts Magazine* (December 1987): 89-93.

Neisser, Judith. "A Magnificent Obsession." *Art and Auction* (December 1987): 108-13.

Ratcliff, Carter. "Artist's Catalogue: Susan Rothenberg—Images on the Edge of Abstraction." *Architectural Digest,* December 1987, 52-58.

1988 Blackwood, Michael (producer). *Four Artists: Robert Ryman, Eva Hesse, Bruce Nauman, Susan Rothenberg,* film. Text and narration by Joan Simon. New York: Michael Blackwood Productions, 1988.

Koscielny, Margaret. *The M. Anwar Kamal Collection of Art—Printmaking: Late Nineteenth and Twentieth Century,* exhibition catalogue. Jacksonville, Fla.: Cummer Gallery of Art, 1988.

1988 Carnegie International, exhibition catalogue. Pittsburgh: The Carnegie Museum of Art, 1988.

1988—The World of Art Today, exhibition catalogue. Milwaukee, Wisc.: Milwaukee Art Museum, 1988.

"Susan Rothenberg," in *Saatchi Collection,* exhibition catalogue. London: Saatchi Collection, 1988.

Works on Paper, exhibition catalogue. San Francisco: John Berggruen Gallery, 1988.

Bass, Ruth. "New York? New York!" *Art Talk,* January 1988, sec. 2, p. 30.

Malen, Lenore. "Susan Rothenberg." *Art News* (January 1988): 151.

Princenthal, Nancy. "Susan Rothenberg at Sperone Westwater." *Art in America* (January 1988): 129.

Schwendenwien, Jude. "Outside Futurism." *Cover Arts New York,* January 1988, 10.
Dunning, Jennifer. "City Ballet Honors American Composers." *New York Times,* 18 January 1988, C14.
Cottingham, Laura. "Susan Rothenberg—Sperone Westwater." *Flash Art International* (January/February 1988): 122-23.
Dorsey, John. "Intuitive Process Guides Rothenberg's Seemingly Frenzied Strokes." *Baltimore Sun,* 23 February 1988, 1E, 2E: 4.
"The Cornell Fine Arts Connection." *Cornell Architecture Art and Planning,* Spring 1988, 4-5.
Gornick, April, Freya Hansell, and Susan Rothenberg. "Three Painters." *Bomb* (Spring 1988): 19-23.
Kazanjian, Dodie. "Lining Up for Art—Waiting Lists Are the Latest Expression of an Overheated Art Market." *House and Garden* (March 1988): 33-34.
Kaufman, Jason Edward. "Motion and Drama Spring from Rothenberg's Paintings." *New York City Tribune,* 2 March 1988, 9.
Rothenberg, Susan. "Diffusions—A Project for *Artforum.*" *Artforum* (April 1988): 118-21.
Brownstein, Joan. "Painter's Return." *Cornell Alumni News,* June 1988, 79.
Kuspit, Donald. "Gordon Matta-Clark—Josh Baer Gallery, Galerie Lelong." *Artforum* (Summer 1988): 132.
Simon, Joan. "Gordon Matta-Clark: Reconstructions." *Arts Magazine* (Summer 1988): 84-87.
Casorati, Cecilia. "Rome and Naples." *Contemporanea—International Art Magazine* (July/August 1988): 16-17.
Rothenberg, Susan. Excerpts from a studio talk. *ICI Newsletter* (New York) (Fall 1988): 4.
"Carnegie International Exhibits New Artistic Developments." *Flash Art News* (supplement to *Flash Art International*) (October 1988): 2.
"Susan Rothenberg." *B.T.—Bijutsu Techo* (October 1988): 118.
Cherubini, Laura. "Susan Rothenberg." *Flash Art* (ed. Italiana) (October-November 1988): 121.

1989 Baker, Kenneth. "Carnegie International." *Artforum* (March 1989): 138-39.
Plagens, Peter. "Under Western Eyes." *Art in America* (January 1989): 33-41.
Tuchman, Phyllis. "Rothenberg's Dancers: Serial Image of Figures in Motion—The Subject of New Murals." *View: The Photojournal of Art,* June/July 1989, 72-75.

1990 *Susan Rothenberg: 15 Years—A Survey,* exhibition catalogue. Essay by Robert Storr. Malmö, Sweden: Rooseum Center for Contemporary Art, 1990.
Susan Rothenberg: Paintings, exhibition catalogue. New York: Sperone Westwater, 1990.
Handy, Ellen. "Mysteries of Motion: Recent Paintings by Susan Rothenberg." *Arts Magazine* (May 1990): 70-74.
Kazanjian, Dodie. "New Image." *Vogue,* May 1990, 292-99, 320, 323.
"Goings on About Town," *New Yorker,* 14 May 1990, 15.
Hughes, Robert. "The New Decadence." *New Republic,* 25 June 1990, 27-38.
Kipphoff, Petra. "Ermälte Bilder." *Die Zeit* (20 July 1990): 47.
Hanson, Alan J. "Susan Rothenberg: Sperone Westwater Gallery." *Contemporanea—International Art Magazine* (September 1990): 99-100.
D'Amato, Brian. "Susan Rothenberg: Sperone Westwater." *Flash Art International* (October 1990): 153-54.
Heartney, Eleanor. "Susan Rothenberg: Sperone Westwater." *Art News* (October 1990): 183.
Sorensen, Ann Lumbye. "Susan Rothenberg: The Rooseum." *Contemporanea—International Art Magazine* (December 1990): 104-5.

INDEX

Page numbers are in Roman type. Illustrations are indicated by page numbers in *italic* type. All works are by Susan Rothenberg unless otherwise noted.

A

Abstract Expressionism, 36
abstraction/representation, conflation of, 23, 49-52, 175 n.28
Africano, Nicholas, 52
Albright-Knox Art Gallery, 10, 18, 173 n.7
Algarve (1975), 39, 117; *43*
Al with Bananas (1984), 132
Ammann, Jean Christophe, 94
"Anti-Illusion: Procedures/Materials" exhibition (Whitney Museum, 1969), 23, 174 n.19
"Johnsian" group, 174 n.19
"Rauschenbergian" group, 174 n.19
Armstrong, Richard, 174 n.19
Arte Povera artists, 49
Asher, Michael, 58
Asian Sex (1982), 108; *109*
Atherton, Peggy, 173 n.9
Atwood, Alan, 11, 153
Axes (1976), 49; *51*

B

Baby Swan Family (1982), 103
Baldessari, John, 58
Bartlett, Jennifer, 22, 52
Baynard, Ed, 174 n.24
Beckley, Bill, 39
Beggar (1982), 108, 117; *107, 112*
Between the Lines, 176 n.46
Beuys, Joseph, 49, 176 n.42
Big and Little Head (1980-81), 85; *86, 100*
Biker (1985), 132, 176 n.48; *133, 134*
Biker (1985, drawing), *135*
Black Head (1980-81), *87*
Blackness (1972), 20
Blue Bars (1982), 108, 117; *105*
Bluebird Wings (1989), 168; *168*
Blue Body, 79, 88, 175 n.33; *79, 100*
Blue Chair, The (1987), 150; *151*
Blue Frontal (1978), 58, 62, 74; *60*
Blue Head (1980-81), *84*
Blue Oval (1981), 108; *100, 101*
Blue U-Turn (1989), 164; *163*
Blue Woman with Frog (1988), 153
Blum, Peter, 173 n.3
boat images, 95-98, 103; *96, 97, 103*
Body Art, 33, 49, 174 n.22
Bone Heads (1989-90), 164; *166, 167*
bone-shaped images, 62, 67, 71, 74, 79, 164; *60, 67, 72, 73, 75, 76, 77, 80, 81, 166*
Borofsky, Jonathan, 58, 176 n.42
Brach, Paul, 13
Brenson, Michael, 150
Bucket of Water (1983-84), 120, 140; *121, 134*
Buddha images, 10, 150, 153, 176 n.55; *159, 160*
Buddha with Bamboo (1988), 153; *160*
Butterfly (1976), 52; *53*

C

California Institute for the Arts (Valencia, CA), 57-58
cave painting figuration, 28, 36, 49
Cherry Pit (1978-79), 62
Clocktower, The, 22, 174 n.18
Cocoon (1981), *112*
color(s). *See* palette (Rothenberg's)
Conceptual Art, 22, 23, 57, 174 n.22
continuous motion images, 120, 123, 128, 132-37, 138-46, 161; *140-45, 147, 150, 152, 154-56*
Corcoran School of Art (Washington, D.C.), 15
Cornell University Fine Arts School, 11-12, 14
Creek, The (1981-82), 95; *95, 96*

D

dance and performance, 11, 19, 21-22, 24, 49, 146, 161
painting and, 49, 146, 161
Diagram of PaineWebber Commission (1987), *157*
Dom, the, 12, 173 n.12
Double Masked Heads (1974), 38; *39*
Double Measure (1977), 33, 52; *56*

drawing(s), 36, 58, 123, 124, 137
relationship of to paintings, 36, 124
"Drawings: The Pluralist Decade" exhibition (1980 Venice Biennale), 94
Duff, John, 19, 23, 26, 28, 174 nn. 19, 24

E

Elizabeth (1984-85), 132; *128*
Etruscan painting, 176 n. 51
Evans, Donald, 11, 173 n. 10

F

Falling Rock (1983), 120
feminist artists, 49, 117-18
First Horse (1974), 27; *27*
Fish Sculpture (1987), 164, 177 n. 60; *164*
Flanders (1976), 40, 52; *42*
Folded Buddha (1987-88), 153; *159*
Food (restaurant), 22, 174 n. 18
For the Light (1978-79), 67; *67, 69*
Formentera (Spain), 14-15
Four Color Horse (1976), 49, 175 n. 27; *50*
Foxes on a Hill (1972), 28-29, 74; *28*
From Buffalo (1976-77), 36; *54*
From Hand to Mouth (1967, Nauman), 117

G

G. T. (1977), 138; *138*
Giacometti, Alberto, 108
"Giotto" blue (Rothenberg's), 15, 17, 108, 153, 164
Girouard, Tina, 19, 174 nn. 18, 19
Glass, Philip, 19, 39
Glueck, Grace, 173 nn. 1, 14, 176 nn. 43, 44, 45, 47
Golden Moment, A (1985), 128; *130*
Grandmother (1983-84), 120-23; *122*
Graves, Morris, 174 n. 24
Graves, Nancy, 19, 23-24
Green, Denise, 52
Green Ray (1984), 146; *119*
Greenwald, Ted, 174 n. 15
Grey Head (1980-81), *83*
Guston, Philip, 71, 74, 176 n. 42
Gyro (1986-87), *143*

H

Half and Half (1985-87), 137-38, 146; *148*
Hall, Susan, 19, 173 n. 15
Hands and Shadows (1978-79), 62; *61. See also* cover
Harris, Ruth, 173 n. 8
Hay, Alex, 19
Hay, Deborah, 19
head image(s), 58, 62; *59, 61, 64. See also* Heads and Hands images
Headlights (1982-83), *112*
Head Roll (1987), *144*
Heads and Hands images, 88, 89-95, 103; *82, 83, 84-87, 90, 93*
Heads at a Tank (1990), 169; *171*
Heilman, Mary, 18, 19, 174 n. 19
Heiss, Alanna, 174 n. 18
Herrera, Hayden, 176 n. 56
Hesse, Eva, 19, 23
Holding the Floor (1985), 132, 137, 140, 146; *136*
horse image(s), 27-40, 47-58, 62-71, 74, 79, 88, 94, 168-69, 172, 174 n. 21, 175 n. 33; *27, 30-32, 37-39, 41-46, 48, 50-57, 65, 168, 170, 171*
fragmentation of, 58, 62, 67-71, 74; *60, 63, 68-72, 75-77*
and human figure, 77, 79; *77, 78, 80, 81*
Hourglass (1982), *112, 114*
Hughes, Robert, 176 n. 51
Hulk, The (1979), 74; *76*
human figures, 77, 79, 89, 98, 103, 118-28, 132; *118, 119, 121, 122, 124, 126-29, 133-35, 136, 139*
fragmentation of, 22, 153, 164; *148, 149, 158, 159, 160*
in motion, 98, 120; *95, 99, 121*
See also portraits; spinners, dancers, vaulters, jugglers
humanism, 24, 120
Hurson, Michael, 175 n. 28
Hydra (Greece), 12

I

I x I (1977), 36, 52; *55*
imagery (Rothenberg's), 47, 49, 175 n. 29, 176 n. 51
boat, 95-98, 103
bone-shaped, 62, 67, 71, 74, 79, 164
Buddha, 150, 153, 176 n. 55
continuous motion, 98, 120, 122, 123, 128, 132-37, 138-46, 161
dreamlike, 103
fragmentation of, 67-71, 74, 103, 153, 164
heads (early), 58, 62
Heads and Hands, 88, 89-95, 103
horse, 7, 27-40, 47-58, 74, 79, 88, 94, 168-69, 172, 174 n. 21, 175 n. 33

human figures, 77, 79, 89, 98, 103, 118-28, 132
scale of, 88, 103
shadow-puppet, 62
spinners, jugglers, dancers, vaulters, 140, 146, 153, 161, 176 nn. 51, 52, 55
"U-turn" form, 162-64, 168
volumetric, 103
X-inscribed, 33-36, 49
See also individual listings
INGspray (1984-85), 128; *128*
Itzig, the Sunday horseman (Freud's), 77, 175 n. 32

J

Jenney, Neil, 19, 23, 52, 173 n. 15, 174 n. 19
Joachimides, Christos, 175 n. 37
Johns, Jasper, 13, 20
Johnson, Miani, 39, 98, 174 n. 24, 177 n. 61
Jonas, Joan, 19, 24
Jones Beach Piece (1970, Jonas), 24, 161; *25*
Juggler #3 (1987-88), *152*
jugglers, 140, 146, 176 n. 52; *152*
Jughead (1980), 89; *90*

K

Katz, Bill, 39
Kazanjian, Dodie, 177 n. 59
Kelpie (1978), 62; *65*
Kounellis, Jannis, 49
Kramer, Hilton, 40, 47, 174 n. 23
Kunsthalle Basel, 94, 98

L

L. R. (1984), 128; *131*
Landry, Dickie, 19, 174 n. 19
Lane, Lois, 52, 174 n. 24
Layering (1975), 40, 52; *41*
Lew, Jeffrey, 39, 174 n. 18
line (Rothenberg's):
as "band," 62-67
as bone shape, 71-74
Lippold, Richard, 19
Little Blue Freak (1982), 108

M

Maggie's Cartwheel (1981-82), 98; *99, 100*
Maggie's Split (1981-82), 98; *95*
Malanga, Gerard, 12-13
Mary I (1974), 33; *34*
Mary II (1974), 33; *34*
Mary III (1974), 33; *34*
Matta (b. Matta-Clark), Gordon, 11, 18, 19, 173 n. 10, 174 n. 18
Minimalism, 13, 14, 22, 24, 36, 47, 120
Mirror Piece (1970, Jonas), 24; *25*
Mr. Bear (1978), 67; *66*
Mondrian (1984), 124-25; *127*
Mondrian Dancing (1984-85), 128; *129*
Mondrian, Piet, 123, 175 n. 27, 176 n. 46
"dynamic equilibrium" of, 125-28
Mondrian series, 124-28
Monk, The (1983), 117, 118, 120, 146; *115*
Morris, Robert, 13, 23
Moskowitz, Robert, 29, 52, 94, 95, 174 n. 21
Motherwell, Robert, 19
Muchnic, Suzanne, 173 n. 2
Mukuhara (1974), 33, 38; *32*
Multiple Splice (1972), 20; *22*
Murray, Elizabeth, 95, 132
My Bones (1979), 74

N

Nabokov, Vladimir, 176 n. 52
Native American sand painting, 49
Nauman, Bruce, 19, 23, 28, 117, 162, 164, 174 n. 22, 176 n. 58
Neo-Expressionism, 94, 117, 118, 120
humanism and, 120
"New Image" and, 94-95
Neo-Minimalism, 120
New Image Painting, 23, 94-95, 175 n. 29
"New Image Painting" exhibition (Whitney Museum, 1978), 52-57, 175 n. 28
"New Spirit in Painting" exhibition (Royal Academy, London, 1980), 94, 175 n. 37
"New Talent" exhibition (Sachs Gallery, 1974), 38
Night Ride (1987), 146; *147*
Nilsen, Lisbet, 173 nn. 4, 6, 174 n. 20, 175 n. 40, 176 n. 41
Nine Sheep (c. 1967-68), 15; *16*
98 Greene Street Loft, 22, 173 n. 15
North Wall (1976), 33, 40

O

1-6 (1988), 153, 161; *154-57*
112 Greene Street, 22, 39, 174 n. 18
Orange Break (1989-90), 164; *165*
Our Lord (1979), 77; *78*

Outline (1978-79), 67; *67, 70*
Overcoat (1982-83), 118; *118*

P

PaineWebber commission (1988), 153, 176 n.55; *154-57*
palette (Rothenberg's), 26, 47, 74, 98, 108, 123, 137, 146, 164, 175 n.27
  early, 17
Papa Cohen (1985), 132
Patches (1982), 111; *112, 113*
Performance Art, 22, 174 n.22. *See also* dance and performance
Pillow (1984), 132, 176 n.47; *132*
Pontiac (1979), 67; *67, 72*
Poons, Larry, 13, 173 n.13
Pop Art, 13, 14, 24
portraits, 162; *131, 132, 138. See also* self-portraits
Post-Minimalism, 22, 24, 47
prints, 57, 175 n.30; *57*
Process Art, 19-20, 22-23, 27

R

Ratcliff, Carter, 49
Rathbone, Eliza, 175 n.31
Rauschenberg, Robert, 19
Red Banner (1979), 74
Red Blush (1984-85), *128*
Red Head (Head within Head) (1978), 88; *59*
Red Head (1980-81), *86*
Red Man (1985-86), 138; *139*
Red Slippers (1981), 89, 146; *91*
Reflections (1981), *112*
Reich, Steve, 19, 39
Rest (1981), *112*
Richenberg, Robert, 11, 174 n.21
Rifkin, Ned, 29, 174 n.21
Rose (1980), 88
Rosenberg, Dr. Joseph, 10, 12
Rosenthal, Norman, 175 n.37
Rothenberg, Adele (mother), 9, 10
Rothenberg, Leonard (father), 9, 10
Rothenberg, Susan:
  attempted move to Canada, 17-18
  birth and childhood in Buffalo, 9-11
  dance and performance interest, 11, 19, 22, 49, 146, 161
  daughter, Maggie, 26, 169
  divorce from George Trakas, 77
  Nancy Graves and, 19, 23-24
  in Greece, 12
  jobs, 20, 174 n.17
  marriage to George Trakas, 25, 57-58, 67, 77
  marriage to Bruce Nauman, 162, 176 n.58
  in New Mexico, 162-72
  in New York, 12-14, 18-20, 88, 92, 98
  as "Orphan Annie," 20, 118
  pictured, *77, 95, 112, 167, 172*
  and psychotherapy, 98, 175 n.39
  in Spain, 14-15
  teaching at California Institute for the Arts (Valencia, CA), 57-58
  in Washington, D.C., 15, 17
  Mary Woronov and, 11, 12, 18, 23, 33
Rothenberg, Susan (art training):
  Atwood, Alan (Cornell), 11, 153
  early, 10-11
  Colby, Victor (Cornell), 12
  at Corcoran School of Art, 15
  at Cornell University Fine Arts School, 11-12, 14
  independent study in New York, 12-14
  Richenberg, Robert (Cornell), 11, 174 n.21
  at State University (Buffalo), 11
  Szabo, Laszlo, 11, 175 n.27
Rothenberg, Susan (studios):
  Franklin St., 88, 98
  New Mexico, 162-72
  Sag Harbor, 175 n.38, 176 n.55
  TriBeCa, 98
  Union Square, 13
  West Broadway, 18-20, 88, 92, 98
Rothenberg, Susan (work of):
  asymmetrical symmetry, 28, *29*, 125-28
  "cave painting" figuration, 28, 36, 49
  Conceptualism and, 22, 23, 57
  drawing(s), 36, 58, 123, 124, 137; relationship of to paintings, 36, 124
  early work, 10-12, 14-17, 19-21, 26-27
  exhibitions: Kunsthalle Basel (1981), 94, 98; "New Image Painting" (1978), 52; "New Spirit in Painting" (1980), 94; "New Talent" (1974), 38; 112 Greene Street, 39-40; Sperone Westwater (1987), 146; Stedelijk Museum (1982), 94, 98, 117; Venice Biennale (1980), 94; Willard Gallery, 40, 49; "Zeitgeist" (1982), 117, 175 n.37. *See also* Selected Exhibition History
  Expressionism and, 36, 47, 94, 117, 118, 120
  figure/ground relationship, 20, 27-30, 33, 38, 39-40, 47, 103, 175 n.29
  "Giotto" blue, 15, 17, 108, 153, 164

halving of compositions, 15, 28, 33
imagery, 47, 49, 175 n.29, 176 n.51; boat, 95-98, 103; bone-shaped, 62, 67, 71, 74, 79, 164; Buddha, 150, 153, 176 n.55; continuous motion, 98, 120, 123, 128, 132-37, 138-46, 161; dreamlike, 103; *102*; fragmentation of, 58-62, 67-71, 74, 103, 153, 164; heads (early), 58, 62; Heads and Hands, 88, 89-95, 103; horse, 7, 29, 47-58, 74, 79, 88, 94, 168-69, 172, 174 n.21, 175 n.33; human figures, 77, 79, 89, 98, 103, 118-28, 132; scale of, 88, 103; shadow-puppet, 62; spinners, jugglers, dancers, vaulters, 140, 146, 153, 161, 176 nn.51, 52, 55; "U-turn" form, 162-64, 168; volumetric, 103; X-inscribed, 33-36, 39, 49. *See also* individual listings
influences: Giacometti, 108; Graves, 19, 23-24; Guston, 71, 74, 176 n.42; Johns, 13, 20, 26; Mondrian, 123-25; Morris (Robert) box, 13; Poons, 13, 173 n.13; Rosenberg, Dr. Joseph, 10; Samaras, 10, 12, 13; Serra, 20, 26; stone Buddha, 10, 153; *Yellow Christ* (Gauguin), 10
interior space, 88-89
line: as "band," 62-67, 88; as bone shape, 71, 74
Mary paintings, 33
materials, 19-20, 26, 95, 98
Minimalism and, 13, 14, 22, 24, 36, 47, 120
Mondrian series, 124-28
painting surface, 19-20, 28, 36, 94, 98, 146
pairing/doubling of images, 28, 33, 89
palette, 26, 47, 74, 98, 108, 123, 137, 146, 164, 175 n.27; early, 17
Performance Art and, 24, 49, 146, 161
Pop Art and, 13, 14, 24
portraits, 162
prints, 57, 175 n.30
Process Art and, 19-20, 22-23, 27
sculpture(s): *Fish Sculpture* (1987), 164; student, 12; study of, 11-12, 173 n.11
self-portraits, 71-77, 89, 103, 175 n.31
"spirit" paintings, 17
titles of, 20, 174 n.16
"weathers" in paintings, 89, 95, 98
See also individual listings
Rubber Balls (1967-68), 15, 29, 146; *14*

S

Sachs Gallery, A. M. (New York), 38, 39
"New Talent" exhibition (1974), 38
Samaras, Lucas, 10, 12, 13
Saret, Alan, 11, 18, 19, 22, 23, 24, 27, 173 n.10
Schjeldahl, Peter, 92, 175 n.31
Schnabel, Julian, 94, 95
Screen Door (c. 1967-68), 15; *16*
sculpture(s), 164, 174 n.11, 177 n.60; *164*
student, 12
study of, 11-12, 173 n.11
Self-Portrait (1982), 103; *104*
self-portraits, 71-77, 89, 103, 175 n.31; *104*
Semmel, John, 62
Serota, Nicholas, 175 n.37
Serra, Richard, 19, 20, 23, 26
shadow-puppet images, 62; *61, 64*
Shapiro, Joel, 23, 29, 174 n.21, 175 n.28
Shea, Judy, 174 n.24
Siena Dos Equis (1975), 39; *45-46*
Silverstreams (1972), 20
Simonds, Charles, 174 n.22
Singer, Michael, 11, 18, 19, 173 n.10
Single Splice (1972), 20
Smith, Roberta, 175 n.29
Smithson, Robert, 19
Smoker (1978-79), 71, 146; *73*
Snowman (1983), 117, 120; *112, 116*
SoHo, 21, 22
Solomon, Alan, 13
Solomon, Holly, 38, 39, 174 n.15
Somebody Else's Hand (1979), *64*
Sonnier, Keith, 19, 23
Speedboat (1981), *112*
speed and motion images, 98, 120; *95, 99, 116, 121*
See also continuous motion images
Sperone, Gian Enzo, 146
Sperone Westwater Gallery (New York), 146
spinners, dancers, vaulters, jugglers (images), 140, 146, 153, 161, 176 nn.51, 52, 55; *140-45, 147, 150, 152, 154-56*
Squeeze (1978-79), 62; *63*
Stable (1974), 33; *37*
Stedelijk Museum (Amsterdam), 94, 98, 117; *100*
Stick in Throat (1978), 62; *61*
Storr, Robert, 94
Stoumen, John, 18
Studies for Head and Hands (c. 1980), *82*
Study: Throw-up Head (1978), 62; *61*
Szabo, Laszlo, 11, 175 n.27

T

Tattoo (1979), 74; *67, 75*
Tenmen (1982), 108; *110-11*

Three Heads (1990), 169; *170*
Three Plus One (1982), 98
Three Trees, 177 n. 61
Tobey, Mark, 174 n. 24
Trakas, George, 24-25, 57-58, 67, 77, 138
Trakas, Maggie (daughter), 26
TriBeCa, 21, 22, 98
Triphammer Bridge (1974), 30, 36-38, 39; *31*
True, David, 175 n. 28
Trumpeter (1984-85), *134*
Tuning Fork (1980), 79; *81*
Two Rays (1981), 98; *97, 112*

U

"U-turn" form, 162-64, 168
Underneath (1970, Jonas), 24
United States (1975), 39, 52, 117; *44*
Universal Limited Art Editions, 176 n. 46, 177 n. 60
Untitled (1974), 33; *30*
Untitled (1976, 39¼×50″), 36; *48*
Untitled (1976, 38½×50″), 36; *48*
Untitled (1977), 57, 175 n. 30; *57*
Untitled (1978, head), *64*
Untitled (1978, shadow-puppet hand), *64*
Untitled (1978-79), *71*
Untitled (1979, 36½×36⅛″), 68
Untitled (1979, 50×38″), 74; *77*
Untitled (AEIOU) (1980), 89; *90*
Untitled (1981, 26¼×23″), *93*
Untitled (1981, 28×17″), *93*
Untitled (1981, 28¼×22½″), *92*
Untitled (1982), *106*
Untitled (1984, 29½×42½″), 123; *124*
Untitled (1984, 47½×31″), *126*
Untitled (1984, 49×37″), *125*
Untitled (1984, 61×42½″), *135*
Untitled (1986, 5×12′), *140*
Untitled (1986, 21×30″), *145*
Untitled (1986, 22×30″), *150*
Untitled (1987, 43½×30″), *142*
Untitled (1987, 22⅛×31″), *142*
Untitled (1987, 11⅞×8⅛″), *145*
Untitled (1987, 20¼×14¼″), *149*
Untitled (1988, 42½×41½″), *158*
Untitled (1989), *162*

V

Van Grevenstein, Alexander, 94
Variability of Similar Forms (Graves), 23
Vaulting (1986-87), *141*
Venice Biennale (1980):
  Aperto section, 94
  "Drawings: the Pluralist Decade" exhibition, 94

W

Wallach, Amei, 176 n. 57
Warhol, Andy, 12-13
  at the Dom, 12, 173 n. 12
Westwater, Angela, 146
White Mountain, 79, 88, 175 n. 33; *79*
White Robe (1974), 38; *38*
Whitney Museum of American Art (New York), 22-23, 52
  "Anti-Illusion: ..." exhibition (1969), 23, 174 n. 19
  "New Image Painting" exhibition (1978), 52-57, 175 n. 28
(W)holes and Parts #4 (1971), *21*
(W)holes and Parts series, 20-21
Wilke, Hannah, 174 n. 22
Willard Gallery (New York), 39, 40, 49, 137, 174 n. 24; *52, 67, 112, 128, 134*
Willard, Marian, 174 n. 24
Wishbone (1979), 79; *80*
Withall (1982), 103; *102*
Woronov, Mary, 11, 12, 18, 23, 33, 173 n. 12
  Andy Warhol and, 12

X

X-inscribed imagery, 33-36, 39, 49; *50, 54, 55, 56*

Y

Yellow Christ (Gauguin), 10

Z

"Zeitgeist" exhibition (Martin-Gropius-Bau, Berlin, 1982), 117, 175 n. 37
Zimmerman, Elyn, 58
Zucker, Joe, 52